ONLY HOPE

# Only Hope

## *Coming of Age under China's One-Child Policy*

---

VANESSA L. FONG

STANFORD UNIVERSITY PRESS
STANFORD, CALIFORNIA
2004

Stanford University Press
Stanford, California
www.sup.org


Library of Congress Cataloging-in-Publication Data

Fong, Vanessa L., 1974–
Only hope : coming of age under China's one-child policy / Vanessa L. Fong.
p. cm.
Includes bibliographical references and index.
ISBN 0-8047-4961-2 (cloth: alk. paper)
ISBN 0-8047-5330-x (pbk.: alk. paper)
1. Teenagers—China—Longitudinal studies. 2. Only child—China—Longitudinal studies. 3. Parent and child—China—Longitudinal studies.
I. Title.
HQ799.C5 F66 2004
305.235'0951—dc22 2003019111

Printed in the United States of America on acid-free, archival-quality paper.

Original Printing 2004

Last figure below indicates year of this printing:
13 12 11 10 09 08

Designed and typeset at Stanford University Press in 10 / 12.5 Palatino.

# Contents

# Tables

# Acknowledgments

I am deeply indebted to the Dalian students and parents who shared their lives and dreams with me, and to the Dalian teachers and administrators who allowed me to teach and conduct research in their schools. The research, writing, and revision process for this book was funded by a Beinecke Brothers Memorial Fellowship, an Andrew W. Mellon Grant for Predissertation Research, a National Science Foundation Graduate Research Fellowship, a grant from the Weatherhead Center at Harvard University, an Eliot Dissertation Completion Fellowship from Harvard University, the Wenner-Glen Foundation for Anthropological Research, and a postdoctoral fellowship at the Population Studies Center of the University of Michigan at Ann Arbor. I am immensely grateful to James L. Watson (my dissertation adviser at Harvard), and my dissertation committee members, Michael Herzfeld and Arthur Kleinman. Their demands for clear writing, solid evidence, and theoretical engagement improved my work immeasurably, and their wisdom, kindness, and generosity continue to inspire me. I thank William R. Jankowiak, James Z. Lee, Martin King Whyte, and an anonymous reviewer at Stanford University Press for carefully reading my entire manuscript and providing detailed, tremendously helpful suggestions. I thank Muriel Bell and Carmen Borbon-Wu at Stanford University Press, for their kindness and advice throughout the publication process. Lawrence Alan Babb, Amrita Basu, Deborah Gewertz, Miriam "Mitzi" Goheen, Hua R. Lan, Jerry Dennerline, Jan Dizard, and Shen Tong were my mentors during my undergraduate years at Amherst College, and they have continued to sharpen my thinking about China, social theory, and life in general. As my writing group partners, Erica James, Manduhai Buyandelgeriyn, and Sonja Plesset provided me with detailed suggestions about various drafts of this book. The conversations and commensality I shared with them were highlights of my graduate student life. Andrew Shryock, Don Nonini, Graeme Lang, Jesook Song, Joan Kleinman, Maris Gillette, Nicole Constable, Shu-Min Huang, Ichiro Numizaki, Rubie Watson, Suhong Chae, Susan Greenhalgh, Ted Bestor, Tianshu Pan, and Twila Tardif gave me immensely valuable advice about various portions of this book. I am grateful for the questions and comments I received from faculty, students, postdoctoral fellows, and others when I presented portions of this book at meetings of the American Anthropological Association and at Harvard University, at the University of California at San Diego, at the University of Michigan at Ann Arbor, at the University of Minnesota at Minneapolis / St. Paul, and at the University of Oregon at Eugene. I thank Amal Fadlalla, Ann McDonald, Amy Young, Belinda Lew, Bernie Perley, Brian Palmer, Calvin Lew, David Kim, David Taylor, Dusty Hoang, Doug Campbell, Elizabeth Karpinski, Fred Errington, Fuji Lozada, Gabriel Taylor, Gary Mason, Hector Davila, Kevin Carr, Kristin Kane, Jana Amoroso, Jennifer Thompson, Jennifer Yan, Julia Huang, Linh Du, Lisa Gourd, Lucia Volk, Lois Mono, Malka Matveev, Maria Solorio, Mark Bryce, Melissa Caldwell, Michael Ru, Matt Crosby, Nicole Newendorp, Nor Chiao, Pilar Montalvo, Priscilla Song, Rachel Murphy, Richard Bryce, Richard Vega, Roberta Bryce, Sean Dang, Sandy Chang, Saroja Dorairajoo, Sisa DeJesus, Steve Slagle, Sue Hilditch, Thomas Malaby, Tiantian Zheng, Tom Bryce, Wen-Ching Sung, Yoel Matveev, Yuechun Song, Yuson Jung, Zongze Hu, and Zeke Taylor for their laughter, compassion, and friendship. Finally, I thank my parents and relatives, who I understood and appreciated much more after doing the research for this book.

# ONLY HOPE

# Introduction

"SOME PEOPLE say singletons are spoiled. Do you agree?" I asked a homeroom of college prep high school seniors in 1999. Because most of them were born after China's one-child policy began in 1979, all but three of the 48 students in the room were singletons.[1]

"Yes, singletons are spoiled," said Tian Xin, a lively, friendly girl. "Singletons' parents don't eat anything, and they let their children eat everything, so children grow fatter and fatter!"

"That's right!" said Luo Jun, a boy known for his sense of humor. "For instance, this classmate here is a singleton," he said, pointing to Shen Na, a slightly plump girl sitting nearby. "So her parents let her eat too much, and that's why she's so fat!" He ducked as she tried to hit him over the head with a textbook, to the delighted laughter of their classmates.

"I don't think singletons are spoiled!" said Sun Pei, an outspoken girl. "We face pressure to get into good colleges so we can get good jobs to support our parents when they're old. We'll have to make a lot of money to support our parents all by ourselves! So our parents are always nagging us to study harder. How can we be spoiled when we're always being scolded for not studying hard enough?"

"My parents think I'm spoiled because I have good food and good clothes, while they had such a hard life, and were so poor while they were growing up," added Li Yue, a cheerful, energetic girl. "But I don't think I'm spoiled. Of course my life is better than theirs in material terms. But I also have to work so much harder in school than they did.

Even on Sunday, my one day off, I spend all day with the tutors my parents hired. I have to study constantly every day!"

"We may be spoiled, but younger children are worse," said Xu Wang, a boy wearing stylish, brand-name clothes instead of the school uniform he was supposed to wear. "We were born in the early 1980s. China didn't even have brand-name clothes or fast food when we were small! So there were limits to how much our parents could spoil us. But younger children have so many more ways to spend their parents' money, so they're even more spoiled than we are!"

"If you could have a sibling, would you want one?" I asked.

"No, because I wouldn't want to share my things," said Sun Pei.

"An older sister would be nice, but a younger brother would be horrible," said Lu Jie, a boy who sometimes played poker during lunch despite school prohibitions. "He would be favored, get all the good food, and leave none for me!"

"It's better for parents to have only one child," said Yu Xu, an earnest girl. "With a lot of children, they won't care about any of them."

"Many families favor one child over others, so I'm glad I don't have siblings," said Zhou Fei, a studious boy. "My family's poor, so they wouldn't be able to support two children."

"I'd like an older brother, because he could teach me about life, and help me out," said Tan Gang, a boy who was often teased for being oversensitive. "In times of failure, an older brother's encouragement would be even more effective than a parent's."

"I'd like an older brother, because he could help me support our parents when they're old," said Feng Yongqin, a girl who usually scored low on tests.

## Children of the One-Child Policy

This is an ethnographic study of the consequences of the world's first state-mandated fertility transition. Because of China's one-child policy, the vast majority of urban Chinese youth born after 1979 are singletons. I spent 27 months between 1997 and 2002 examining the effects of near-universal singleton status on the subjectivities, experiences, and aspirations of teenagers in Dalian, a large coastal city in northeastern China.[2] I found that what mattered most was not their singleton status per se, but rather the fact that they were singletons in a society used to large families. China's one-child policy was designed to create a generation of ambitious, well-educated children who would lead their country into the First World. This strategy has succeeded, but at a price. Heavy parental investment enabled many singletons to attain First World living standards and educational opportunities. But singletons' ambitions often clashed with the limitations of their Third World parents and society. Children of China's one-child policy became First World people too quickly for their families and society to keep up. They faced intense parental pressure and competition for elite status in the educational system and the job market, as well as the accusation that they were spoiled because they had unrealistically high expectations. This situation was common among young people in many societies with declining fertility, but it was especially intense in Chinese cities because of the abruptness and near-universality of the fertility transition hastened by the one-child policy. My study of Chinese singletons highlights how the cultural model of modernization associated with the fertility transition is both a cause and an effect of the unrealistically high expectations often said to characterize modern youth worldwide.

Modernization is not only an economic program, but also a cultural model internalized by those hoping to rise to the top of the capitalist world system. When this cultural model is adopted by the bulk of a population, large families that invest little in each child are replaced with small families that invest heavily in each child. This process, which demographers call the "fertility transition,"[3] has been documented in all First World societies[4] and many Third World societies aspiring to join the First World.[5] China, however, is the only society where the fertility transition was hastened by strictly enforced birth quotas. Rather than waiting for modernization to produce low fertility, the Chinese state has used low fertility as a means to accelerate modernization. In 1970, when population control policies began, China's total fertility rate[6] was 5.8 births per woman; in 1980, two years after the start of the one-child policy, China's total fertility rate was down to 2.3 births per woman.[7] Rural residents had higher fertility than urban residents even before the one-child policy, and families with two or more children remained the norm in rural areas, where the need for sons to provide farm labor, protection from crime, and old age support made the one-child policy difficult to enforce.[8] In urban areas, however, most children born after 1979 had no siblings.[9] Many urban Dalian singletons were the grandchildren of rural migrants. These singletons' parents were not only the first generation in their families to be constrained by the one-child policy, but also the first generation to be subjected to the modernizing forces of urban life. The combination of these factors created a stark contrast between the large families of those born in the 1950s and the small families of those born in the 1980s. Among the high school and junior high school students I surveyed in 1999, 94 percent[10] of respondents were singletons, while 81 percent[11] of respondents' fathers and 82 percent[12] of respondents' mothers had at least three siblings.

Most studies of China's one-child policy have focused on its demographic effects.[13] While such studies present powerful portraits of the scale and scope of China's state-mandated fertility transition, they provide little insight into the lives of the singletons that transition produced. Studies of the one-child policy's social effects have explored parents' responses to the one-child policy,[14] compared the personalities of singleton and non-singleton children,[15] and detailed particular aspects of singletons' childhood consumption patterns.[16] Missing, however, is an ethnography that examines the subjectivities and experiences of Chinese singletons as they come of age. In this book, I address the question of what it is like to grow up as a singleton in a society used to large families.

## Research Methods

I could have conducted my study in just about any Chinese city, since the rate of compliance with the one-child policy was high in most urban areas of China. I chose Dalian because its local dialects were very similar to Mandarin Chinese (my native dialect, as well as China's official dialect), and because it had an extensive bus system that allowed me to get around quickly despite my inability to ride a bicycle and my unwillingness to rely on taxi rides that could prevent me from traveling with people who could not afford them.

My research methods consisted primarily of a survey and participant observation in homes and classrooms. I worked in Dalian as an unpaid English conversation teacher at a vocational high school, a junior high school, and a non-keypoint college prep high school in exchange for the opportunity to survey students and observe their classes and other activities. In the case of the junior high school and the college prep high school, I simply walked in and introduced myself to school administrators, who were convinced of my legitimacy after seeing a letter from the office of Harvard University's Dean of Students that certified my enrollment at Harvard, and after asking their English teachers to verify that I was fluent in English. In the case of the vocational high school, I was introduced to administrators by a friend who had been the college professor of some of the school's teachers.

Held during periods that were normally used for study hall, the English conversation classes I offered consisted of English language games and lively discussions of whatever topics the students wanted to discuss. I visited some homerooms (*banji*) once a week, some once a month, and some once a year. I also spent several days each month sitting in homerooms, observing students' activities throughout the day. Each homeroom consisted of 40–60 students who sat at their desks during the bulk of the school day, while different teachers came in to teach different subjects.

In 1999, I conducted a survey of most of the homerooms in grades 10–11 at the vocational high school and all of the homerooms in grades 8–9 at the junior high school and grades 10–12 at the regular college prep high school. I received completed surveys from most of the students attending the schools where I taught. A comparison of my survey sample with school enrollment lists shows that 9 percent[17] of students in the homerooms I surveyed either refused to fill out my survey or were not in class at the time I conducted the survey. In each homeroom I surveyed, I explained my research, distributed the survey, had students fill it out, and answered questions about the survey questions and my research. Whenever I refer to findings from "my survey" or "the author's 1999 survey" in this book, I am referring to this survey, which asked 2,273 students about their attitudes, educational histories, consumption patterns, family structures, socioeconomic backgrounds, and interactions with their parents. Each survey question had a different number of respondents, since not every respondent wrote a legible answer to every survey question, and since 191 students received incomplete surveys because of photocopying errors. I have excluded missing data from all percentage calculations based on my survey.

According to my survey results, all respondents were between the ages of 13 and 20, 94 percent[18] of them had no siblings, 5 percent[19] had one sibling,[20] and 98 percent[21] were Han, the ethnic group that comprised 92 percent[22] of the Chinese population and 84 percent of Liaoning Province[23] in 2000. The average age of survey respondents was 16.[24] The average age of survey respondents' mothers was 43,[25] and the average age of their fathers was 45.[26] Each school contributed about a third of the respondents to my survey.[27] The junior high school and college prep high school had balanced gender ratios, while respondents from the vocational high school were 71 percent[28] female because their school specialized in female-dominated majors such as business and tourism. Thus, my total survey sample is 58 percent[29] female. I break my statistical findings down by gender or school only when dealing with survey responses that vary significantly by gender or school.

The first people I got to know in Dalian were teachers, students, and administrators at the schools where I taught, and random staff members, businesspeople, and fellow customers I met at shops, markets, malls, parks, restaurants, bus stops, post offices, internet cafes, and photocopying service centers. After these initial contacts introduced me to their friends, relatives, and acquaintances as a "Chinese American doctoral student," I received many invitations to go to teenagers' homes to tutor them in English or provide information about how to go abroad. I received even more invitations after several Dalian newspapers and television stations publicized my work as an unpaid English teacher. During the bulk of my fieldwork, I lived with a junior high school student I tutored, his factory worker father, and his mother, who invited me to live with her family after several long conversations at the small shop where she worked as a salesclerk after retiring from her factory. I also lived with eight other families for periods ranging from a few days to several weeks.

In response to the questions that most people asked me when we first met, I gave answers that highlighted how I fit Chinese cultural models of the kind of life story someone like me should have: "I was born in Taiwan. I'm a singleton. When I was three years old, my parents took me to America, where I attended primary school, junior high school, college, and a graduate program in anthropology. Now I'm here to do research for my doctoral dissertation." I explained that I was doing "social research" (*shehui diaocha*), a term made respectable by a tradition of Chinese sociology identified both with academic professionalism and with the Chinese state's efforts at social reform.[30] While I told the truth about my autobiographical details, I did not present them in the same way I usually did to people in the United States, in terms of a series of choices made in an idiosyncratic quest for a unique personal identity. Rather, I packaged my background into the same kind of narrative commonly used by urban Dalian people my age to describe their own life stories, and presented myself as a successful conformist who followed what was widely recognized as a laudable academic path to upward mobility. I tried to be very noncommittal about my ethnopolitical identity. I was called everything from "American" (*meiguoren*) to "foreigner" (*waiguoren*) to "foreign student" (*waiguo liuxuesheng*) to "imitation foreign devil" (*jia yangguizi*) to "banana person" (*xiangjiaoren*) to "Chinese with U.S. citizenship" (*meiji huaren*) to "Chinese descendant" (*huayi*) to "patriotic overseas Chinese" (*aiguo huaqiao*) to "Taiwan compatriot" (*Taiwan tongbao*) to "Chinese student returned from study abroad" (*zhongguo liuxuesheng*). When asked to choose between these labels, I said that I would accept any label my questioners deemed appropriate. When asked, "Are you Chinese or American?" I replied, "Both." When asked, "If there were a war between China and America, who would you support?" I replied "Neither, because I would not support war." When pressed further, I explained that I adhered to a concept of identity as fluid, shifting, subjective, and fragmented, and expounded on anthropological theories of ethnicity and nationalism. With this explanation, I usually managed to change the subject, either to further discussions of anthropological theories and case studies from all over the world for those who were interested, or to something unrelated to my ethnopolitical loyalties for those who were bored.

While many urban Dalian residents seemed fascinated with my academic and ethnopolitical background, it was primarily my role as an English teacher that led them to invite me into their homes, schools, and lives. Most people addressed me as "Teacher Fong" when we first met. English was vital for success in the educational system, the job market, and efforts to go abroad. College and high school entrance exams included difficult foreign language tests. Though students were allowed to take these tests in Japanese or Russian instead of English, few schools offered courses in languages other than English, which was taught as a core subject at the college, high school, junior high school, and elementary schools attended by most urban Chinese students born in the 1980s and 1990s. Many instruction manuals, research materials, scientific textbooks, and Internet websites were available only in English. As the dominant language of the First World, English was seen as the most versatile foreign language, since even foreigners from non-Anglophone countries were likely to have studied English. Most employers gave preference to applicants with a good command of English. Non-Asians living in Dalian told me that they were often approached by strangers who wanted to practice speaking English. Teenagers used the term *waiyu*, which means "foreign language," as a synonym for "English" (*yingyu*), and sometimes said things like "He speaks both *waiyu* and Japanese."

Most tutors were local high school teachers or college students. As a doctoral student from an American university, I was considered better qualified than most other English tutors, and my refusal to accept payment was icing on the cake. I was swamped with requests for tutoring. I granted those requests that seemed most likely to contribute to my goal of having equal numbers of teenaged boys and girls from a wide range of achievement levels and socioeconomic backgrounds represented among the students I tutored. Over the course of my fieldwork, I was invited to the homes of 107 young people, usually to provide tutoring or advice about how they might get opportunities to study or work abroad. Because of time constraints, however, I lost touch with most of them after one or several visits. I maintained long-term friendships only with the 31 families that developed the strongest rapport with me. The rapport that transformed members of these families from acquaintances into friends was based on intersubjective factors (such as trust, emotional compatibility, and a shared sense of humor) that did not seem to correlate with quantifiable variables like income, occupational status, or educational attainment. Thus, the sample of 31 families that I ended up befriending was about as socioeconomically diverse as my original sample of 107 families. I visited these 31 families on a regular basis, and still keep in touch with them by telephone and e-mail. All but two of them were single-child nuclear or stem families. Most of their children were teenagers at the time I met them, though the youngest was 10 and the oldest was 28.

To avoid commodifying my friendship with students and parents and to prevent them from feeling that they could not afford my company, I refused payment for my tutoring. I explained that their teaching me about Chinese life was more than enough compensation for my teaching them about American life and the English language. Most students readily accepted this explanation, but most parents did not. Often, when I tutored a student for the first time, I had to fight off parents who tried to give me money by shoving it in my pocket or backpack. One mother chased me down the street and threw money at me; another dropped money from the window of her fourth-floor apartment once I had reached the street below. When forced to take money, I returned it or presented its equivalent in gifts of fruit, chocolate, or study materials at my next visit. Gradually, parents realized that my refusal of money was genuine, and not the usual pretense required by courtesy norms. They became comfortable with this once we had established long-term relationships of generalized reciprocity. I accepted gifts such as books, clothes, souvenirs, and hair accessories that were presented as tokens of friendship, and reciprocated with tokens of similar economic value and social meaning on later occasions. Meals created superb research opportunities and warm commensal sentiments, so I accepted invitations to eat whenever possible, and sometimes brought fruit or chocolate as my contribution to holiday feasts.

Students at the schools I studied did not want their classmates to know that I tutored them in their homes, for fear of being perceived as recipients of favoritism in the English conversation classes I taught. They asked me to maintain the same discretion that was expected when they received private tutoring from their regular teachers. Powerful cadres wanted me to be discreet about the fact that I tutored their children, and thus prevent my less powerful friends from asking them for favors by invoking my name or asking me to request favors on their behalf. Many people wanted me to spend more time with them and less with others. Some elite parents disapproved of how I "wasted time" associating with non-elite families. Some non-elite students and parents suspected me of providing greater assistance to families that might be able to give me valuable gifts and favors. Many people told me that it was fine for me to write and publish about their perspectives and experiences as long as they were not personally identifiable, but asked that I avoid talking about them with anyone who knew them. To minimize jealousies, indiscretions, and gossip, I told people as little as possible about my relationships with others in Dalian.[31] By cultivating a habit of discretion about my social networks, I also made it less likely that they would be affected if I got into trouble.

I always carried a small notebook in my pocket, and frequently took notes. I spoke with people in Chinese if they had no ability or desire to practice English, and in a combination of English and Chinese if they had some English ability and wanted to practice it. Dalian people almost always spoke to each other in Mandarin Chinese or Dalian area dialects, regardless of their knowledge of foreign languages or other dialects of Chinese. In this book, I have translated everything that was said in Chinese, broken English, or a combination of Chinese and English into fluent American English.[32] Quoted dialogues represent conversations that I jotted down either while they were spoken or several hours afterwards.

Some adults became nervous, and many teenagers made fun of me, the first time they saw me take out my notebook. Businesspeople feared that I might be an undercover journalist or official trying to expose their illegal business practices. I explained that my constant note-taking was part of my dissertation research, offered to stop taking notes if it made them uncomfortable, and promised that I would never identify them by their real names or easily identifiable details in anything I published (except for the names of public figures that I never met, and the names of authors whose published work I cite, all names in this book are pseudonyms). After they got to know me well enough to feel that I was harmless, most people got used to my note-taking, and ignored it.

The sample of students I surveyed or befriended did not contain enough non-singletons to provide an adequate basis for extensive comparisons with singletons. Therefore, this book is primarily about the experiences of single-child families. My observations and surveys of the small number of two-child families in my sample led me to believe that two-child families experienced many of the same pressures and dilemmas that one-child families experienced, with slightly less intensity. While a comparison of singleton respondents with respondents who had one sibling indicated that singleton status correlated with greater freedom from household chores and respondents' belief that parents spoiled them, the correlations were small (see Table 1). The difference between having one sibling and having no siblings was incremental rather than absolute. Parental pressure and investment were diluted when shared by two children, but still considerably more intense than when shared by four children. The key issue I explore in this book is therefore not the difference between one-child families and two-child families, but rather the difference between the small families of late 1990s teenagers and the much larger families of their parents.

## A City of Migrants

Dalian is young by Chinese standards. Previously the site of small, sparsely populated fishing villages, Dalian's existence as a port city began when Russia started building Dalian's harbor in 1899, after acquiring the area that became Dalian as part of the Liaodong Leasehold in 1898. This area was transferred to Japan in 1905 as a result of the Russo-Japanese War of 1904. The Soviet Union took the area from Japan in 1945, and returned it to China in 1954. Almost all the Japanese and Russian colonizers left by the time China regained official control over Dalian, which developed into a center of heavy industry, attracting migrants from the nearby countryside and from throughout northeastern China and Shandong Province. The population of the three urban and

TABLE 1
Household Chores Done by Singleton Respondents and Those with One Sibling

| | Singleton | One sibling |
|---|---|---|
| Percentage who indicated they cooked | 13% ($N$ = 2,030)* | 20% ($N$ = 118)* |
| Percentage who indicated they cleaned | 45% ($N$ = 2,032)* | 55% ($N$ = 118)* |
| Percentage who indicated they did laundry | 37% ($N$ = 2,027)** | 51% ($N$ = 118)** |
| Percentage who indicated they were "spoiled" (*guan*) by at least one parent | 67% ($N$ = 1,992)** | 54% ($N$ = 114)** |

SOURCE: The author's 1999 survey.
* $p < 0.05$; ** $p < 0.01$.

two semi-urban districts of Dalian increased from 559,010 in 1949 to 1,977,214 in 1999.[33] In addition, the population of the rural counties, small towns, and semi-rural areas[34] under the jurisdiction of Dalian's government increased from 1,943,176 in 1949 to 3,455,199 in 1999.[35] Archives maintained by Dalian's governmental bureaus usually classified Zhongshan, Xigang, and Shahekou (the three completely urban districts) and Ganjingzi and Lushunkou (the two partly urban, partly rural districts) as the urban center (*shinei*) of the Dalian area. I use the term "urban Dalian" to refer to these five districts (where I did most of my research), and the term "Dalian area" to refer to the administrative area known as Dalian City (*Dalian Shi*), which lumps the five districts of urban Dalian with the rural and semi-rural areas of Jinzhou District, Kaifa District, Wafangdian City, Pulandian City, Zhuanghe City, and Changhai County. While urban Dalian occupied 1,062 square kilometers (roughly the size of Hong Kong), the Dalian area occupied 12,574 square kilometers (roughly the size of the Bahamas).[36]

Many urban Dalian residents were sent to nearby rural areas (often their own natal or ancestral villages) during the Cultural Revolution (1966–1976), but most returned to urban Dalian by the 1980s. Dalian's urbanization intensified after China's economic reforms began in the late 1970s. Dalian's government invested heavily in an extensive, efficient bus system that connected every part of urban Dalian, and in the replacement of farmland, wilderness areas, and decrepit housing with modern high-rise apartment buildings. When real estate developers demolished a building, they had to give its residents payment or new housing in exchange for their old homes. Many residents welcomed such deals, which enabled them to move into newer, more comfortable housing. Because of its short history, ethnic homogeneity, extensive bus system, and rapid housing development, urban Dalian had no slums or ghettos. Some wealthy company managers lived across the street from impoverished workers they had recently laid off.

In 1999, urban Dalian ranked as the second most populous urban area in Liaoning Province, and the fourteenth most populous urban area in China.[37] Dalian had much in common with other large Chinese cities. Because of their migration histories, though, many Dalian families experienced even more rapid modernization, urbanization, fertility decline, and upward mobility than their counterparts in older Chinese cities. In the 1990s, when the Chinese government started dismantling policies that had protected state enterprises from global market forces, many cities—particularly those in the northern industrial "rust belt"—began to suffer widespread unemployment. Geographically and economically part of the "rust belt," Dalian was not spared the blows of economic restructuring; 34 percent[38] of the respondents to my survey indicated that they had at least one parent who was laid off or retired. Still, as a port city with pleasant parks and beaches, strong trade networks, a well-developed transportation infrastructure, and ambitious, progressive officials, Dalian weathered these blows better than most of its inland counterparts.

To attract foreign and domestic investment, trade, and tourism, Dalian officials dubbed their city the "Hong Kong of the North," and spent the 1990s transforming Dalian from a center of heavy industry into a "city of soccer and fashion" by aggressively expanding the service sector to compensate for unemployment in the industrial sector. Dalian's government invested heavily in the development of malls, hotels, parks, squares, beaches, sports, schools, paved roads, communications, entertainment, tourist attractions, public transportation, and high-rise office buildings.[39] The government's efforts succeeded in keeping the local economy relatively strong despite the factory bankruptcies that caused many middle-aged people to lose their jobs, pensions, and health insurance. Thus, even while their parents became unemployed and unemployable, young people were able to find work in rapidly expanding, high-paying service sector fields such as tourism, hospitality, education, commerce, catering, finance, trade, business, and communications.

Most urban Dalian residents were children or grandchildren of migrants from less developed areas of China. Among respondents to my survey, 7 percent[40] had at least one parent born in the countryside, 92 percent[41] had at least one parent who had lived in the countryside, 43 percent[42] had at least one grandparent who had worked as a farmer,[43] and 66 percent[44] indicated that their *jiguan* (paternal grandfather's hometown) was not in urban Dalian or any of its surrounding rural areas. Like rural residents, migrants from the countryside were likely to have high fertility rates. Unlike families in older cities that began their transition from high to low fertility as soon as birth control technologies became widely available in the 1960s, most urban Dalian families did not start their fertility transitions until the 1970s, when population control policies began. The fertility transition was thus even more abrupt in urban Dalian than in older Chinese cities.

## The Capitalist World System and the Cultural Model of Modernization

The ambitions of students I knew in urban Dalian derived from their internalization of the cultural model of modernization (*xiandaihua*). Cognitive psychologists[45] and psychological anthropologists[46] have proposed that human motivations arise from cultural models (also called "schemas" or "scripts") that create narratives, expectations, and goals out of the chaos of experience. As Claudia Strauss and Naomi Quinn have argued,[47] cultural models can be embodied and taken for granted, like what Pierre Bourdieu called "habitus";[48] unlike habitus, however, cultural models can be consciously perceived. An individual's actions are motivated by interactions between countless cultural models with varying degrees of psychological force. These cultural models can promote, contradict, or invoke each other. Failure to attain the goals generated by particularly powerful cultural models causes suffering, while the attainment of those goals causes happiness. The content and motivational force of any given cultural model is determined by a combination of cultural meanings and individual experiences, and subject to change in response to changing circumstances. Meanings, experiences, and circumstances are in turn shaped by social, political, and economic forces.

The political and economic forces that have made the cultural model of modernization salient for many individuals worldwide can best be understood with reference to Immanuel Wallerstein's analysis of the "capitalist world system."[49] Beginning with the emergence of capitalism in Western Europe during the fifteenth century, this system spread until it encompassed almost every area of the world. The capitalist world system is based on an international division of labor that divides the world into "core," "peripheral," and "semi-peripheral" regions. Core regions dominate, extracting raw materials and cheap labor from peripheral regions. Declining core regions and rising peripheral regions are considered "semi-peripheral"; they exploit peripheral regions, but are also exploited by core regions. Peripheral regions sometimes become core regions and vice versa. There can also be core and peripheral areas within each country.[50] Despite the historical variability of various nations' ranking within the capitalist world system, however, this system is ultimately defined by the inequalities that structure relations between regions. By the end of the twentieth century, the core regions (now known as the First World) had used a combination of military force, imperialism, colonization, and trade to incorporate just about all other regions into the capitalist world system.

This system promotes the cultural model of modernization, which motivates people to desire First World affluence and believe that participation in a modern economy will enable them to attain that affluence. A modern economy is characterized by high-density urban living conditions, long hours of work away from home for women as well as men, a system that prevents children from engaging in economically productive labor, a competitive job market that demands a long and expensive period of formal education, and constant growth in the production and consumption of goods and services. These factors promote low fertility by making the rearing and education of children extremely costly to their parents. These factors are also promoted by low fertility, which improves children's ability to compete in the capitalist world system by enabling them to get a heavily concentrated dose of parental investment. While the conditions of a modern economy are designed to maximize the efficient production and control of the labor power needed by capitalism,[51] the development of a modern economy can also be the goal of regimes with strongly anti-capitalist ideologies (including socialism, communism, and Maoism) that nevertheless aim to compete with capitalist regimes. Though the development of a modern economy does not guarantee success in the capitalist world system, it is a condition that must be met before a society can even have a chance at attaining the dominant position enjoyed by core regions. Most individuals worldwide want to attain that dominance because it will help them attain prestige, pleasure, security, affluence, and good health, all of which are goals of powerful cultural models that existed even before the establishment of the capitalist world system. Individuals living in a society isolated from the capitalist world system could attain those goals by following local cultural models of religion, politics, kinship, and economic production. But once a society is incorporated into the capitalist world system, standards of prestige, pleasure, security, affluence, and good health are redefined and inflated, so that modernization becomes the best, and sometimes the only, means of reaching these goals.

Max Weber wrote that "A man does not 'by nature' wish to earn more and more money, but simply to live as he is accustomed to live and earn as much as is necessary for that purpose."[52] Marshall Sahlins has argued that the capitalist world system makes people feel poor by convincing them that they have "Infinite Needs."[53] Though not as carefree as the hunter-gatherers that Sahlins called the "original affluent society," most Chinese people at least did not desire the rapid technological growth that the cultural model of modernization could bring until they were confronted with the superior military and economic power of First World countries during the nineteenth century.[54] China was first integrated into the capitalist world system during the Opium War (1839–1842), when The British government forced the Chinese government to allow the sale of opium in China. Beginning with its defeat in the Opium War, the Chinese government made a series of concessions of money, territory, sovereignty, and trade rights to a variety of foreign countries, including Austria, England, France, Germany, Italy, Japan, Russia, Spain, and the United States. The social, political, and economic problems caused by these concessions led to the fall of the Qing dynasty in 1911. The Nationalist-dominated government that replaced the Qing dynasty was in turn replaced in 1949 by Mao Zedong's Communist government, after a bitter civil war. Under the Maoist government, China joined the Soviet bloc, which tried to establish a socialist world system separate from the capitalist world system. Despite its Marxist ideology, however, the socialist world system bore many similarities to its capitalist counterpart, including a hierarchy based on the extent to which member societies had adopted a modern economy. Disillusioned,

Chinese leaders promoted autarky during the 1960s in an attempt to remove China from all world systems. Mao Zedong's government (1949–1976) severely restricted foreign trade, travel, and information that might cause yearnings for First World living standards. In their introduction to a volume on the role of Western European and North American imports as status symbols in Latin American societies, Benjamin Orlove and Arnold J. Bauer argued that, unlike Latin America, Eastern Europe, and some parts of the Middle East, China had escaped the allure of European and North American goods by avoiding the "strong Europeanization of elites and other groups."[55] Maoist leaders hoped that autarky would keep Chinese people from internalizing a cultural model of modernization that would make them feel impoverished.

This strategy worked on some parents I knew in urban Dalian, who bitterly contrasted their 1990s "poverty" with their 1960s "affluence." At first I found this perplexing in light of the fact that they were materially much better off than they had been prior to the post-Mao economic reforms. When Li Na's mother told me, "I never thought I would be this poor. I'm glad we weren't allowed to have more than one child because as it is we can barely support the one we have," I pointed out that her family now had a color television, a telephone, a washing machine, their own bathroom, and meat at nearly every meal, all of which she had on other occasions told me were unimaginable in her own childhood. She replied,

> Of course we didn't have these things, but no one else did either, so we didn't even think about them. My Pa was the only one working, and he had my Ma and the three of us children to support, but we were still better off than a lot of families that had more children. Now both my husband and I are working, but we can barely support one child. When I was a child, schooling was almost free. Now Li Na comes home asking for more money for school fees every few weeks. She sees a friend with name brand clothing and wants it too. Our neighbors have home theater systems, and it's embarrassing that we don't. I never felt this poor when I was small.

Yet Maoist attempts to maintain autarky ultimately failed because Maoist leaders were themselves motivated by the cultural model of modernization. This cultural model made them want to "catch up" with the industrial and military standards of the First World by implementing drastic policies like the Great Leap Forward, which caused three years of devastating famine (1959–1961). After Mao Zedong's death in 1976, Chinese leaders stopped resisting integration into the capitalist world system. Instead, they sought to raise China's position within this system by developing the same modern economy that propelled the core regions to dominance. While the selling of cheap labor to the First World was a major source of economic growth, Chinese leaders did not see it as the ultimate goal of China's integration into the capitalist world system. Rather, they saw it as a short-term means to their long-term goal of having China gain a dominant position in the capitalist world system, not as a purveyor of cheap labor, but as a center of finance, technology, and highly educated, well-paid professionals able to compete on an even footing with their First World counterparts. Though they have managed to transform China from a peripheral region to a semi-peripheral one, Chinese leaders will not be satisfied until China joins the First World as a core region. Instead of allowing the Chinese population to keep producing cheap labor by maintaining high fertility patterns, the Chinese state enforced a rapid fertility transition designed to cultivate a generation of "high-quality" people with the resources and ambition to join the global elite. While this strategy was most effective in urban areas, it was also targeted at the countryside, where fertility limitation policies clashed sharply with rural cultural models that emphasized the need for sons to work the land, provide protection from crime, and support their parents in old age.

Though the state-controlled media continued to encourage patriotism, they also presented glamorous images of the First World, partly because such images were popular with the audience, and partly because learning from the First World was a state-sanctioned modernization strategy. Magazines, newspapers, and television programs featured First World experts, First World sports and entertainment news, positive reports about how things were done in the First World, and news about successful Chinese projects modeled on similar projects abroad. Teenagers focused on the positive aspects of life abroad, such as the luxuriousness of cars, housing, and commodities, even when the media also presented negative aspects, such as crime, poverty, and racism.

"You see, not all Americans are rich," I told vocational high school student Liu Yang as we watched a news segment about an American slum in 1998.

"Really? Then why are there so many cars parked in that slum?" he rejoined. "In China, not even well-off families can afford a car."

Commodities and name brands produced by companies from the First World were perceived to be of higher quality than those produced by Chinese companies, and even those that were not of higher quality basked in the halo effect of those that were. Chinese businesses tried to enhance their appeal by emphasizing the foreign connections (real or fictitious) of their products by putting the flags, maps, place names, and historical figures of developed countries on their signs and advertisements and on the products themselves. Some wealthy people bought products with foreign name brands rather than Chinese ones whenever possible, even though foreign brands were more expensive than Chinese brands. As vocational high school student Zheng Yi said to his parents in 2000, "Why would I want a Chinese brand when all Chinese brands are just poor imitations of foreign brands?"

The fanciest department stores, supermarkets, malls, hotels, and eateries in urban Dalian were at least partly owned by foreign companies. Because salaries abroad were many times higher than salaries for similar work in China, those who returned from working abroad were extremely wealthy by Chinese standards, as were those who received remittances from family members who lived abroad. Many students and parents told me that "anyone who returns from abroad is coated with gold." They often saw foreign tourists, businesspeople, and even students spending money freely at the fanciest stores, hotels, and restaurants. First World money was prestigious because of its stability and high exchange value, because of its association with an alluring world of foreign wealth, and because of the legal and economic obstacles that kept it out of the hands of ordinary people.[56] Unable to obtain real U.S. dollars, some teenagers bought clothing, pens, posters, and decorations with images of U.S. dollars on them. Chinese people who worked in at least partially foreign-owned companies or in fields such as shipping, trade, travel, translation, and tourism had much higher salaries than their counterparts working for Chinese employers who did not deal with the First World. Those fluent in First World languages got the best jobs, and those who returned from study abroad got much better jobs than they would have gotten with comparable Chinese education.

Bombarded by images of First World lifestyles, teenagers often talked about the inferiority of their lives in comparison with the lives of people in the First World. Urban Dalian people were much better off than most Chinese people, and China was better off than many other Third World societies. Yet even relatively wealthy urban Dalian people complained about being "poor," and lamented that China was "hell" compared to the First World, which was "heaven." They judged their own socioeconomic conditions not only by comparison with those of others around them, but also by comparison with those of the First World. Everyday conversations in urban Dalian were peppered with references to the gap between life in China and life abroad. At first I thought this was because of my presence, but after a while I noticed that even strangers in buses and shops who did not know about my American identity talked to each other about how "Chinese people are poor, unlike foreigners," and "This is just how Chinese people have to live." Some teenagers also admitted that they made invidious comparisons between life in China and life abroad even when I was not around. After centuries of conflict and negotiation, the core regions of the capitalist world system had finally succeeded in forcing Chinese people to internalize the cultural model of modernization.

Chinese leaders presented mandatory low fertility, rising inequalities, and the loss of jobs, pensions, and medical insurance as sacrifices that Chinese people had to make for the construction of a modern economy that would eventually bring First World affluence. Many teenagers and their parents complained that such sacrifices were excessive or unfairly distributed. No one, however, questioned the desirability of First World affluence itself. The people I knew in urban Dalian had internalized the capitalist world system's tendency to rank all places by their respective levels of modernization. Within China, urban areas ranked above rural areas, and wealthier cities ranked above less wealthy ones. Dalian ranked above most other places in China, but still below Shanghai, Beijing, and many cities in the fast-developing South. All developed countries ranked above China, and were conflated under the term *waiguo*. This term literally meant "foreign countries," but its use in everyday conversations approximated the English term "First World," lumping together all societies more developed than China, and excluding all those with development levels less than or equal to China's.[57] Despite the Chinese government's friendly relations with many Third World countries, the existence of countries less developed than China was ignored in popular discourses on "foreign countries."

French demographer Alfred Sauvy coined the term "Third World" (*tiers monde*) in 1952, when he published an article in the leftist French newspaper *L'Observateur* that drew an analogy between the non-industrialized countries and the "Third Estate" (*tiers état*), which in pre-revolutionary France referred to commoners (the "First Estate" consisted of clergymen, and the "Second Estate" consisted of the nobility).[58] By the 1970s, the term "Third World" was widely used in Western discourse to refer to the peripheral regions of the world.[59] During the Cold War, the term "Third World" referred especially to peripheral regions that were not aligned with either the capitalist bloc ("First World") or the socialist bloc ("Second World"). China was sometimes considered part of the "Second World," but that term and the alternative world system it implied disappeared with the collapse of the Soviet Union.

I use the term "First World" to represent the prestige, affluence, and core region status that people I knew in urban Dalian desired, and the term "Third World" to represent the poverty and peripheral region status that they saw as characteristic of China. Though they themselves did not use these terms, they frequently talked about how China was a "poor" (*qiong*), "backward" (*luohou*) "developing country" (*fazhanzhong guojia*) that needed to "develop" (*fazhan*) and "modernize" (*xiandaihua*) in order to "catch up to" (*ganshang*) "rich / developed countries," (*fada guojia*), which were also known as "advanced countries" (*xianjin guojia*) or simply as "foreign countries" (*waiguo*). These classifications did not necessarily coincide with geopolitical boundaries. When talking about "foreign countries" (*waiguo*), they seldom mentioned African, South Asian, Latin American, or Pacific Islander societies, but sometimes drew examples from Hong Kong, Macao, and Taiwan (territories that they adamantly maintained were part of China). As terms that refer more to living conditions than to specific geographical areas or political entities, "First World" and "Third World" are the English phrases that best capture popular Chinese ideas about the "haves" and "have-nots" of the world.

As a globally widespread dream of orderly progress toward First World conditions, the cultural model of modernization differs from "modernity," a term which anthropologists[60] have used to describe the diverse, unpredictable, often undesirable situations various individuals and societies experience in the capitalist world system. Though different modernities vary in the degree to which they adhere to the ideal path outlined by the cultural model of modernization, this cultural model is still perceived as a program with clear goals and predictable outcomes. Studies of many impoverished areas worldwide[61] (including some rural areas of China)[62] have reported despair and disillusionment with the promises of modernization. Most people I knew in urban Dalian, however, still believed in those promises. Rather than attributing the suffering caused by the Great Leap Forward famine (1959–1961), the Cultural Revolution (1966–1976), and the growing inequalities of the post-Mao era (1976–present) to the cultural model of modernization itself, they perceived such suffering as the result of Chinese people's failure to adhere closely enough to the path that First World societies took to the top of the capitalist world system. Despite the problems it caused, the cultural model of modernization remained credible because it did seem to be delivering on its promise of upward mobility, particularly for residents of relatively prosperous cities like Dalian. Unlike societies that experienced more widespread disillusionment about the cultural model of modernization, China has enjoyed high economic growth rates since it adopted this model in the 1950s.[63] Ironically, the fact that China managed to maintain its upward mobility in the capitalist world system even while many other Third World and postsocialist societies experienced devastating declines was due at least partly to the Chinese government's autarkic tendencies, which protected China from neocolonialism, economic dependency, and the "austerity," "shock therapy," and "structural adjustment" modernization schemes imposed by organizations like the World Bank and the International Monetary Fund.[64]

People I knew in urban Dalian defined "modernization" in the same way First World modernization theorists[65] did: as progress toward the adoption of a modern economy that is likely to improve a society's position in the capitalist world system. Such progress could be measured objectively by statistical indicators of health, education, living standards, and per capita Gross Domestic Product, and subjectively by the degree of a society's cultural resemblance to the core region countries widely acknowledged as "developed" and "modern." Anthropologists have criticized terms like "development," "modernization," and "the postsocialist transition" for promoting pernicious and erroneous assumptions about a desirable, inevitable, universal, and unilinear evolution toward the conditions of the First World.[66] But these were the very assumptions that people I knew in urban Dalian embraced in their quest to join the First World. Though they resented the fact that China was far behind the First World according to the cultural model of modernization, they accepted this cultural model as the only reality possible. As David Harvey has argued, global capitalism has managed to convince many people worldwide that "There is no alternative."[67] In China, as in many societies caught in the capitalist world system, the cultural model of modernization enjoyed the status of what Pierre Bourdieu called "doxa," the "self-evident and natural order which goes without saying and therefore goes unquestioned."[68]

## Representations

Chapter 1 of this book focuses on how the cultural model of modernization affected the lives of eight teenagers, while the other chapters explore how political, economic, and demographic factors have made that cultural model salient for many teenagers and parents in urban Dalian. Chapter 2 examines the role of the fertility transition as an integral part of the cultural model of modernization. Chapter 3 shows how the educational system became a crucible of competition for the elite status singletons were socialized to expect. Chapter 4 explores the implications of low fertility for cultural models of love, filial duty, and parental investment. Chapter 5 discusses how singletons were accused of being "spoiled" and "unable to adjust" when their high expectations clashed with the limited opportunities available to them.

My portrait of the demographic patterns prevalent among single-child families in urban Dalian is based on statistical records published by Chinese governmental bureaus[69] and on the results of my survey. My portrait of the individual lives that helped produce these demographic patterns is based on participant observation. Demographic statistics are useful for characterizing the broad patterns that emerge from the diverse strategies of individual agents. Ethnography is useful for providing glimpses of the agency, emotions, and cultural models of individuals. By combining qualitative and quantitative approaches, I hope to capture the nuances of individual experiences and subjectivities without losing sight of the patterns that structure and constrain them.

The schools where I conducted my survey enrolled students from a wide variety of socioeconomic backgrounds, though the most disadvantaged teenagers (such as those who were disabled or lacked urban registration) and the most elite teenagers (who were more likely to attend private schools, keypoint high schools, or study abroad programs) were underrepresented. Because of the mid-level statuses of the schools where I conducted research, demographic findings based on my survey did not differ drastically from those based on census data and official records published by Dalian's government.[70] Dalian's educational system divided high schools into six ranks of prestige. The non-keypoint college prep high school I surveyed belonged in the second most prestigious category, and the vocational high school I surveyed belonged in the fifth most prestigious category. The junior high school I surveyed had the widest range of achievement levels and socioeconomic statuses, since it admitted all primary school graduates in its neighborhood without considering their exam scores or ability to pay. It was generally considered an average junior high school.[71] Almost all urban Dalian teenagers attended primary and junior high schools, and most went on to secondary education as well (see Chapter 3 for more about Dalian's educational categories and school enrollment rates).

The tutoring and information I provided was only useful to those who believed they had some chance of going abroad, scoring high enough on an entrance exam to get into colleges or high schools (most of which required foreign language skills), or getting work that required English skills. I suspect that this belief was widespread among urban singletons, since 66 percent of respondents to my survey[72] indicated that they had been tutored in a foreign language at some point in their lives, 88 percent[73] indicated that they took private afterschool classes or were tutored by people other than their parents at some point in their lives, and I seldom heard of urban singletons who considered it futile to study English. Still, I cannot claim to have known families from all areas of China's socioeconomic pyramid. Like my survey sample, my ethnographic sample does not include youth from the hyper-elite top or the impoverished bottom of that pyramid.

Teenagers frequently talked about wanting to become "wealthy" (*fuyü* or *you qian*), "big money" (*dakuan*), "cadres" (*ganbu*), "officials" (*guan*), "managers" (*jingli*), "white collar" (*bai ling*), or "intellectuals" (*zhishifenzi*). I use the term "elite" to refer to people in any of these high-status categories, and the term "non-elite" to refer to everyone else.[74] Though some families I knew were wealthy by Chinese standards, none were wealthy by First World standards. I was told that a small number of high officials, high-level employees in foreign companies, and owners of extremely successful Chinese companies had incomes that would be high even by First World standards, but none of them happened to be part of my social network.

Almost all the students I knew had urban residential registration (*hukou*) by the time I met them. A few had been born in rural areas, but inherited urban registration from their mothers, who gave birth to them while living in rural areas during the Cultural Revolution (1966–1976). As Aihwa Ong has observed,[75] states grant different kinds of citizenship to different categories of people. In China, rural citizens had far fewer rights to good living conditions than urban citizens.[76] Since 1962, Chinese cities have strictly enforced China's 1958 Regulations on Household Registration, which were designed to keep rural migrants from flooding cities.[77] Urban registration was reserved for those living in cities in 1954, those whose mothers had urban registration, those whose employers were willing and able to secure urban registration for them, and those who received urban registration as part of special deals with the government (such as those that occurred when rural land was requisitioned for urban use).[78] Migration was heavily restricted because each city's government provided food, clothing, health care, housing, schooling, pensions, and work only for its own citizens. By the 1990s, however, it was possible to obtain these things from the private market, and some state enterprises were also willing to hire rural citizens for jobs that urban citizens were unwilling to take. Still, rural citizens were severely hindered by their ineligibility for state subsidies and good jobs. Prior to the 1990s, children inherited the registration of their mothers, and not their fathers. Neighborhood committee cadres told me that the purpose of this law was to discourage rural women from marrying urban men to gain urban registration for themselves and their children. Because of strong traditions of patrilocality, particularly in the countryside, rural men were not as likely as rural women to practice this strategy. As part of broad nationwide reforms,[79] however, the rules were changed in the 1990s to allow children to inherit either parent's residential registration, and to allow rural citizens who purchased urban housing to apply for urban registration. Still, most of the rural citizens living in urban Dalian could not attend school, but rather worked in fields shunned by urban citizens, like construction and housekeeping. Since the 1980s, rural citizens have been estimated to constitute 10–30 percent of the people living in major Chinese cities.[80] Rural migrants tended to be working-age men and unmarried working-age women; children, elderly parents, and wives were left behind to tend farmland. Many migrants retained land rights in their home villages, and returned to their land during long holidays, planting and harvest seasons, and periods of unemployment. Most rural citizens could not afford to send their children to urban schools, since even the least expensive urban schools (primary schools, junior high schools, and college prep high schools) demanded extra fees from students who lacked urban registration. In addition, many rural schools did not teach students enough to enable them to compete with urban students on high school or college entrance exams. When I visited the natal villages of some students' parents, I met rural teenagers who talked about going to urban areas much as urban teenagers talked about going abroad. Though many of the urban citizens I knew were just a generation or two removed from their rural origins, their world was vastly different from the rural world inhabited by the villagers they left behind. Even urban citizens with rural relatives usually limited their interactions with those relatives to a few visits per year. My arguments about the experiences of urban citizens do not necessarily apply to the experiences of rural citizens, who constituted 64 percent[81] of the Chinese population in 2000.

My survey results were useful for providing a broad portrait of the socioeconomic and demographic characteristics of the people I studied. This portrait served as a reality check against what I learned from participant observation. Many students I knew, for instance, claimed that "everyone else" had cellular phones and computers when trying to persuade their parents to purchase these goods. Yet only 33 percent[82] of respondents to my survey indicated that their families owned cellular phones, and only 13 percent[83] indicated that their families owned computers. Ethnographic research also served as a reality check against my survey findings. For instance, I learned by talking with students that the income data I had collected with my survey was largely false, since wealthier respondents tended to under-report their parents' incomes by excluding gifts, bribes, and illegal business profits, and respondents with unemployed parents tended to report the incomes their parents earned prior to becoming unemployed. Some respondents admitted to me after I befriended them that they had felt embarrassed about reporting unusually high or low parental incomes, and therefore left the survey question about income blank or reported inaccurate but socially appropriate figures.

As many critics have pointed out, statistics and ethnography are both flawed methods of representing reality.[84] Because they are flawed in different ways, though, statistical and ethnographic representations can complement each other and provide a better provisional understanding of a reality that will always be too complex, varied, and subjective to be fully captured on paper. The cultural models and material circumstances of respondents to my survey and the people I knew seemed to be shared by the majority of their counterparts in urban Dalian and other large Chinese cities.[85] By no means, however, should my account of the experiences and subjectivities of people I knew in urban Dalian be seen as representative of the entirety of Chinese social life. The stories I tell here cannot even be representative of the whole of any individual's subjectivity. Rather, they merely represent fragments of life that I glimpsed at particular moments during the course of fieldwork. Still, while these stories should not be seen as representative, they can be seen as illustrative of the everyday dilemmas and concerns that tend to produce and be produced by a modern economy. While the hopes, fears, and experiences of each family and each individual are unique, they also resonate with the perils and possibilities faced by many others in similar positions throughout the capitalist world system.

## Global Processes, Local Experiences

By exploring the social, economic, and psychological consequences of China's one-child policy, this book reveals how parents and children are affected by the fertility transition, a process that has taken place in most societies worldwide. Because it was unusually sudden and extreme, the fertility transition caused by China's one-child policy presents an especially stark example of how the cultural model of modernization can shape individual lives. While they bear particularities unique to China, to urban Dalian, and to the families I got to know, many of the experiences portrayed in this book are also shared by low-fertility families worldwide. The fertility transition is an integral part of the cultural model of modernization that has been adopted by all First World societies and most Third World societies. While the Chinese state is unique in the ruthless effectiveness of its direct efforts to create a fertility transition, other states have promoted fertility transitions indirectly, by adopting the modern economy necessary for success in the capitalist world system. As David Harvey has argued, individual and national "choices" about reproduction and family life in the capitalist world system are actually determined by the political economy of capitalism, which "continuously strives to shape bodies to its own requirements."[86]

Each individual's relationship to the capitalist world system is shaped by the interactions of a unique set of subjectivities, experiences, and cultural models. Still, the degree and range of individual variations are limited by the mutually supportive forces of the fertility transition, the cultural model of modernization, the modern economy, and the capitalist world system. These forces enjoy what Antonio Gramsci,[87] Pierre Bourdieu,[88] and Jean Comaroff and John Comaroff[89] have called "hegemonic" power. Most people caught in the capitalist world system pursue strategies that end up reinforcing the hegemony of these forces, which pervade their consciousness so deeply that they take it for granted. This does not mean that they lack agency; it just means that their agency is shaped and constrained by the capitalist world system. People I knew in urban Dalian sometimes resisted the demands of that system by refusing to study hard, limit fertility, invest in education, or seek high-paying work, but such resistance was too infrequent, self-defeating, and disorganized to result in social change.[90] Most of the time, they followed the cultural model of modernization: They studied hard, limited fertility, invested heavily in education, and sought high-paying work. Some of them achieved their goal of upward mobility, and the sum of their actions helped to achieve their goal of raising China's status in the capitalist world system. Successful students and parents saw themselves as highly effective agents who bent circumstances to their will; the fact that their will was in turn shaped by the cultural model of modernization perpetuated by the capitalist world system does not nullify the fact of their agency.

At the dawn of the twenty-first century, most people worldwide were motivated by the cultural model of modernization. Societies now known as part of the First World had a head start in the establishment of the modern economy that helped them become core regions, and peripheral societies now known as part of the Third World are struggling to catch up. This pattern has caused many people worldwide (including people I knew in urban Dalian) to assume that modernization was an inevitable process of unilinear evolution. Yet there was nothing inevitable about the rise and spread of the modern economy, which became globally dominant because of a particular set of historical circumstances. These circumstances were rooted not only in invention of industrial technologies, but also in the practices of conquest, colonialism, imperialism, exploitation, and impoverishment perpetuated by the societies that modernized early on the societies that modernized late. Recognizing modernization as the only way to avoid being trampled by the First World, Third World people have struggled to become like First World people as quickly as possible. Chinese officials hoped that the fertility transition produced by the one-child policy would hasten the establishment of a modern economy that would improve China's position in the capitalist world system.

## When Little Emperors Grow Up

Small families tend to socialize children to accept the cultural model of modernization. Chinese leaders promulgated the one-child policy in order to produce a generation with First World consumption and education patterns. Unlike a child who must share family resources with many siblings, a singleton enjoys a heavily concentrated dose of parental investment. Consequently, Chinese singletons have been socialized with the same high expectations, consumption demands, and educational aspirations as youth in the First World. However, because of the extraordinary abruptness and universality of the fertility transition that was hastened by the one-child policy, Chinese singletons also face unusually high levels of parental pressure and competition for elite status in the educational system and job market.

In contrast, Chinese parents who had large numbers of children during the 1950s and 1960s socialized most of their children with neither the aspiration nor the resources to win elite status. Inequalities between the elite and non-elite were smaller in the political economy of socialism, so fewer students and parents felt that trying to win elite status was worth the effort. It was also not essential for every child to win a high-paying job, since the cost of providing parents with old age support would be shared by many siblings, and poorer siblings could get help from wealthier siblings during hard times. While some elite families practiced low fertility and high parental investment, most non-elite families did not. While some parents focused heavy investment and aspirations on one or two especially talented sons, they still allowed daughters and less-talented sons to grow up with the expectation that they would not become part of the elite. While some talented sons of elite, low-fertility parents experienced the same kind of pressure and investment common in single-child families, most people born in the 1950s did not. Thus, competition for elite education and work was not nearly as intense in the 1960s and 1970s as it was in the 1990s.

Most urban Chinese youth born in the 1980s were singletons socialized to become part of the elite. In addition to being the sole focus of parental love and pride, singletons were expected to be the main source of their parents' post-retirement income, medical payments, and nursing care. Many of them will also have to support children, grandparents, parents-in-law, and grandparents-in-law. In a modern economy that promotes increasingly large inequalities, only an elite job can supply enough income to enable one person to provide so many dependents with a respectable lifestyle. Thus, just about all singletons aspired to win elite jobs, usually through academic achievement. The universality of singletons' aspirations for elite status produced rapid diploma inflation and fierce competition in the educational system and the job market. Parents invested the bulk of family resources in their singletons in order to give them every possible advantage in the race for upward mobility. Teenagers talked about how "society is a contest where people eat people." The stakes are especially high because, if singletons lose out in the competition for socioeconomic status, their parents will have no other children to fall back on, and a singleton who falls into poverty will have no siblings to turn to for help.

The population aging caused by the fertility transition has outpaced China's efforts to develop a social security system to provide support for its elderly. Singletons are likely to bear alone the burdens of elder care that were once shared by many siblings. On top of that, these burdens have intensified because of post-Mao economic reforms, which caused 25 percent of survey respondents' mothers[91] and 12 percent of survey respondents' fathers[92] to lose their jobs. State officials assumed that retired people would be supported primarily by their children rather than by medical insurance and pension plans, which were reduced, eliminated, or allowed to lag behind inflation as part of efforts to make state enterprises more competitive in the capitalist world system. Since the highest-paying, most prestigious jobs were reserved for graduates of the post-Mao educational system, many singletons were their families' last best hope for upward mobility.

Chinese adults created a lexicon for expressing their discomfort with the high expectations of the rising generation of singletons. Singletons (*dushengzinü*) were "little suns" (*xiao taiyang*) because their parents' lives revolved around them. Parents "doted" (*chong*) on them, "drowned them with love" (*ni'ai*), and "spoiled them till they were bad" (*ba tamen guan huai le*). Singletons developed such high expectations that they "lacked the ability to adjust to their environment" (*meiyou shiying nengli*). They became haughty, demanding "little emperors" (*xiao huangdi*). This last term was especially popular in both the Chinese and the international media, as it conjured up the comical image of a small child lording it over worshipful adults. It was assumed that singletons were spoiled because they got a more concentrated dose of parental attention than children with siblings. Yet parental attention did not consist solely of love, support, and pampering. It also consisted of discipline, demands, and expectations.

Chinese singletons were called "little emperors" because their parents spoiled them just as the imperial court once spoiled its emperors. But there were strings attached to the good living conditions singletons enjoyed. Chinese emperors were pampered, but they also had a duty to bring glory and prosperity to their empire. So it was with the "little emperors" created by China's one-child policy.

CHAPTER 1

# "The Next Few Months Will Determine Your Future"

## *Eight Teenagers' Stories*

THIS CHAPTER introduces some of the main characters of this book by following eight singletons on their journeys through Dalian's late 1990s educational system. Born between 1979 and 1984, they belong to a generation that consists primarily of singletons. I hope that these eight stories will serve as illustrations of the complex, varied, and changing ways individuals dealt with their circumstances and cultural models. To illustrate as broad a range of circumstances as possible, I have chosen to focus this chapter on teenagers who were the most "high-achieving," "low-achieving," "poor," or "wealthy" among all the urban Dalian teenagers I knew, most of whom had socioeconomic statuses and achievement levels that lay somewhere in between the extremes exemplified by the subjects of this chapter.

The wealthy teenagers and their parents, teachers, friends, and relatives identified them as "wealthy" (*fuyü*), "having good conditions" (*tiaojian hao*), and "having money" (*you qian*). Each of them had at least one parent in a managerial position, an apartment with at least four rooms in addition to the kitchen and bathroom, and at least two of three goods widely considered to be "luxuries" (the computer, the air conditioner, and the microwave oven). These teenagers were wealthy only when compared with the vast majority of people in China. None of their families owned cars. They lived well in China, but their households' annual incomes were still less than the annual tuitions charged by most First World colleges. I estimated that each "wealthy" household had an annual income (including salaries, pensions, subsidies, bribes, gifts, and business profits) that was at least 30,000 yuan (US$3,750), but still well below US$13,880, the United States federal government's official 1999 poverty line for an American family of three.[1]

The poor teenagers identified themselves as "poor" (*qiong*), "experiencing difficulty" (*kunnan*), and "not having money" (*meiyou qian*), and were identifed as such by their parents, teachers, friends, and relatives. Each of these teenagers had at least one unemployed parent and lived in a one-room apartment with no computer, air conditioner, or microwave oven. I estimated that each of their families had a 1999 annual income (including salaries, pensions, subsidies, gifts, and profits from peddling) that was between 7,200 yuan (US$900) and 18,000 yuan (US$2,250).

According to information collected by China's National Bureau of Statistics from Chinese work units, the average 1999 annual salary in China was 8,346 yuan (US$1,043).[2] According to information collected by Dalian City's Archives Office from Dalian area employers, the average 1999 annual salary in the Dalian area was 9,443 yuan (US$1,180).[3] According to a representative sample survey[4] conducted in Chinese cities by China's National Bureau of Statistics in 1999, the average annual per capita income was 5,889 yuan (US$736) for all respondents, 12,148 yuan (US$1,519) for the wealthiest ten percent of respondents, and 2,647 yuan (US$331) for the poorest ten percent of respondents.[5] According to a 1999 representative sample survey[6] conducted by Dalian City's government, the annual per capita income in urban Dalian was 6,274 yuan (US$784) for all respondents, 11,767 yuan (US$1,471) for the wealthiest ten percent of respondents, and 3,018 yuan (US$377) for the poorest ten percent of respondents. Like my survey, these surveys probably underestimated incomes because respondents were unlikely to report illegal, informal, or untaxed income (such as bribes, gifts, subsidies, and business profits). People told me about these kinds of income only after they got to know me very well, and I doubt that even those I knew best told me about all their income. Since my knowledge about incomes was incomplete, my classification of families described in this chapter as "wealthy" or "poor" is based partly on the consumption patterns I observed, partly on how these families classified themselves and were classified by others who knew them, and partly on what I knew of their official and unofficial incomes.

My classification of teenagers as high-achieving or low-achieving was likewise based partly on what I knew about their class rankings, exam scores, and school placements, and partly on how they were described by themselves and by their parents, teachers, friends, and relatives. The low-achieving teenagers described in this chapter usually ranked in the bottom half of their classes, and were often described by themselves and others as "lazy" (*lan*), "unable to sit still" (*zuo bu zhu*), "unable to be disciplined" (*guan bu liao*), "greedy for leisure" (*tan wanr*), and "bad at studying" (*xuexi bu hao*). The high-achieving teenagers usually ranked in the top half of their classes and (with the exception of Wang Song) were often described by themselves and others as "hardworking" (*nuli*), "assiduous" (*keku*), and "good at studying" (*xuexi hao*).

Each of the stories in this chapter was shaped by a different combination of the three most significant factors in stratification: gender, academic achievement, and socioeconomic background. I do not, however, mean to suggest that these teenagers are representative of all Chinese youth of the same gender, achievement level, and socioeconomic background. Rather, I present their stories to illustrate a few of the ways these factors can shape individual subjectivities, experiences, and opportunities, while recognizing that countless other stories remain untold.

## Yang Shu, a Wealthy, Low-Achieving Girl

While browsing through a rack of dresses at a downtown clothing store in 1998, I caught the eye of the storeowner, a striking, elegantly attired woman in her 40s. "What are you looking for?" she asked eagerly.

"Something nice that I can wear to a wedding," I said.

"Whose wedding?"

"My student's."

"You're a teacher?"

Storeowners liked to inquire about the personal lives of their customers, both to build rapport and to develop their marketing strategies. I also wanted to learn more about her, especially since she seemed old enough to have a teenaged child. So I engaged in a lengthy conversation with her, in the process revealing my background.

As was sometimes the case, this revelation led to a request for tutoring. "My daughter doesn't like to study, but she's smart," she said. "If Yang Shu gets interested in her studies, she'll be a top student. But Chinese teaching methods are too dull. I've gotten many tutors for her before, but they couldn't get her interested, and when she's not interested, she won't study. Maybe you can get her interested in English with foreign teaching methods."

A few days later, I met Yang Shu's mother at her store right before it closed, and we took a bus to her apartment. Yang Shu was playing a computer game with her best friend Sun Wei. With their identical ponytails and matching jeans and blouses, the two girls looked like sisters.

"Lazy girls!" Yang Shu's mother chided them. "The other ninth graders spend all their time studying. But what do you do? You play computer games!"

"I was just teaching Sun Wei how to use the computer," Yang Shu explained sheepishly.

"Teacher Fong can teach you about computers, and pure American English. She's the Chinese American I told you about," Yang Shu's mother said.

"I'm pleased to meet you!" I said in English.

"What did she say?" Sun Wei asked Yang Shu in Chinese. Yang Shu shrugged, and they both started laughing.

"Do you want to learn English?" I asked in English.

They laughed even more. "We can't understand you!" Yang Shu said in Chinese.

"Do you want to learn English?" I repeated in Chinese.

"Yes!" the girls shouted in English, relieved that I could speak Chinese.

"You have a lot to learn from Teacher Fong. Value this opportunity!" Yang Shu's mother said as she went to the kitchen to make dinner. The girls proceeded to grill me in Chinese about American movies and music.

"Where's your Pa?" I asked Yang Shu as we sat down to dinner.

"He's away on a business trip," Yang Shu replied. Months later, after I grew closer to Yang Shu and her mother, they told me the truth: When Yang Shu was in fifth grade, her parents divorced. He remarried, but still paid child support for Yang Shu. In addition, he gave her spending money and expensive gifts.

"My parents were glad that I married a company manager, but I realized what he was really like when he started beating me and having affairs," Yang Shu's mother told me. "I was glad to be rid of him. I pity his new wife."

I visited Yang Shu and Sun Wei several times a month. I tried using games and stories to teach them grammar and vocabulary words from their textbooks, but even such tactics could not hold their attention for long. I had somewhat more success teaching them the English words in computer games and the English-language movies they watched on Yang Shu's large-screen VCD (Video Compact Disc) player. Yang Shu sometimes invited her boyfriend Jiang Yi, Sun Wei, Sun Wei's boyfriend Teng Fei, and me over to sing karaoke on her home entertainment system. Other times, we went together to malls, restaurants, and video game parlors. The teenagers' parents encouraged them to take me along on outings, hoping that I would serve as a chaperone. "Don't tell my Ma how I am with Jiang Yi!" Yang Shu warned me.

"What do you think of my daughter's little friend?" Yang Shu's mother asked me one day as we chatted in her store.

"Sun Wei's very nice," I responded evasively, pretending not to know that the term "little friend" was a euphemism for "boyfriend."

Recognizing my discomfort, Yang Shu's mother laughed. "That little thing told you not to tell me how she is with Jiang Yi, didn't she? Her homeroom teacher already told me. I've told my daughter not to waste her time on boys, but she does it anyway. There's nothing I can do to stop her. I just want to know what you think of him."

"He's very nice too," I said.

"What good is that? I hear he's an even worse student than she is. He's a waste of her time. The school prohibits dating for a reason. She's just a child! What use is it for her to have a 'little friend'? She's smarter than anyone else in her class, but she's wasting all her potential. She should hold on tightly to her time and use it to study for the entrance exam. Tell her that. Maybe she'll listen to you."

I told Yang Shu that I agreed with her mother that she should spend more time preparing for the high school entrance exam. "Just make a decision to study hard these last few months before the exam," I advised her. "After that, you can play all summer long."

"I know," Yang Shu said. "But I just need to relax sometimes. Some people get so nervous about the exam that they end up panicking and doing worse than they would have if they had relaxed, like I'm doing."

I was watching a TV show with Yang Shu when her mother came home in tears from the parents' meeting at Yang Shu's school. "You ranked near the bottom of your class!" she yelled at Yang Shu. "I was so embarrassed, I couldn't even look at the other parents. I wanted to run out of the room. How do you expect to get into a college prep high school with such low scores? Do you think your Pa will help you? One of these days he'll have a child with his new wife, and he'll forget all about you. And if you score too low, there's no amount of money that will make a college prep high school take you."

"What use are college prep high schools?" Yang Shu replied. "I hear that even college graduates can't find jobs these days."

"If even college graduates can't find jobs, how do you expect to find a job?" her mother sobbed. "Do you expect me to support you the rest of my life? Do you just want to take over my store after I'm old and bedridden? There's no future in that! I want something better for you!"

"Don't worry," Yang Shu said. "I'll think of a way to get ahead no matter what happens on the exam."

"How?" her mother demanded. "How will you get a good job if you don't study hard? Do you expect to sit at home all day while a rich husband supports you? You might get a man to marry you just for your looks, but after a while he'll just be annoyed at you and say you're no use. Then you'll fight and he'll divorce you. Then what will you do?"

Hoping to keep their friendship group together, Yang Shu, her boyfriend Jiang Yi, Sun Wei, and her boyfriend Teng Fei selected the same college prep, professional, and vocational high schools as their top choices.

When the time came, Yang Shu's mother left a relative in charge of the store and spent both days of the high school entrance exam standing in the rain outside the exam hall, along with hundreds of parents waiting for their children to come out for meal breaks.

Yang Shu only scored high enough to qualify for a vocational high school that was not even her top choice. She was willing to enroll at that school, but her parents sent her to a private boarding school instead. This school accepted any student whose parents could pay 7,000 yuan (US$875) per year for tuition. "I like this school because it's strict, and has the style of an army training camp," Yang Shu's mother told me. "My daughter's smart, and she'll be a good student once she grows up and understands things. This school hires the best teachers, and the curriculum is the same as the kind at the college prep high schools. If she still doesn't get into college after that, I'll send her to college abroad. She'll get further abroad, where what matters is ability, not just exam scores."

Soon after Yang Shu enrolled at the private high school, Yang Shu's mother told me that her clothing store was not doing well. She faced stiff competition from the American superstore Wal-Mart and the French superstore Carrefour, both of which opened in Dalian in 2000, to a flood of customers. "The superstores are robbing me of my customers," she told me. "They have better prices, selection, locations, and atmospheres, and people like shopping for clothes, food, and household goods all at one store. How can I compete?"

On top of that, consumer demand was falling. "Now so many people are unemployed, no one can afford new clothes," she lamented. "They used to come to me for the latest fashions, but now they'd rather just wear clothes from last year, or ten years ago. And some of these unemployed people have started their own businesses, selling cheap, low quality clothes. So customers expect me to sell my high quality clothes at the same low prices, and I have to sell at a loss!"

She was consoled, however, by Yang Shu's apparently increased devotion to her studies. "I knew it was a good idea to send her to the private school," Yang Shu's mother told me. "It's giving her the discipline that I never had time to give her." Yang Shu's mother was pleased that her daughter had finally broken up with her boyfriend. "She's finally growing up and realizing that she shouldn't waste time playing around with a boy!"

Yang Shu was less pleased. She told her mother that she chose to break up with Jiang Yi because she wanted to focus on her studies. But she told me that Jiang Yi had dumped her because he had fallen for a girl at his vocational high school. "How could he be so fickle!" she sobbed to me. "I was nicer to him than I was to myself. But then he forgot about me as soon as we stopped attending the same school. I thought he loved me! I can't believe I was so foolish. I should have listened to my Ma! She said that men are unreliable, and she was right! Maybe if I hadn't wasted so much time playing around with Jiang Yi, I'd be in a college prep high school, getting a better and less expensive education. From now on, I'll just focus on studying. I never want to have a 'little friend' again!"

Yang Shu worried about her family's future. Not only was her mother's business faltering, her father's income was also falling because of his company's financial troubles. "I have to get into college," she told me. "I used to think I could rely on my parents and my friends, but now I know that I can only rely on myself."

## Sun Wei, a Poor, Low-Achieving Girl

Yang Shu and Sun Wei had been best friends since first grade, when they shared a desk and chatted so much that no teacher ever allowed them to sit together again. They lived on the same street, and walked to and from school together every day. Yang Shu ate dinner at Sun Wei's home when Yang Shu's mother had to work late at her store. Sun Wei went to Yang Shu's home to play computer games, sing karaoke, or watch movies and cable TV shows on a large-screen television that could also be used to view VCDs. All Sun Wei's family had was a small television with poor reception and no cable. Yang Shu and Sun Wei loved "My Fair Princess" (*Huanzhu Gege*), a hit soap opera based on Taiwan writer Qiong Yao's mainly fictional novels about the adventures of the eighteenth-century Manchu Emperor Qianlong's long-lost daughter Imperial Fern and her best friend Little Swallow, a mischievous orphan girl adopted by Qianlong and courted by his son Fifth Prince. Yang Shu nicknamed Sun Wei "Little Swallow," and Sun Wei nicknamed Yang Shu "Imperial Fern."

I could see the resemblance. Sun Wei had Little Swallow's liveliness and blithe disregard of adversity, and Yang Shu had Imperial Fern's grace and elite parentage. As in the case of Little Swallow and Imperial Fern, Yang Shu's boyfriend Jiang Yi and Sun Wei's boyfriend Teng Fei were best friends as well, and the two couples went everywhere in a merry quartet.

Sun Wei's parents refused to follow their daughter's homeroom teacher's advice that they forbid Sun Wei to see her boyfriend. "I know your friends are important to you, and I know you can't be with the rest of them without also being with Teng Fei," Sun Wei's mother told her. "Just make sure you're always with the group and never alone with him."

Sun Wei's parents were amused by their daughter's nickname. However, Sun Wei's father reminded her, "You can't be as carefree as Little Swallow, because you're not an orphan. You have parents who have sacrificed a lot for you, and you have to repay us by studying hard."

After losing her factory job, Sun Wei's mother had used her sister's connections to get hired as a street sweeper, only to quit soon afterwards because her kidney problems, high blood pressure, and chronic fatigue made it impossible for her to work on her feet all day. Sun Wei's father still worked at the factory that laid his wife off, but his pay was frequently late, and sometimes did not arrive at all. When Sun Wei was not home, her parents skipped meals to save money. Their gaunt, pale faces contrasted sharply with their daughter's round, rosy cheeks.

Sun Wei wanted to study, but she had difficulty sitting still. "I've tried, but I just can't get the knowledge into my head!" she told her parents. "Our home is too crowded. I can't stand it. I'll go over to Yang Shu's place to study. It's better over there!"

Though they liked her friends, Sun Wei's parents worried that she had picked up their poor study habits. "Your friends don't have to worry about getting an education, because they have rich and powerful parents who can provide for them. What do you have, but us?" her father said.

When hanging out at the mall, Sun Wei and her friends took turns treating the whole group to meals and snacks. Though Sun Wei only took her turn when getting the least expensive treats, such as popsicles or drinks, even these generated a need for spending money that Sun Wei's parents found burdensome. "Can't you all just bring thermoses of water from home?" her mother asked.

"That's not the point!" Sun Wei cried. "When you go out, you're supposed to have treats. My friends are always treating me to expensive meals! I have to at least treat them to popsicles!"

"If you study hard, you'll get a good job and earn lots of money, and then you can treat your friends to banquets at fancy restaurants!" her father said. "Wouldn't that be nice?"

Sun Wei usually managed to restrain herself from buying things at the mall while shopping with her friends. But one day, she pleaded with her mother, "Yang Shu and I found stylish black shoes that fit us perfectly! But Yang Shu says she won't buy a pair unless I do, because she doesn't want me to be jealous. Please give me the money to buy them!"

"Yang Shu's Ma runs a store," Sun Wei's mother said. "Couldn't she get shoes for both of you at a discount?"

"No! She sells clothes, not shoes, and maybe there's no more of this particular style and size left anywhere else in the city! Besides, I'd be embarrassed to ask her Ma to do anything like that. Please give me the money!"

"I'll give you the money if you rank in the top ten in your class on the next test," Sun Wei's mother said.

"By that time, someone else will have bought our shoes!" Sun Wei protested. "But if you give me the money now, I promise I'll study harder than I've ever studied before, and I'll score very high, if not in the top ten, then at least higher than I did on the last test!"

Sun Wei's mother relented and gave her the money. "Mama, I love you!" Sun Wei cried, and danced around her tiny apartment with the money in her hand.

True to her word, Sun Wei studied harder than ever before. "Even when I can't stand it, I force myself to stare at my books, until I fall asleep over them," she told me. On the next test, she ranked 28th in her class of 53. She usually ranked in the 30s, so her parents were elated by the improvement in her score. "Keep this up, and you'll certainly get into a college prep high school," her mother said gleefully.

As the high school entrance exam drew near, Sun Wei's mother grew increasingly anxious. She asked friends and relatives for advice on what kinds of food she should prepare to stimulate Sun Wei's brain and enhance her energy in preparation for the exam. She put extra effort and money into creating especially delicious meals for Sun Wei, and refused to let her help with chores. "The next few months will determine your future," she told Sun Wei. "Every minute should be spent on your studies."

The anxiety took a toll on Sun Wei's mother's already bad health. A few weeks before the exam, she saw a doctor who said that her kidney problems and high blood pressure were serious enough to require hospitalization. She refused because she worried that her absence would cause Sun Wei to do badly on the high school entrance exam. The doctor prescribed Western pharmaceuticals to improve her kidney function and lower her blood pressure, but she purchased less expensive Chinese herbal medications instead. When I gave her money to help with medical expenses, she spent most of it on special foods and dietary supplements to prepare Sun Wei for the exam.

While I waited with Sun Wei's mother for Sun Wei and Yang Shu to come home from school, Sun Wei's mother's sister came by to visit. "Sun Wei's exam is important, but so is your health," she chided Sun Wei's mother. "You should be hospitalized. Sun Wei can take care of herself. You shouldn't sacrifice your body just to stay around her."

"If I stay in the hospital, Sun Wei will be anxious, and she won't be able to concentrate on her studies," Sun Wei's mother replied. "She might get upset, she might become malnourished because her Pa is such a bad cook, she might waste time doing chores, or she might just spend all her time playing around with her friends instead of studying," Sun Wei's mother said. "I can't abandon my daughter at the most critical time of her life. I have just one child, and I love her more than I love my own life."

Nervous about an anticipated wave of layoffs at his factory, Sun Wei's father did not dare ask for time off on Sun Wei's exam days. "But you don't need to be there for her exam either," he told his wife. "Don't risk your health to do that. It's not like you could take the exam for her. She'll be fine on her own, and if she needs anything, she can ask Yang Shu's Ma."

"She'll need her own Ma," Sun Wei's mother said resolutely. "What if she gets sick? What if she runs out of the exam hall in tears? How could I not be there for her?"

Yang Shu and Sun Wei wore their matching, stylish black shoes to the high school entrance exam. Sun Wei's mother felt ill as we waited outside the exam hall in the wind and rain, but she refused to go home as Yang Shu's mother and I suggested. Sun Wei's mother was heartened when her daughter came out smiling, saying the exam was easier than she had expected.

Sun Wei's mother was hospitalized for a week after the exam. Against her protests, her husband paid for doctors to give her expensive intravenous Western medications to lower her blood pressure. "It's my fault," Sun Wei told me sadly. "My Ma wouldn't have been so anxious if I were a good student." While her friends celebrated their graduation from junior high school, Sun Wei spent all week beside her mother's hospital bed.

Sun Wei scored higher on the high school entrance exam than she had usually scored on practice tests, but not high enough to get into a college prep or professional high school. Though disappointed, Sun Wei's parents could not blame her. "Sun Wei really gave her best effort in the last few months before the exam," her mother said. "She shouldn't have spent so much time playing around before, but there's nothing we can do about that now."

Sun Wei was accepted to her top-choice vocational high school. "If she studies hard from now on, she can get a degree through an adult education college or the college equivalency exams, and she'll still get a good job," her father said.

Sun Wei was frustrated to hear that a classmate who had scored lower than her got into a college prep high school through a combination of bribes, connections, and extra fees. Sun Wei's parents had none of these resources. They depended on loans and gifts from friends and relatives just to pay for the vocational high school's tuition of 2,000 yuan (US$250) per year.

Sun Wei and Yang Shu wept as they bid each other farewell right before Yang Shu got in the long-distance bus to her boarding school. "Don't forget Little Swallow!" Sun Wei cried as the bus drove away.

In vocational school, Sun Wei missed the tight circle of friends she had in junior high school. "I've made some new friends, but I still miss my old friends," Sun Wei said. "Junior high school friendships are less complicated, and more real, than high school friendships." She was still dating Teng Fei, who had gotten his parents to send him to her vocational high school just so he could continue to be with her. But Sun Wei's parents were more suspicious of her relationship with Teng Fei now that Yang Shu and Jiang Yi were no longer around.

"Never go out alone with him," Sun Wei's mother warned her. "Things can happen if you're alone with a boy. Your chastity will be your capital when it's time for you to marry, and that's at least ten years away! There's no guarantee you'll be with Teng Fei for that long! And at this point, you don't even know how successful he'll be. He's a nice boy, but he's bad at studying, and maybe all he knows is how to spend his parents' money."

"Stop nagging," Sun Wei replied. "I'm a good girl. I'm having fun with Teng Fei, but I understand things. I'll be careful. Don't worry."

Sun Wei was angry with Jiang Yi for dumping Yang Shu, and Teng Fei also disapproved. Still, Teng Fei remained friends with Jiang Yi, and this caused tension between him and Yang Shu. Sun Wei and Yang Shu still called and visited each other during vacations, but they no longer went out together with Jiang Yi and Teng Fei. Fearing what might happen if their daughter went out alone with her boyfriend, Sun Wei's parents seldom let her see Teng Fei outside of school.

Though she had just been an average student in her junior high school, Sun Wei was one of the better students at her vocational high school. Though this was at least partly because vocational high schools had fewer high-achieving students than junior high schools, Sun Wei's parents preferred to emphasize that Sun Wei was "studying hard because she finally grew up and understood things."

Sun Wei's parents depended on gifts and loans from friends and relatives to pay for Sun Wei's tuition, and also for expensive weekend classes to prepare her for the adult education college entrance exam. "Sun Wei made some mistakes when she was small and didn't understand things, but now that she knows the importance of studying, we want her to get as much education as she can," Sun Wei's father told me.

Sun Wei hoped that she could attend adult education college classes at night, and work during the day. "When I see my Ma trying to peddle things on the street despite the weakness in her body, it makes me want to cry," she told me. "I feel so impatient. I want to start earning money so I can stop being a burden on my parents, and start improving their lives."

## Teng Fei, a Wealthy, Low-Achieving Boy

Sun Wei's boyfriend Teng Fei sometimes treated Sun Wei, Yang Shu, Yang Shu's boyfriend Jiang Yi, and me to meals at his parents' restaurant. Sometimes, at Teng Fei's parents' request, I gave English lessons to all four friends before or after the meal.

Sun Wei and Yang Shu sometimes called Teng Fei "Fifth Prince," after Little Swallow's true love. "You should get your eyes checked if you think I look like Fifth Prince," he told them with typical self-deprecating humor. Short and bespectacled, Teng Fei looked nothing like Alec Su (Su Youpeng), the movie star from Taiwan who played Fifth Prince. Even Sun Wei teased Teng Fei about his nerdy appearance, though she loved him for his affable, easygoing personality.

Teng Fei's parents paid no attention to his homeroom teacher's recommendation that they force him to end his romance with Sun Wei. "Other parents scold their children for having 'little friends,' but their children keep doing it anyway. They just stop telling their parents anything," Teng Fei's mother told me. "I never scold Teng Fei, so he tells me everything. This way, at least I'll be able to give him advice."

Teng Fei's father approved of Sun Wei because she was "a good girl" and a better student than Teng Fei: "Maybe she'll make him study harder," he told me. Still, he warned him against taking the relationship too seriously. "You're just children," he said. "Who knows what will happen in the future?"

Sun Wei adored Teng Fei. "He has such a good temper," she told me. "Even when I hit him or scold him, he just smiles!"

At first, I thought Teng Fei was a good student because he seemed to listen intently to my English lessons even when his friends tried to distract me with jokes and banter in Chinese. However, when I quizzed them, he got even fewer answers right than his friends did. "Don't nod and pretend that you understand," I chided him. "Tell me if you have questions!" He just smiled.

Teng Fei's parents spent most of their time running the restaurant. "I'm glad I have such a good son," Teng Fei's mother told me. "My heart can be at rest, because I know he won't get into trouble." When he was not spending time with his friends, he usually watched television or played computer games at home. Unlike many other low-achieving boys, he was quiet and never got into fights at school.

Still, Teng Fei's parents worried about his low scores. They hired college students to tutor him, but his scores never improved. He usually ranked at the bottom of his class. "How do you expect to get into a good high school if you don't study?" Teng Fei's mother demanded as we waited for his friends to return from a shopping trip.

"Do I really need to go to high school?" he asked. "Why can't I just help you run the restaurant after I graduate?"

"Foolish child!" his mother exclaimed. "You'll need an education to run the restaurant! Otherwise, you'll be cheated into bankruptcy the moment we hand it to you!"

"But you only had a junior high school education, and you're doing fine," Teng Fei rejoined.

"Your generation is different from ours! These days, you need a good education just to survive. No one will respect you if you don't have an education."

"My real friends will respect me no matter what, and I don't care what anyone else thinks."

"That's just what a little child would say! My little treasure doesn't understand anything," his mother lamented to me. "When will he understand?"

"When you buy me a cellular phone, then I'll understand!"

"He's so cute!" she said to me as she pulled him onto her lap and hugged him. He looked embarrassed.

Teng Fei's parents could not afford to leave their restaurant all two days of the high school entrance exam, but they took taxis to drop him off and pick him up. They prepared special meals for him in their restaurant's kitchen.

Teng Fei scored too low to get into the vocational high school that had accepted Sun Wei, but his parents got him in anyway after paying some extra fees. "I could just have him help with the restaurant, but that would be a waste of his potential," Teng Fei's father told me. "I want him to get as much education as he can. Maybe I'll send him abroad for college, so he can start his own restaurant abroad. Didn't you say that foreigners like Chinese food?"

Like Yang Shu's mother's clothing store, Teng Fei's parents' restaurant suffered from increasing competition and decreasing consumer demand. "Chinese people no longer like Chinese food," Teng Fei's mother complained to me. "There are so many restaurants now, the rich customers are getting picky. They want new tastes, Western or Japanese food, or Chinese regional specialties. And the poor customers don't even come anymore because they're unemployed or think they might lose their jobs soon, so they have to save money."

"It's fine for us to keep the restaurant going," Teng Fei's father said. "We're old, and we just need to earn enough to live on. But we don't want Teng Fei to help with the restaurant. He's young, so we want something better for him."

"Maybe he could develop himself abroad," Teng Fei's mother said. "Tell me, is it easy to open a restaurant in America? How much would it cost to get started? How much profit could you make?"

"I don't know much about the restaurant business, but I'd guess it costs tens of thousands of U.S. dollars at the very least," I answered.

"I've heard of people going abroad as students, working part-time as waiters, and gradually learning and saving enough to open their own restaurants," Teng Fei's mother said.

"I guess some people do that, but it's not that easy," I said. "Waiters barely earn enough to cover their living expenses."

"Teng Fei doesn't have to go into the restaurant business," Teng Fei's father said. "Maybe he could start a business in computers or trade. He could stay here in Dalian, or maybe he could go to a bigger city to develop himself, or go abroad. We just want him to do something he's good at, and something he likes. We're willing to invest whatever capital we can, but he has to be the one to get it going."

Teng Fei was one of the lowest-scoring students in his vocational high school, just as he was in his junior high school. His parents continued to hire tutors for him. Sun Wei and I tutored him as well. Teng Fei humored us, but his rankings seldom improved.

"What do you want to do when you grow up?" I asked.

"I don't know," Teng Fei replied. "I'd like to go abroad or get a job in a foreign company in Dalian, if I can. Or I could just help my parents with the restaurant."

## Yu Tao, a Poor, Low-Achieving Boy

I first heard about Yu Tao from his maternal aunt, the mother of Li Jian, a junior high school student I tutored. "Do you want to end up like your cousin Yu Tao?" she asked Li Jian whenever he asked for permission to go out with his friends. "Yu Tao always went out with his friends when he was your age. Are they any help to him now?"

When I asked who Yu Tao was, Li Jian's mother told me his story. She used to baby-sit him when he was a toddler. He had a "wild" (*pi*) streak even then. Though his wildness had not stopped him from getting above-average test scores in primary school, he "learned to be bad" (*xuehuai*) from a group of undisciplined boys he met in junior high school. Together, they ditched school to go to malls and video game parlors. They had girlfriends despite school prohibitions. They spent so much time socializing that they had no time to study. Worst of all, they got into fights with other boys.

"My sister kept getting called to Yu Tao's school for meetings with teachers about Yu Tao's behavior. Sometimes she had to pay for other boys' medical expenses after Yu Tao injured them. I feel sorry for her, but it's also her own fault for spoiling Yu Tao like she does. If my son cared more about his friends than about his own parents, I'd beat him till he couldn't walk," Li Jian's mother said with a meaningful glance at her own son.

On the high school entrance exam of 1998, Yu Tao just barely scored high enough to get into a technical high school that prepared students for factory work. Though his parents had both lost their factory jobs and were peddling soap, shampoo, toilet paper, and other household supplies on the streets to supplement the unemployment payments of about 300 yuan (US$38) per month that they each received from their former employers and the poverty subsidy of 39 yuan (US$5) per month that their household received from street committee social workers, they managed to borrow enough money from friends and relatives to pay for Yu Tao's schooling, which cost about 2,000 yuan (US$250) per year. But Yu Tao frequently ditched school to spend time with his friends. Some of them had not been admitted by any high school. After just one semester of technical high school, Yu Tao dropped out. He applied for many jobs, but could not get hired anywhere. He refused to help his parents peddle goods because it would embarrass him in front of his friends. He claimed that his friends paid for his meals when they went out, and even gave him spending money. His parents were terrified that he was actually getting the money through crime, and their suspicions were confirmed when his former junior high school teacher called them to report that Yu Tao and his friends had been using beatings and threats to extort money from younger boys who were still at the junior high school. Yu Tao's parents begged the teacher and the victims' parents not to call the police. They agreed after Yu Tao's parents and the other bullies' parents paid them twice the amount their sons had extorted.

Yu Tao was still unemployed when I met him and his parents at a Labor Day (May 1) reunion of Li Jian's maternal kin in 1999. Unlike most other teenagers I knew in urban Dalian, Yu Tao was muscular and heavily tanned from the many hours he spent playing soccer and basketball with his friends. Yu Tao's mother begged her siblings and their spouses to help him find work. They promised to try, though they were all poor workers or struggling owners of small businesses with few connections to potential employers.

"Could you be my sponsor to go to America?" Yu Tao asked me. "I'll do any kind of work, even if it's hard."

"Now you're saying you're willing to do hard work?" his father asked him sarcastically after I said that I had no power to get him a work visa to the United States. "Why didn't you just finish school if you were willing to work?"

"I don't want to be a factory worker in China," Yu Tao replied. "All the factories in China are going bankrupt, anyway. There's no future in that."

"And you have a fine future now!" his father snapped. "We skipped meals so you could buy textbooks, and we almost froze to death hawking goods in the cold to save money for your tuition, because all our hopes were pinned on you. And how have you repaid us?"

"Don't worry," Yu Tao said coolly. "I'm going to start a business with my friends, and we're going to be rich."

Some of Yu Tao's aunts and uncles snickered, but Yu Tao's mother came to his defense. "Don't laugh! My son is smart. If he had spent on his studies just a tiny bit of the effort he devoted to playing around, he would have been an excellent student! Once he grows up and starts understanding things, he'll succeed. It's the wild but smart boys who grow up to become rich businessmen."

After meeting me, Yu Tao's parents sometimes sent their son to Li Jian's home to join in the English lessons I gave Li Jian. Yu Tao liked talking with me about American lifestyles. He grilled me about how much various kinds of cars cost in the United States. However, whenever I tried to explain the rules of English grammar and spelling, Yu Tao's attention wandered, and he started bantering with Li Jian, much to Li Jian's parents' dismay. Eventually, Li Jian's mother told her sister to stop sending Yu Tao over for my lessons. "He's distracting Li Jian," she said. "Besides, Yu Tao's too far behind to learn anything, anyway."

Yu Tao's parents invited me to their small, cramped apartment for dinner a few times. When I complimented Yu Tao on a delicious roast pork dish he had made, his mother said to me, "My son's really good at cooking, and he likes doing it, too. Could you get him a job in a restaurant in America? Maybe if you ask your friends and your parents' friends if they know anyone who owns a restaurant. Or he could work as a cook in one of your professors' homes." I replied that I did not have any connections with Americans who needed cooks.

Yu Tao's father's brother helped get Yu Tao hired as a night watchman at a factory, but he was fired after a few weeks for speaking disrespectfully to his supervisor.

Yu Tao was still unemployed when I bumped into his father at a bus stop a few months after Yu Tao was fired from his night watchman job. "How's Yu Tao doing?" I asked.

"How would I know?" he growled. "He won't even talk to me. When I try to give him advice, he laughs at me. When he was small, I could beat him. But now that he's bigger than me, I can't do anything, because what if he hits me back? He loves spending money, but he refuses to think about the future. What kind of future can a boy like him have? I wish I had a daughter instead."

A few months after that, the father of one of Yu Tao's friends hired Yu Tao as a waiter at his restaurant, but fired him after just a few weeks because he was often late for work.

Yu Tao's parents borrowed money to pay for classes to prepare Yu Tao for the college equivalency exams. He failed every exam he took. This was not surprising, since even college prep high school graduates frequently failed those exams, and Yu Tao had dropped out of his technical high school after just one semester.

"I have a favor to ask you," Yu Tao's mother said to me when I called her after I had returned to the United States in 2000. "It's all right if you can't grant it, but just hear me out."

"What is it?"

"Some of Yu Tao's friends have gone abroad, and he's anxious to do the same. We've heard that all one needs to get a visa is a foreign friend who can write a letter of invitation. Can you do that for us? You won't have to spend a cent on him. We'll borrow money for the plane ticket, and he'll get a job to support himself as soon as he gets there."

"It's not that simple," I said. "A letter from me would be useless. A letter from a school admitting him or employer willing to hire him might be useful, but I have no power to get that for him. Besides, the American government only issues work visas for Chinese people with special abilities most Americans don't have. It's hard to get a visa for someone who hasn't even finished high school, and if he comes on a student visa, you'd have to pay hundreds of thousands of yuan every year to support him, because the American government doesn't let foreign students work enough to pay for their tuition and living expenses."

"What about the Chinese immigrants in the movie *Be There or Be Square*? They weren't students and they didn't have special abilities, so how did they get to America?" she asked.

"I don't know!" I replied. "Maybe they went illegally, or maybe they received visas to reunite with family members, or maybe they started out as students or tourists and found ways to stay. Anyway, it's just a movie. It's not necessarily accurate."

"You really have no way of getting him to America?" she pressed.

"Really," I said.

"All right, I just wanted to ask," she said. "Yu Tao wants to talk with you." She spoke a few inaudible words to Yu Tao before handing the phone to him.

"Hi Yu Tao, how are you doing?" I asked.

"Just average," he said.

"How are your studies going?" I asked.

"Just average," he said.

"Have you been able to find a job?" I asked.

"No," he replied. "There are just too many high school and college graduates here, so I can't compete for the good jobs. I don't want to get a bad job here because it won't pay off. But I'm willing to do any job abroad because a year's wages abroad are equal to ten years' wages in China. If I can just work for a few years in America, I'll have enough money to come back and start my own business."

"You wouldn't be able to save that much here," I said. "The wages here may be ten times higher than in China, but so are the expenses. With little English ability and not even a high school diploma, you'd have at least as much difficulty finding a job here as you have in China. And any job you get would pay a wage that barely covers your living expenses."

"I could still save enough money to be rich in China," he insisted after I gave him estimates of wages, rents, and food prices in the United States. "I'll work 80 hours a week, eat plain rice every day, and rent the smallest, worst room I can find. I'll find a way to save money, if you just give me a chance to work in America."

"I don't have the ability to do that," I said. "I'm not a school admissions officer, or an employer, or an immediate family member of yours, so American officials won't pay any attention to me if I ask them to give you a visa."

"Couldn't you tell them I'm your brother?" he asked. "Or ask your parents or professors to help? I'm pleading with you."

"I can't do anything illegal," I said. "If the law changes, or if I see an opportunity for you to come here, I'll tell you, but I don't think that's likely."

"Please try your best," he said. "I don't have a future in China."

## Lin Lin, a Wealthy, High-Achieving Girl

"How long will this take?" Lin Lin asked her parents impatiently as they prepared to take her and me to a fancy restaurant.

"It'll just be a few hours," her father said. "The food will be delicious, and you'll learn a lot from Teacher Fong."

"I know, but the traffic is jammed because it's rush hour, we won't be able to find a taxi, and that restaurant takes a long time to prepare its dishes," Lin Lin said. "I have a test this week. You should go first, and I'll take a taxi over in an hour, after the traffic is less congested and the food has arrived."

"All right," her mother said, and gave her money for her solo taxi trip.

"Why don't we just walk to a restaurant nearby?" I suggested.

"All the nearby restaurants are unsanitary," Lin Lin's father replied. "Besides, this restaurant has very authentic Beijing-style roast duck, and we want you to know what the very best Chinese food is like."

I went with Lin Lin's parents to the restaurant by taxi. They told me about Lin Lin's strong work ethic and high score on the Test of English as a Foreign Language. "We don't think she'll have the opportunity to develop her abilities fully in China," her mother said. "We want her to go to college in America."

Lin Lin's mother had invited me to dinner after getting my phone number from her friend, the father of an adult education college student I tutored. I had arrived at Lin Lin's home hoping to enjoy a home-cooked meal, which I generally preferred as a form of commensalism more useful to my research and less expensive for my hosts than a restaurant meal. But Lin Lin's parents, both company managers, were too busy to cook that day.

Lin Lin's timing was on the mark. She showed up at the restaurant right after the delicate slices of roasted duck meat with fragrant, crispy skin arrived on our table. Speaking in halting but grammatically correct English, she asked me detailed questions about American life, and told me about the schedule she hoped to keep. "Tonight, I will study one hour, to look at the wrong answers on my math exam," she said. "Then, I will study one hour, to do math problems. Then, I will study one hour, to learn English vocabulary. Then, I will do English exam problems. I want to stay awake till half past twelve." I complimented her on her devotion to her studies. "I have to work hard, because I'm not smart," she said.

"How's her English? Would she have trouble living in America?" her parents asked.

"Her English is really good, and she'd do fine in America," I replied. "But can you really afford to pay for an American college education?"

"We've saved money, and we'll borrow more if that's what it takes to send her to America," Lin Lin's mother said. "We just have one child, and all our hopes are pinned on her."

I explained the costs of living and tuition in the United States, and the dearth of scholarships for Chinese students at the undergraduate level. I suggested that it would be less expensive for her to attend a prestigious Chinese university and then apply to American graduate programs, which were more likely to give Chinese students full scholarships or work as teaching or research assistants. After consulting with friends and relatives, Lin Lin and her parents decided to take my advice.

When the time came for Lin Lin to apply to Chinese universities, her parents debated over whether she should select a local university as her top choice among first-rate four-year universities, or whether she should aim for a more prestigious university in a different city. They sought advice from me and from their friends, relatives, and co-workers about which Chinese universities were most likely to enhance a student's chances of getting accepted to an American graduate program with full financial support. While higher-ranked universities in other parts of China might enhance her chances of going abroad, those universities were more selective, and had smaller quotas for students from the Dalian area. The local university had lower minimum score requirements, especially for local students. Moreover, Lin Lin's mother had a friend who was a professor at that university. Even if Lin Lin scored below the cutoff, she might still get accepted with help from this friend. With their extensive social networks, Lin Lin's parents would also be able to help Lin Lin in myriad other ways if she stayed in Dalian. In the end, they told her to select the local university because it was the safest choice. Lin Lin agreed.

Despite their busy schedules, Lin Lin's parents both took time off from work to stay with her all three days of the college entrance exam of 1999. After we saw Lin Lin off into the exam hall, I accompanied her parents as they took a taxi to McDonald's, waited in line to get Happy Meals to go, and then took a taxi back to the exam hall to wait for Lin Lin to come out on her lunch break. Lin Lin came out smiling, and gave her mother a detailed account of how she did on various parts of the exam as they walked hand in hand to the taxi, where Lin Lin's father stayed to prevent other families from taking it. They had the taxi drive them home so that Lin Lin could eat her Happy Meal in their air-conditioned apartment.

Lin Lin scored well above the cutoff for first-rate four-year university programs, and was easily accepted by the local university. She and her parents regretted that they had aimed too low.

After the college entrance exam, her parents invited me to their home for meals on several occasions. Lin Lin told me that she was relieved that she had scored as high on her college entrance exam as she usually scored on practice tests. "I used to have poor psychological quality," she said. "I was always ranked near the top of my junior high school, and all my teachers said I would have no problem getting into a keypoint high school. But I panicked during the high school entrance exam, and scored below the keypoint high school cutoff. I cried for weeks afterwards. I didn't want to live. My parents had to pay so much money to get me into a keypoint high school, and they had to ask for help from people who knew the principal. So I felt a burden in my heart, and I was determined to prove that I was worthy of all that."

With the exam over, Lin Lin could at last spend time with her friends without feeling guilty about neglecting her studies. "I spent every winter and summer break since first grade getting tutored or going to extra classes," she told me. "This is the first real holiday I've ever had!" She particularly relished going to restaurants and shopping malls with her friends from high school. She started buying fashionable clothes. Though she had always kept her hair boyishly short because she feared that washing and brushing longer hair would take time away from her studies, she now resolved to let it grow long enough to hold a popular hairstyle.

Her parents gave her a hundred yuan (US$13) each time she went out. "We want her to play and be happy," her mother told me. "She's earned it." They warned her, however, not to spend time alone with her male best friend. Though Lin Lin insisted that she had never had a boyfriend, and that she and this boy were "brothers" (*gemenr*) her parents warned her against "letting something develop" with him. "You want to go abroad, so don't get distracted," her mother cautioned her.

Lin Lin looked forward to college all summer. After she enrolled, however, she told me she felt disappointed. She tried living in a dormitory for a few months, but soon found that she could not stand sharing a small dorm room with seven other girls. She was surprised that they were not as disciplined as she had imagined students at a first-rate university would be. They chatted so much that she could not concentrate on her studies. She missed her computer, her comfortable bed, and her quiet, spacious room. So she moved back home, and commuted to her university.

After I returned to the United States, Lin Lin and her parents continued to ask me for advice about getting Lin Lin into an American graduate school. Lin Lin's mother recounted stories she had heard about others who had gone abroad. "My co-worker told me that her friend's daughter went to America as a graduate student," she told me. "She married a Chinese American, they both got jobs in computer programming, and just a few years later, they bought a house and two cars, with no help from their parents. How many years would it take to save enough money to buy a house and two cars in China? Now they're trying to bring her parents over to America too."

"I want her to be able to develop her abilities, but it's hard for a smart but quiet girl like her to rise up high in China," her father said. "I want her to come back to serve the motherland. But I want her to be able to do it on her own terms. I don't want her to be held back because she doesn't know how to flatter people, or because her parents don't have the right connections. Why is it that Chinese people abroad can win Nobel prizes, but not Chinese people in China? Anyone who has studied abroad is coated in gold. They're treated differently from the rest. That's what I want for her."

Lin Lin wanted to go abroad, but she also worried about the difficulty of winning a scholarship. "My parents might be able to send me abroad without a scholarship if they borrow from all their friends and relatives, but I wouldn't want them to take on such a burden," she said. "I only want to go if I can get a scholarship on the basis of my own ability. Otherwise, I'll just look for a job in China. I won't need to go abroad if I can find a good job here. China is developing fast, so maybe in the future I'll be able to earn as much in China as I could abroad."

## Hu Ying, a Poor, High-Achieving Girl

As I hurried home from the college prep high school one cold December day in 1998, a girl with large, bright eyes and a determined expression ran after me. It was Hu Ying, one of hundreds of students I taught at that school. "Teacher Fong . . . " she called out.

"Hello!" I replied.

She paused to gather her breath and her courage, and then blurted out shyly, "Will you be my English tutor?"

"Okay!" I replied enthusiastically. After discussing where and when I would meet her, she asked nervously how much I would charge for tutoring her. "I don't let your school pay me to teach English, so how could I charge you for tutoring?" I replied. "Like I said in class, I'm here to do research. I just want to learn more about you and your family."

We met at the school on Sunday, her only day off, and took a bus to her apartment. In addition to a tiny, poorly ventilated kitchen and a bathroom with a floor toilet that had to be flushed with tubs of water carried from the kitchen sink, there was one cramped but neat and clean room that served as the bedroom, living room, dining room, and Hu Ying's study. It contained a few cabinets, a small couch, a bed that Hu Ying and her parents all slept on at night, and a dinner table that also served as Hu Ying's desk.

We spent the morning sitting at the table, going over mistakes she had made on practice tests and homework assignments. She asked me to explain the rules of syntax, spelling, and grammar underlying each answer she failed to get right. We tried conversing in English, though we switched to Chinese whenever our conversations got too interesting to rely just on the English words she knew. When she could not remember words she had previously memorized, she sighed with frustration and said, "I'm too stupid."

At noon, Hu Ying's mother came back, dragging the large bag of socks and knit caps she failed to sell at a stall she had rented in the outdoor market. Hu Ying introduced me to her mother as we helped her drag the bag in.

"It's not worth it. You're freezing and exhausted, but you're struggling just to avoid losing money," Hu Ying chided her mother, a 49-year-old worker who had been given early retirement from her factory.

"It's better than just staying at home!" her mother replied. "If I can make just a few more yuan a day, that's a few more yuan I can save for your college tuition. After you finish college and get a good job, you can support me, but until then I have to do everything I can to make money to send you to college."

Hu Ying's mother talked with me for a while about her hopes for Hu Ying. Then Hu Ying's father returned from exercising with his friends. After Hu Ying introduced me to her father, a 50-year-old factory worker, he boasted about Hu Ying's studiousness. "I don't know how I ended up with a daughter who loves to study," he said. "Maybe I would have been a good student too if my family hadn't been so poor that I had to start working when I was 15."

Hu Ying cleared the table of her study materials as her parents prepared dishes of bean sprouts, leeks, mushrooms, chopped pork, and chicken drumsticks that were considerably more expensive than what they ate when there was no guest. Over lunch, I told Hu Ying's parents about my research and my life in the United States, and they told me about their admiration for American people and dislike of American imperialism.

After lunch, as I prepared to leave, Hu Ying's mother put a 50-yuan note (US$6) in my hand. It was one-eighth of her monthly pension. I gave it back to her. She stuffed it in my pocket. I took it out, tried to stuff it in her hand, and then threw it on the table when she backed away. She snatched it up and tried to stuff it in my backpack. "Take it, take it!" she insisted, while I dodged and struggled. After a few minutes, I managed to get out the door without the money. "See you next week!" I grinned triumphantly at Hu Ying and her parents, shut the door, and ran off before they could come out after me.

I tutored Hu Ying in English every weekend until she took the college entrance exam. As she and her parents got to know me, they realized that my refusal of money was genuine, and stopped trying to make me take it. Eventually, we became close enough that they sometimes let me eat the same simple meals of rice and leftovers they often ate. Hu Ying diligently plowed through the excruciatingly boring fill-in-the-blank and multiple-choice questions in her workbooks. She forced herself to stay up studying long after her parents had fallen asleep. She borrowed textbooks from friends to avoid the expense of buying them.

During study hall at school, Hu Ying hunched over her books even while other students chatted. She was grateful for her homeroom teacher's efforts to keep everyone quiet. "My homeroom teacher's strict, but only because she has high hopes for us, just like for her own child," Hu Ying told me.

Hu Ying seldom went out with her friends, most of whom were also studious. "I don't have time to play around, so I can't make friends with classmates who don't study well," she told me. She told me that she had never had a boyfriend. Her test scores were sometimes among the top five in her class of 52 students.

She dreamed of getting into a good college that would lead to a prestigious, high-paying job. "I want to get a good job so I can buy my parents a nice apartment," she said after seeing a relative's large new apartment. "They've had hard lives, and I want them to be happy in their old age. I also want the kind of job that would let me respect myself. I don't want to just work as a waitress."

Though she was one of the most disciplined teenagers I knew, Hu Ying told me that she had been "as wild and naughty as a boy" when she was a child. "My Pa had wanted a son, so I wanted to climb trees and jump off walls even better than the boys could, just to please him," she told me. "But as I grew up, I realized that I would never be a boy, no matter how many trees and walls I climbed, and that my Pa was happiest when I did well in school. So I worked hard to become a top student in my junior high school."

Hu Ying had missed the cutoff for "publicly funded" (*gongfei*) students at a better college prep high school by just two points. She had the option of going to that school as a "self-funded" (*zifei*) student. With enough money and connections, she might even have gotten into a keypoint high school. Understanding that her parents could not afford those options, however, she had rejected them and dedicated herself to studying as hard as she could at her own high school. "If I had really wanted to study at a better high school, my parents would have come up with the money somehow, even if they had to borrow it from friends and relatives," she told me. "But I felt it wasn't worth it. Spending that much money would have put a lot of psychological pressure on me, and that might have made me panic during the college entrance exam," she told me. Though she had not panicked during the college entrance exam she took after she graduated in 1998, she had still scored too low to get into any of the colleges she had selected as her top choices. Therefore, she was repeating her senior year at the time I met her.

Hu Ying's two best friends from junior high school had both gone on to keypoint high schools and first-rate universities. Hu Ying attended another friend's college graduation in the summer of 1998, and found it exhilarating. "A group of women graduates were singing the song 'Come, 1998', and it seemed so appropriate," Hu Ying told me. "When I was watching them, I thought, 'I must go to college!'"

Hu Ying's father could not take time off from work, but her mother and maternal aunt accompanied her all three days of the college entrance exam. They brought bags of pears, apples, bananas, and steamed buns for her to snack on while waiting for the exam hall to open, but Hu Ying was so nervous that she could only drink water. Over the three days of the exam, they took special care to prepare mild meals that were not likely to give her indigestion, but she was too nervous to eat much.

Some of Hu Ying's classmates took the adult education college entrance exam so that they would have a backup option if they failed to get into a regular college. Hu Ying, however, refused to do so. "I've heard that adult education colleges aren't as fair as regular colleges. I know students who got into better adult education colleges through connections, even though they scored lower than others who got into worse colleges. I don't want to waste my energy. For me, it's a regular college or nothing!"

When it was time to apply to colleges, parents of college prep high school seniors milked their social networks for information about colleges and majors. Some seniors told me that they barely had time to look at their college application materials before they were snatched away by their parents, who took full responsibility for deciding which majors and colleges their children should apply to.

Hu Ying, however, relied almost entirely on her friends and teachers for advice. Her parents could not do much to help her, as they and most of their friends and relatives were factory workers with no connections to the educational system.

"What kinds of majors are suitable for a girl?" she asked me.

"I'm not sure," I said. "Just choose something you'll enjoy and be good at."

"You should apply for the Maritime University," her mother suggested. "I hear all its women graduates end up as customs officers, wearing uniforms and caps."

"No, only a few get those jobs," Hu Ying said. "How could the government have enough money to give jobs to every graduate? Besides, I'm sure I didn't score high enough to be accepted by that university."

When I called her the night before the college application form was due, she had still not decided on her top choice colleges and majors. After she submitted her application, she told me that she had decided at the last minute to select education departments as her top choices because they charged the least tuition. A few days, later, however, she heard from a friend that those departments required interviews by a deadline that had long passed. Horrified that she had wasted her top choices on them, Hu Ying rushed to the district education office to change her application. After scolding Hu Ying until she burst into tears, a staff member there allowed her to fill out a new application.

Hu Ying's parents griped so much about regular colleges' annual tuition of 2000–3,000 yuan (US$250-US$375) that she did not even dare to mention that she might have the option of paying 8,000 yuan (US $1,000) a year for admission to a four-year college as a privately funded student even if she scored below the cutoff. The day before she had to decide whether to apply for that option, however, her father told her, "My friends were all talking about the new option for privately funded students, and they said I'd be a fool to deny it to such a studious daughter. I think they're right. So if you want to be a privately funded student, I'll find a way to get the money together."

Wracked with indecision, Hu Ying spent the day thinking her options over and discussing them with her parents. When I visited her the day after the deadline for signing up as a privately funded student had passed, she told me, "We decided it wasn't worth it. My parents' lives are hard enough as it is. Their lives will be unbearable if they have to pay 10,000 yuan a year for me, and owe so much money to so many people. And who knows what might happen? Right now the colleges claim that anyone who pays extra to get in will be treated just like other students, but maybe things will change once I'm there. Maybe I'd have to pay extra for room and board as well, and only get the worst teachers, and have the fact that I paid extra to get in stamped on my diploma. Besides, I don't want to buy exam scores with money."

Hu Ying scored just under the cutoff for four-year colleges. Some classmates whose scores were even lower than Hu Ying's official score were accepted by a four-year college that had lowered its cutoff after not getting enough qualified applicants. When she heard about this, she reproached herself for not having made that college her top choice. She was easily accepted by her top choice among junior colleges, a school that was a day away by train. Her mother and maternal aunt took the train with her to help her move into her dorm. Whenever Hu Ying came back home on vacation, her parents prepared elaborate meals for her and showered her with gifts. Hu Ying's mother cried each time she saw Hu Ying off at the train station.

Like many students at her junior college, Hu Ying took extra classes to prepare for college equivalency exams that could get her a four-year college degree. The exams were so difficult, however, that she and her classmates failed most of them. Still, they continued to take the exams every semester, hoping that they would eventually pass all 15 exams and qualify for the four-year degree.

"I want to get as much education as I can," Hu Ying told me. "I'd like to get a four-year degree, and then maybe even a master's degree. I want to get a job that's interesting and pays well. I'm a child of poor workers, but I want my future child to be the child of an intellectual."

Hu Ying's mother found work as a janitor. She worked six days a week for only 350 yuan (US$44) a month, but it was more than she could make by peddling goods in the outdoor market.

Hu Ying got a part-time job from an instant noodle company, surveying local storekeepers about the kinds of instant noodles they carried. She earned 2.50 yuan (US$0.31) for each survey she got a storekeeper to fill out. "It's not a lot, but it's nice spending money, and I like not having to ask my parents for money all the time," she told me when I called her from the United States. "Besides, it's interesting work, and a new experience!"

Though Hu Ying's parents had difficulty earning enough money for her tuition and living expenses, they were not happy when she told them about her new job. "It's not worth wasting precious study time to earn a few yuan," her mother said. Hu Ying came to agree as the semester wore on and she became busier, so she quit her job.

A high school friend of Hu Ying's college roommate offered to let Hu Ying stay for free in her dorm room in Beijing so that Hu Ying could attend a prestigious English language institute during the summer. "Their GRE and TOEFL preparation classes cost thousands of yuan, but I'd only have to pay 580 yuan for a regular English class," Hu Ying told me. "My Ma doesn't want me to go because she thinks it's too expensive, and I could learn English in Dalian for much cheaper, and she's also worried about me going to Beijing alone. But I really want to go! It's the best English language institute in China! When will I get another opportunity like this? And I've never been out of my province, and I so much want to see my country's capital!"

Hu Ying eventually persuaded her parents that the opportunity was too valuable to pass up. Hu Ying was thrilled. As soon as she arrived in

Beijing, she took a bus to Tiananmen Square, and waited there all through the night to see the flag-raising ceremony at 5:00 AM the next morning. She eagerly attended the English language institute's classes, during which she sat in an auditorium with about 500 other students, listening to inspirational lectures about the English language and First World cultures by teachers who had grown up in China but became fluent in English after studying abroad.

Hu Ying was awed by the dedication of her classmates at the English language institute, some of whom attended China's top universities. "They're so grand, and I seem so small compared to them," she told me. "As I walked through an area of Beijing full of famous universities, I saw endless waves of well-educated people my age, and I wondered how I could ever get a good job with so much competition."

## Wang Song, a Wealthy, Sometimes High-Achieving Boy

I was introduced to Wang Song, a keypoint college prep high school senior, by his maternal uncle, the father of an adult education college student I tutored. Wang Song's father was an engineer, and his mother was an accountant. They asked me to tutor Wang Song in English.

Wang Song's parents complained that he was lazy. Wang Song admitted that he did not always study as much as he should. To me, however, it seemed that he studied all the time. Each time I visited him, he showed me reams of practice exams he had completed, and asked me to explain the grammatical rules underlying all the questions he had gotten wrong. He seldom went out with his friends on weekends. When his parents visited their friends and relatives during Spring Festival, he stayed home to study, even though it meant missing out on socializing, delicious feasts, gift money, and marathon poker and mahjong sessions. His parents prepared fancy meals in their spacious dining room whenever I visited, but he always gulped down his food in less than twenty minutes, and went back to his room to study, leaving his parents and me to linger over the meal for another hour.

Still, his parents scolded him for not studying enough. "Everyone is trying to get into college," his mother reminded him. "The top-scoring students are not going to rest. You may be studying harder than ever before, but so are they. You can't just study harder than you've ever studied. You also have to study harder than everyone else has ever studied."

"If you get into a good college, I'll be completely carefree," his father said. "I care more about your future than anything else. You're my only worry. If you fail to get into college, it'll hurt me more than if my company fired me."

Wang Song's test performance was uneven. On several tests, he had ranked among the top ten students in his homeroom, to his parents' delight. On other tests, however, he ranked in the middle or even the bottom of his class. "Sometimes I think my scores drop when I study too hard, and get too anxious," he told me. "It's my parents' fault for nagging me so much. During the test, I hear their nagging in my mind, so I get upset and distracted."

As they stood outside the exam hall, waiting for the start of the college entrance exam of 1999, his parents seemed more nervous than he was. He chatted with some friends, but his parents insisted that he open his books and do some cramming during the last minutes before the exam began. "I've studied as much as I can," Wang Song said. "Now it's up to fate."

"Don't be so nonchalant!" his mother said. "We both took time off from work to be with you today, and we're not going to leave until you do. If the exam questions seem hard and you feel like giving up, think about your parents standing out here in the heat and humidity, waiting for you. Think of how much your parents have sacrificed for you. Think of how much your parents care for you."

After the exam, Wang Song was uncertain how he had performed. "I can't remember which answers I put down!" he cried when he looked at an answer book designed to help students estimate their scores. Unable to estimate his score, he and his parents agonized over which schools he should make his top choices. They knew from his high school tests that he was capable of getting a wide range of scores. In the end, his parents told him to gamble on assuming that he had scored high enough to get into a top-ranked college.

"We don't want him to waste his time at a bad college," his father told me. "If he doesn't get in anywhere, he can retake the exam again next year."

They lost their gamble. Wang Song scored below the cutoffs of all his top-choice colleges. His score was even lower than the cutoff for privately funded (*minban*) students.

"Wang Song's Pa and I cried when we learned his score at midnight, but Wang Song didn't seem to react," Wang Song's mother told me when I called to ask about his score. "He said it was fate, and that we shouldn't worry about it. But his Pa and I couldn't fall asleep. We were worried that Wang Song would do something drastic, and wanted to console him. We went into his room, only to find that he was cheerfully playing a videogame!"

The next morning, Wang Song went out to play soccer with his friends from junior high school. His parents' relief at his lack of suicidal tendencies gradually turned to annoyance at his nonchalance. "He doesn't think about the future," Wang Song's father told me. "He doesn't care about anything besides playing around."

Wang Song had a different explanation. "I want to get rid of my pain," he told me. "My friends from junior high school didn't even get into college prep high schools, and this year they didn't even make it to adult education colleges. Yet they're still alive, and playing soccer! Being with them is relaxing. My parents think life is not worth living if you can't get into a good college. If I had their attitude, I really wouldn't be able to live!"

Wang Song's parents wanted him to spend another year in high school and then retake the entrance exam. Wang Song refused. "I'll kill myself before I go through that hell for another year!" he said. His parents scolded him and pleaded with him, but they eventually realized that they could not force him to do it. Wang Song was eventually admitted to a low-ranked junior college, but neither he nor his parents thought it was worth it for him to enroll. Wang Song told his parents that he was sick of the Chinese educational system, and wanted to study abroad. They reluctantly agreed to try to send him abroad. In the meantime, they enrolled him in private English classes.

"Now that he's not in school, he doesn't care about studying anymore," his father complained to me. "He thinks we can support him all his life!"

"My parents think I have no regrets, and that they're the only ones who are feeling the bitterness of my failure," Wang Song told me in the privacy of his room. "But I'm suffering, too. I'm suffering more than they are! It's my future that's at stake, after all! I just don't want to let them know how much I regret not studying harder, because I don't want them to say they were right all along, and that I should have listened to them. They were right, but they shouldn't have nagged at me in such an annoying way. They gave me too much pressure, and I couldn't stand it. That's the real reason I did so poorly on the exam."

For the first few months after his parents agreed to prepare to send him abroad, Wang Song was glad to be free of the sleepless, high-pressure schedule he kept during high school. Though he was taking private English classes, he still had plenty of time to play video games and soccer with his friends. Gradually, however, he grew listless. "In high school, a teacher who really cared about us kept saying that, once we were out of school, we would regret every minute of time we wasted during school, because we can never get that time back again," he told me. "I didn't pay attention to her then, but now I realize she was right. I didn't study as much as I should have. Now I regret that. I knew my parents were depending on me, but I let them down."

Wang Song's regrets deepened after his father fell down the stairs of his apartment building and broke his leg. Soon afterwards, his mother had to go to the hospital because of a bad cold, which he attributed to the stress she experienced while taking care of his father. "I'm sad," he said. "It was all because I was arguing with him, and I got him so angry that he didn't look where he was going! He could have died in that fall. If he had died, I would have killed myself. I didn't realize how much I loved my parents until they ended up in the hospital. Now I think about how they're getting old, and how they won't be here forever. I've resolved to stop fighting with them. They're good people, and I'll miss them after they die. If I keep fighting with them, then after they die, I'll regret not having been a good son while they were still alive."

Wang Song and his parents tried to decide between the United Kingdom, France, Germany, Ireland, Australia, Japan, Canada, and the United States as his possible destinations. But none of those countries seemed entirely satisfactory. If he went to Japan, France, or Germany, he would have to enroll in language programs rather than regular college programs, and it would take many expensive years before his language ability would be good enough to gain him admission to regular college programs. Australia, Canada, the United Kingdom, and the United States would not allow him to work enough to pay for more than a small fraction of his tuition and living expenses. Ireland might allow him to work enough to support himself while studying, but he heard from a friend who had gone to Ireland that one had to work long, exhausting hours at dull, repetitive jobs to earn enough to support oneself there. Most importantly, Wang Song worried about how going abroad would burden his parents. "They'd be happier if I attend a good college in China, because I'd be nearby, and they wouldn't have to pay so much money to support me. Yet they're willing to use all their savings to satisfy my desire to go abroad, because they really care for me. Would I be doing right by them if I go?"

He eventually decided that the answer was "no." To his parents' delight, he agreed to retake his senior year, and try his luck on China's college entrance exam again. "I didn't think I'd see things this way, but I miss being a student," he told me. "I miss being with classmates, and knowing what I had to do every minute of every day. Now I'm just a 'youth of society,' and I don't like that. I don't want to be like those boys who hang out on the street all the time, with no hope and no future."

## Chen Jun, a Poor, High-Achieving Boy

I met Chen Jun in 1999, at an extended family gathering for his paternal grandfather's birthday celebration, to which I had been invited by Chen Jun's paternal cousin, a vocational high school student I tutored. Chen Jun's parents asked me to tutor their son as well.

Chen Jun had always been the top student in his junior high school class. "No one else in my class scored as high as I did on practice tests, so I thought it wasn't necessary to work any harder," he said. "I didn't know how bad my junior high school was, or how many other good students there were in other schools. So failing to get into a keypoint college prep high school was my punishment." He did not even get into his regular college prep high school's keypoint class, which provided top teachers and extra homework for its highest-scoring students and also for other students who paid an extra 1000 yuan (US$125) per year. Chen Jun's parents were willing to pay the extra money to get him into that class, but Chen Jun talked them out of it. "It wasn't worth it," he told me. "As long as I work hard, it doesn't matter which class I'm in."

Chen Jun took the warnings of his parents and teachers seriously, and never dated. "There are many boys who ruin their futures by spending all their time chasing girls," he told me. "I'm not going to waste time on anything that won't help me get into college."

I went to Chen Jun's home every other week to help him go over the questions he had gotten wrong in his English workbooks and practice tests. Though he was bored by multiple-choice questions about the finer points of grammar and syntax, he enjoyed the English language passages in the reading comprehension tests. He asked me if I had been to Hawaii, Disneyland, and other places that he had read about in his English textbooks. "I hope that someday I'll be able to see all these places. I want to travel all over the world, work at lots of different jobs, and send my parents money so they can buy a big apartment and have everything they ever wanted," he said.

One day, I arrived at Chen Jun's home for a tutoring session before Chen Jun had gotten back from school, and found that both of his parents were crying.

"What happened?" I asked.

They explained that Chen Jun's father had just learned that he would lose his job. "After 27 years working for the factory, it's come to this," he said, with tears streaming down his face. "I'm going to kill my boss," he said. "Why should I let him live if he won't let me live?"

"Don't even think about that," his wife said. "It wouldn't solve anything. And it's not just your boss's fault. All the factories are going bankrupt."

"Chairman Mao would not have let this happen," he said. "Now Heaven has no eyes."

Chen Jun's mother strategized about how to keep her own job. "Wasn't there an official pronouncement that factories could not lay off workers whose spouses are already unemployed?" she asked hopefully.

Chen Jun's father pointed out many cases that contradicted this "pronouncement." Chen Jun's mother said she would tell everyone at her factory that her husband had lost his job. "Even if there wasn't a pronouncement, at least they'll feel sorry for me. Maybe that'll protect me from the next wave of layoffs."

They debated over whether to tell Chen Jun about his father's layoff. "He might become too upset to do well on the college entrance exam," his mother said.

"He'll figure out that I've lost my job, even if we try to keep it a secret," his father said. "I can't hide this. Do you want me to go off and play mahjong every day and tell him I was at work?"

Chen Jun took the news calmly when he got home from school. "Don't be upset," he consoled his father. "I promise I'll work even harder to get into college, so I can get a good job and earn money. Then, you can just retire and relax."

At Chen Jun's maternal grandmother's birthday party, Chen Jun's mother begged her siblings and their spouses to help her husband find work. They said they would try, and the wealthier ones also offered to help Chen Jun with his tuition if he was accepted by a college.

Most seniors at Chen Jun's high school knew that they were unlikely to get into regular colleges, so they took the entrance exam for adult education college programs, which were less selective and prestigious. Chen Jun, however, refused to do this. "Anyone can get into an adult education college, and bosses know that, so the degree's not useful enough to be worth putting my parents in debt," he said. "If I don't get into a regular college, I'll try to get a job, any job, from anyone who will hire me. Then, after I save enough money, I can go to adult education college or take the college equivalency exams."

Chen Jun seemed to be in a bad mood during our last tutoring session, a month before the college entrance exam. I asked him what was wrong. "Yesterday, my homeroom teacher told our whole class, 'In all the years I've been a teacher, I've never had a student from my homeroom make it to a four-year college. What makes you think you're any different?'" Chen Jun fumed. "How could a teacher say that? And wasn't it his own fault that none of his students ever succeeded? I was so angry at him. After that, no one in my class wanted to study. Everyone just talked and played poker during study hall, and he didn't care. I tried to study, but I kept getting distracted because all the other students were talking and playing around."

"You'll have to ignore them and study on your own," I said. Chen Jun agreed, but he seemed morose and had difficulty concentrating.

I visited Chen Jun's college entrance exam site early in the morning of July 8, 1999, before going to visit the exam sites of my other students. It rained while we stood around waiting for the exam hall to open, so Chen Jun's parents took turns holding an umbrella over him while he took one last look through his textbooks. When I wished him luck, he raised his head briefly to nod at me and then continued to pore over the open textbook he clutched in his hands.

After the exam, Chen Jun went over the exam booklet carefully, trying to estimate his score. "I keep coming up with impossibly high scores," he said. "I'm just deluding myself." When filling out his college application form, he picked the least selective schools as his top choices. He never even told his parents about the new option for privately funded (*minban*) students. "With my Pa unemployed, there's no way we could afford that, even with loans from all our relatives," he told me.

The day after the exam scores were released, I got a call from Chen Jun's mother. "Chen Jun scored above the four-year college cutoff!" she crowed. "He's sure to get into his top-choice school!" She invited me to a dinner to celebrate Chen Jun's achievement.

Chen Jun, his parents, fourteen of their relatives, and I crowded into Chen Jun's family's one-room apartment for the dinner. Chen Jun ate at the table along with his cousins and me, while his parents, aunts, and uncles ate on the bed or the floor. Chen Jun was the only student from his homeroom who scored high enough to be accepted by a regular four-year college. "Now my despicable homeroom teacher won't have to tell another class that none of his students ever made it to a four-year college," Chen Jun told us triumphantly. "He doesn't deserve the glory I've brought him, but at least I've saved his future students from the despair I felt."

## Systems, Cultural Models, and Individual Lives

The stories in this chapter illustrate how teenagers learned various aspects of the cultural model of modernization. Teenagers' responses to this cultural model varied with their personalities, family situations, and their socioeconomic and academic assets. Sun Wei, Hu Ying, and Chen Jun intensely desired academic credentials that could raise them and their parents out of poverty. Secure in his belief that he could maintain his high standard of living by taking over his parents' restaurant business, Teng Fei seemed less driven. Yang Shu's attitude was similar to Teng Fei's when I first met her, but became more like those of Sun Wei, Hu Ying, and Chen Jun as her parents' fortunes declined. Lin Lin's academic excellence opened up the possibility that she could win a job that would make her elite even by First World standards, so she wanted to attain upward mobility by going abroad, even though her parents were already elite by Chinese standards. Like other teenagers, Yu Tao dreamed of getting a college equivalency degree or going abroad; because he lacked academic ability and economic resources, however, he could only channel his aspirations into crime and low-income work. Yu Tao grew increasingly desperate as all these strategies continued to fail. Wang Song started out trying to gain elite status through achievement in China's educational system. When he failed to get into a four-year college, however, he began to see study abroad as the best means to elite status, even though his parents wanted him to retake his senior year and the college entrance exam. However, as he did more research about study abroad, he learned more about the hardships it would impose on him and his parents. His father's injury and his mother's illness also reminded him of his filial duty. In addition, Wang Song missed being in high school. Because of all these factors, Wang Song changed his mind once again, and agreed to follow his parents' wishes.

Ruth Behar has argued that "A life history narrative should allow one to see the subjective mapping of experience, the working out of a culture and a social system that is often obscured in a typified account."[7] Lila Abu-Lughod observed that detailed portrayals of the lives of individuals help the reader to see them "not as automatons programmed according to 'cultural' rules or acting out social roles, but as people going through life wondering what they should do, making mistakes, being opinionated, vacillating, trying to make themselves look good, enduring tragic personal losses, enjoying others, and finding moments of laughter."[8] In support of the "tactical humanism"[9] advocated by anthropologists like Behar and Abu-Lughod, I wrote this chapter to highlight the variations, complexities, and contingencies of urban Dalian teenagers' interactions with the cultural models and political economy I will describe in subsequent chapters. In the chapters that follow this one, I will illustrate the causes and effects of the fertility transition, the cultural model of modernization, and the capitalist world system with scenes and quotations chosen for their effectiveness as examples of the points I make. To avoid distracting readers from these broad patterns, I will refrain from detailing the rich histories and individual idiosyncrasies behind each example. I hope, however, that the reader will remember that every example was taken out of the context of lives as complex as those portrayed in this chapter.

# CHAPTER 2

# Great Expectations

## *Singletons as the Vanguard of Modernization*

TO GENERATE excitement about the return of the Portuguese colony Macao to Chinese rule on December 20, 1999, the state-controlled Chinese media broadcast features portraying Macao as a glittering model of Chinese success in the capitalist world system. As we watched a televised feature about a hospital in Macao where elderly people could get free medical care, the food vendor I was visiting grew angry. "Look at them, they're in heaven!" he cried. "They don't even need children to support them. They can live worry-free. Look at how beautiful and modern their free hospital is. Unlike here, where no one cares about us. When we have no money for a hospital stay, we'll just die. When I'm old and ill, I'll just go and lie on the street and die, and the government will get rid of my body once it starts to rot. We are in the 18th level of hell compared to people abroad. It would have been better not to show us how rich people in Macao are. Just seeing how well they live, and how good their social services are, makes us feel poor."

"The main problem here is that there are too many people," said his 20-year-old son Han Dong, an adult education college student. "People in Macao don't have a lot of children, so of course they're rich. In the future, people here will be just as rich, since everyone in my generation's a singleton. How could China have gotten rich in the past, with every generation doubling the population?"

Han Dong drew on the cultural model of low fertility commonly promoted by the population control propaganda disseminated by the media, workplace political meetings, and politics classes at school. China's one-child policy is based on the principle that it is easier to modernize a smaller group—whether it be a family or a nation—than a larger group. The fewer people there are, the more resources there will be for each person. Chinese population experts have been careful to distinguish this principle from British economist Thomas Malthus's warning[1] that overpopulation will lead to famine. Though he advocated family planning and population control, the late paramount Chinese leader Mao Zedong also vilified "Malthusianism" as an affront to his belief that socialist modernization could eliminate poverty.[2] Even in the final decades of the twentieth century, Chinese Communists adhered to Mao Zedong's portrayal of "Malthusianism" as an ideology used by capitalists to absolve themselves of guilt for letting impoverished people starve to death. Rather than presenting the one-child policy as a means to prevent famine, Chinese officials in charge of population control have emphasized that it is a way to increase the "quality" (*suzhi*) of the Chinese people by applying to birth planning (*jihua shengyu*) the same discipline they applied to economic planning (*jihua jingji*). As then Deputy Prime Minister Chen Muhua wrote in the official government newspaper *People's Daily* (*Renmin Ribao*) in 1979, "The purpose of family planning and of controlling population growth is to promote the four modernizations and to improve the people's standard of living."[3] At the national level, a smaller population would allow each person to enjoy a larger share of national resources, such as jobs, housing, education, food, water, and land. At the familial level, singletons who had family resources all to themselves would be healthier, wealthier, and better educated than siblings who had to compete with each other for parental investment.

## Fertility Limitation Policies

Contraceptive technology has enjoyed official approval in the People's Republic of China since 1954, though it did not become widely available till 1962.[4] Fertility limitation was voluntary until 1970, when Premier Zhou Enlai initiated a population control campaign with Mao Zedong's blessing. This campaign limited each couple to two children, but it was unevenly enforced.[5] Stricter enforcement of family planning laws began in 1978, when government officials set a population target of no more than 1.2 billion people by the year 2000, and decided that a nationwide one-child policy was the only way to reach this goal.[6] Despite widespread rural resistance that led to a de facto two-child policy in the countryside, the state came close to attaining that goal: A nationwide census[7] counted a population of 1,265,830,000 people in the year 2000.[8]

The initial emergence of fertility limitation policies during the 1970s was due primarily to top Chinese leaders' desire to conserve national resources and increase the efficiency of economic planning.[9] Chinese leaders have continued to emphasize this desire to international audiences concerned about conservation, environmentalism, and overpopulation.[10] In their efforts to convince families to obey the one-child policy, however, local officials have focused more on portraying low fertility as an integral component of the cultural model of modernization.[11] To families aspiring to succeed in the capitalist world system, this cultural model had much more motivational force than invocations of their patriotic duty to help conserve national resources. The idea that low fertility would lead to personal as well as national modernization was part of fertility limitation propaganda as early as 1976, when the People's Health Press published the script for a kindergarten skit[12] in which one child lamented to another child:

> I have a host of older brothers and sisters,
> And also have a younger sister named Hsiao-fang.
> I am not a good talker, and merely make random remarks.
> Father and mother are busy at their work;
> Our family affairs are in a complete jumble;
> Older brothers and sisters are of no avail.
> They bother mother until she is truly frustrated.
> I, Hsiao-kang, am like a little sheep;
> I run around as I please and bump into everything.
> My little friends tattle on me;
> So when I get home, I shall surely get slapped.
> You who are called Hsiao-an, let me ask you:
> Why is your family able to study and to criticize
> While my family from day to night is always in one big mess,
> And is always in a meaningless uproar?

Hsiao-an, who had only one sibling, responded that these problems were due to Hsiao-kang's parents' failure to limit their fertility. Hsiao-kang agreed, and the two children then said in unison:

> Family planning is good.
> It is beneficial to grasping revolution and promoting production.
> Let us study Marxism-Leninism-Mao Tsetung Thought,
> Diligently, fervently, and with a strong will for struggle,
> Like a dashing general, for the Three Great Revolutions.

It is beneficial to preparedness for war and preparedness against natural disasters;
The national economic plan will be guaranteed;
Mothers and children will be healthy, their bodies strong;
Future revolutionary generations will grow up hardy and vigorous.
Dear uncles and aunts, listen to what we have to say:
Remember in your hearts Chairman Mao's teachings;
You must do well in carrying out family planning,
And contribute strength to consolidating the dictatorship of the proletariat.

After the economic reforms began in 1978, the idea that low fertility would promote modernization became an increasingly important component of national as well as local officials' rationales for fertility limitation policies. On July 8, 1978, leaders of the Family Planning Office of the State Council published an article in the *People's Daily* (*Renmin Ribao*) that emphasized the urgency of population control. "We hold that although human beings are primarily producers, they are also consumers," the article argued. "If we do not implement planned population control and let the population increase uncontrollably, rapid population growth is bound to put a heavy burden on the state and the people, cripple the national economy, adversely affect the state's construction, the people's living standards and their health, and slow down the progress of the four modernizations."[13] Demographers involved in drafting China's population control policies argued in *Population Theory* (*Renkou Lilun*), a treatise published in December 1978, that population control "will have a beneficial impact and serve to accelerate the rise in the level of technical equipment of the workers, realize the four modernizations, and raise labor productivity."[14] Careful to avoid Malthusian overtones, these demographers wrote, "We are not worried about not having enough food to eat. That we want to control the rate of population growth is not at all because the increase in the means of livelihood cannot keep up with population growth. It is because we want to bring the function of people into full play, to build socialism at a still quicker pace, and to raise the level of the people's material and cultural life at a still faster speed. In a word, we are not concerned about 'not having enough to eat' or being 'unable to feed the population,' but want to enable the people of the whole country to live still better, even more beautifully, and still more meaningfully."[15] Despite the draconian measures sometimes employed to ensure compliance, the Chinese government has tried to portray its population policy not as a desperate measure to avert disaster, but rather as a rational, enlightened government's careful plan to improve the lives of its people.

In contrast, most other contributors to the global discourse on China's one-child policy have emphasized its human costs. Scholars have documented the suffering of women who long for additional children, are blamed by husbands and parents-in-law for giving birth to daughters instead of sons, and face fines, arrest, surveillance, mandatory contraception, gynecological exams, abortions, and sterilizations, and the loss of benefits or jobs.[16] Political activists opposing the one-child policy have focused on abuses such as infanticide and violent, physically coercive abortions or sterilization.[17] Demographers have found an increasingly skewed Chinese gender ratio, which may result from female infanticide, parents' refusal to register daughters, parents' abandonment or lethal neglect of daughters, sex selective abortions, or some combination of these factors.[18] Even some Chinese officials and intellectuals have acknowledged problems caused by the one-child policy.[19] Most rural Chinese officials, including those of villages near urban Dalian, have dealt with widespread resistance against the policy by legalizing second births, and by limiting enforcement efforts to sporadic campaigns against families with unusually large numbers of children.[20]

Because they lived in a city where the promises of the cultural model of modernization seemed within reach, people I knew in urban Dalian expressed views that were closer to those of the Chinese government than those of the one-child policy's critics. These critics have focused primarily on problems in rural areas, where the establishment of a modern economy lagged far behind the fertility transition, and parental desire for high fertility clashed sharply with fertility limitation policies. In urban areas, however, the clash was less severe. While some parents I knew in urban Dalian expressed disapproval of enforcement tactics associated with the one-child policy, their tone conveyed annoyance rather than agony. Many parents told me that, during the early years of their marriages, they had wanted at least two or three children, including one of each gender. Born in the 1950s, these parents had many siblings and were socialized to expect high fertility. Still, when recalling clashes between state policy and their own fertility preferences, they spoke far less bitterly than when they spoke about other sources of suffering, such as the Great Leap Forward famine (1959–1961), the Cultural Revolution (1966–1976), and the loss of jobs, pensions, and medical insurance during the 1990s.

Some parents recalled being angry at the work unit and neighborhood committee cadres who enforced birth control policies with surveillance, compulsory contraception, physical examinations, a strict birth permit system, and the power to punish those who insisted on having second children with fines or the loss of benefits and jobs. Fertility limitation policies depended on these enforcement tactics during the 1970s and 1980s, when parental desire for high fertility was still strong. By the 1990s, however, most parents' attitudes had changed, to the point where vigorous enforcement was no longer necessary to ensure compliance with the one-child policy. Some families became wealthy enough to consider fines and bribes for an extra birth a manageable expense. Enforcement tactics that had frightened families in the 1980s seemed tolerable by the 1990s. The loss of jobs and benefits was not so threatening to those who faced layoffs and factory bankruptcies anyway, or to those who could get work in the rapidly expanding private or foreign-funded sectors, where state policies were often ignored. As political and economic incentives for enforcing the one-child policy declined, cadres became less enthusiastic about tracking down illegal pregnancies. Even cadres who continued to enforce the one-child policy focused on local residents rather than on migrants or visitors. Therefore, as transportation grew more affordable and residential registration rules loosened, it became possible to escape surveillance by staying with a friend or relative in a different part of China for the duration of one's pregnancy. I knew several parents who had violated the one-child policy but suffered no consequences besides the payment of fines that were far less than what many parents spent on educational expenses over the course of a child's life.[21]

Yet, even under these conditions, few people I knew in urban Dalian considered an illegal second birth worth the trouble. By the time I started my fieldwork in 1997, most of them had come to agree with the rationale behind the one-child policy. Many parents told me that, even without a one-child policy, they would not have enough time, money, and energy to raise more than one child. Even parents who told me that they resented the one-child policy's constraints on their own desire for more children said they believed the policy was necessary for making China wealthy and modern. Many blamed their own childhood poverty on the large size of their natal families. Some told me that, though they had wanted more children in the early 1980s, the rapid inflation of educational expenses and consumption standards in the 1990s made them glad they had only one child. In 2000, the father of Lu Jing, a vocational high school student, teased her by saying, "If I had known how much you would cost, I wouldn't have wanted any children at all!"

Singletons themselves were even more comfortable with the cultural model of low fertility. While singletons sometimes talked about how nice it would be to have siblings for companionship in the present and for help with the burden of supporting elderly parents in the future, they also told me they were glad they did not have to compete with siblings for family resources. "My parents had to borrow money from all their friends and relatives just to pay for tuition at my junior college," Zheng Bohua told me in 2000. "If they had another child, there's no way they could have come up with enough money for both of us to go to college." Though the one-child policy allowed a couple consisting of two singletons to have up to two children, 32 percent of the girls[22] and 16 percent of the boys[23] I surveyed indicated that they hoped to remain childless all their lives.

During the Spring Festival of 2000, Zheng Yi, a vocational high school student, took me to a family reunion at his maternal grandparents' home, a one-room apartment where his mother and her seven siblings had grown up. Zheng Yi and his cousins, all singletons, had trouble imagining how a family of ten could have lived in that one room.

"How could humans have lived that way?" Zheng Yi's cousin Chen Yan asked.

"They must have lived like pigs crowded together in a sty," Zheng Yi's cousin Chen Xin replied.

## Low Fertility as Part of the Cultural Model of Modernization

Like Hill Gates[24] and Cecilia Milwertz,[25] I found that the one-child policy did not result in extreme resistance or enforcement in urban areas, where desire for high fertility was far less intense than in rural areas. Low resistance to the one-child policy in cities like Dalian can be attributed to the rapid pace with which people in such cities have internalized the same cultural model of modernization that has caused fertility decline in many societies worldwide. Theories of fertility transition have suggested that a society's fertility rate usually correlates with the degree to which it has adopted a modern economy, in which child mortality is low, most people live in urban environments where children consume a lot more than they produce, most mothers as well as fathers work at jobs incompatible with childrearing, and extensive education is widespread for both genders and seen as the road to socioeconomic success. None of these conditions guarantees low fertility; indeed, some scholars have documented cases[26] in which one or more of these conditions did not cause fertility decline. Still, in many societies, these conditions tend to be produced by low fertility, and cause people to want to limit their fertility. Along with low fertility, these conditions are mutually reinforcing components of a modern economy, which can exist under socialism and postsocialism as well as capitalism. Here, I discuss how and why the conditions of a modern economy have promoted and been promoted by low fertility in a wide range of areas.

Children with fewer siblings tend to enjoy more concentrated parental investment, and thus be less prone to the high child mortality rates that accompany the shortages of food and healthcare often experienced by large families in the Third World. Low child mortality in turn promotes low fertility. Classic fertility transition theory[27] holds that, when child mortality declines, parents feel less compelled to bear large numbers of children to ensure that they have at least a few surviving children. Based on her early 1990s research in the Gambia, Caroline Bledsoe has argued that rural African women practiced high fertility because they felt it was necessary to their goal of ending up with enough surviving children to support them and earn the gratitude of their marital families.[28] Bledsoe, Paul Leslie,[29] and Bruce Winterhalder[30] have argued that fertility decisions are often based on parents' desire for insurance against unpredictable factors like child mortality. A. Roberto Frisancho, Jane E. Klayman, and Jorge Matos found that impoverished parents' desire to compensate for high child mortality by maintaining high fertility contributed to a symbiotic relationship between high fertility, high childhood mortality, and low socioeconomic status among urban Peruvians[31] they studied in 1973.[32] According to Nancy Scheper-Hughes, impoverished women[33] in a 1980s Brazilian shantytown who had an average of 9.5 pregnancies (and 4.2 children who survived to age 5) maintained high fertility in order to compensate for the fact that 36–41 percent of their children died within a year after birth.[34] High fertility in turn led to high child mortality by diminishing resources for all the children in a family, and especially for the least-favored children. Middle-class women[35] in the same city, on the other hand, limited their fertility because they knew that all their children would be likely to survive; therefore, they had an average of three pregnancies and three surviving children, all of whom enjoyed good living conditions.[36]

Demographic theorists[37] have also argued that parents are likely to want few children in an urban environment, where children cannot contribute much to family income even though they cost a lot of time and money to raise and educate. Based on research conducted between 1974 and 1976, Robert A. LeVine and his co-authors found that Gusiii people of Kenya wanted as many children as possible to provide labor as well as prestige for their parents.[38] Based on his 1981–1982 fieldwork, Thomas Fricke found that Nepalese villagers attributed their desire for many children to a familial mode of production that made children valuable social and economic resources.[39] Philippe Ariès suggested that "Malthusianism or birth-control" in eighteenth-century Europe was a reaction to the rise of the child-centered family that developed as schooling became institutionalized.[40] Based on their early 1980s research, John Knodel and his co-authors attributed Thailand's fertility transition partly to the high costs of enabling children to keep up with rapidly rising standards of education and consumption.[41] Harry Oshima attributed the fertility transitions in Japan, Taiwan, Hong Kong, Singapore, and South Korea to the rising costs of education associated with industrialization.[42] Drawing on evidence from Ireland, Java, the United States, Alaskan Eskimos, Mexico, Guatemala, Liberia, Tunisia, Botswana, Ghana, Gambia, and Sierra Leone, W. Penn Handwerker argued that fertility tends to fall when "changes in opportunity structure and the labor market increasingly reward educationally-acquired skills and perspectives, for these changes have the effect of sharply limiting or eliminating the expected intergenerational income flows both from children, and from the social relationships created by or through the use of children."[43]

The concentrated parental investment characteristic of low-fertility parents produces highly educated children. Studies conducted in the United States, China, and Thailand have found correlations between educational attainment and small sibsets, sometimes even after controlling for socioeconomic status.[44] An increase in the proportion of children who are well educated results in diploma inflation, which in turn promotes lower fertility by increasing the length and expense of children's education. Long years of schooling delay marriage and childbearing. The longer women wait before starting families, the fewer opportunities they have to bear children.

Daughters with few siblings are more likely to be encouraged to pursue advanced education and demanding careers that in turn tend to reduce fertility. Highly educated daughters have significant incentives to use their time to pursue prestigious and well-compensated work rather than using it to bear and rear large numbers of children. Studies conducted in Nigeria in the 1980s and 1990s found that increased schooling empowered women to actualize their desire for lower fertility,[45] and that schoolgirls used contraception to prevent pregnancies that could lead to marriage because they wanted to get enough education to gain upward mobility.[46] Schooling is also likely to cause women to learn childrearing practices that reduce infant mortality and thus reduce the need to have large numbers of children, as Robert A. LeVine and his co-authors found in a study conducted in Mexico in 1983[47] and in studies conducted in Nepal between 1996 and 1998 and in Venezuela between 1993 and 1995.[48]

Fertility is especially low when most women are expected to work at jobs incompatible with childrearing. Based on analysis of a 1968–1973 survey of U.S. women, Diane H. Felmlee found that a high rate of employment was one of the strongest correlates of low fertility among women.[49] Shirley Burggraf documented the high economic disadvantages of having children in the United States during the late twentieth century.[50] Hill Gates found that economic disincentives—especially those relating to maternal time that could be used to earn money—led capital-owning Chinese women of 1980s Taiwan and Chengdu to prefer low fertility.[51] Kathleen Gerson documented the hard choices U.S. women faced in balancing the trade-offs between work, marriage, and motherhood during the 1970s,[52] and Arlie Hochschild documented how hard it was for dual career U.S. couples to care for even one or two children in the 1980s.[53] Based on his analysis of U.S. economic and demographic data from 1950 to 1980, William Sander found inverse correlations between fertility and women's earning ability.[54] In a random sample of 300 white middle-class American women who were living in the Los Angeles area and between the ages of 35 and 45 during the 1980s, greater education was associated with fewer children, a desire for fewer children, and a decreased likelihood of ever being married.[55] This pattern was also documented by the Kinsey report on American women of the early twentieth century.[56]

In societies where women previously had little access to paid work, the adoption of a modern economy tends to increase women's employment rates. Parental bias against daughters tends to decrease when daughters are seen as capable of earning money. This pattern was documented by Charles Stafford based on his fieldwork in late 1980s Taiwan,[57] and by Sunita Kishor,[58] Mark Rosenweig and T. Paul Schultz,[59] and Mamta Murthi and her co-authors,[60] who based their conclusions on a comparison of the gender ratios in various districts of India during the 1970s and 1980s. By increasing the value of daughters, a modern economy can make parents less likely to keep having children until they have a son.

Few societies had fertility rates close to replacement level (2.1 births per woman) prior to the establishment of a modern economy. Even before China had fully adopted this economy, however, China's total fertility rate had dropped close to replacement level, and cities like Dalian had fertility rates even lower than those found in most First World cities. Since 1980, China has had a total fertility rate of about two births per woman, and the total fertility rate among women married after 1978 in cities like Dalian is close to one birth per woman.[61] Some elite urban parents had low fertility even before population control policies began.[62] Even without a one-child policy, modernization and urbanization could have produced a fertility transition in cities like Dalian, and eventually throughout all of China. But it would probably have been more gradual, just as it was in the First World. The one-child policy purposefully speeded up China's fertility transition in order to speed up China's journey to the First World.

## Bringing the First World to China

As products of a fertility limitation policy designed to create First World citizens, urban Dalian teenagers took seriously their widely recognized role as the vanguard of modernization in their families and society. They were socialized to believe that they deserved to live in First World conditions. Their parents tried to provide them with such conditions, even when the expense resulted in great parental sacrifice. Teenagers wanted the same name brands, high living standards, prestigious education, and good jobs enjoyed by their First World counterparts. They were frustrated by the gap between the "backwardness" (*luohou*) of their nation and the modernity of the First World. Many talked about wanting to "develop abroad" (*zai waiguo fazhan*). They believed that going to a developed country would be a shortcut to attaining the goals generated by the cultural model of modernization. Teenagers like Lin Lin, Yu Tao, and Wang Song wanted to study and work in the First World, not only to fulfill their personal dream of upward mobility, but also to fulfill their filial dream of making their parents proud and enabling their parents to retire in luxury. They were ambivalent about whether they wanted to settle down permanently in the First World or just gain enough cultural and economic capital to enable them to live under First World conditions after returning to China.

While graduates of top Chinese universities could get fellowships and jobs abroad by applying directly to foreign companies and universities, most would-be emigrants had to rely on private companies of varying degrees of legality that sprang up during the 1990s to meet the demand for opportunities to go abroad. In exchange for large fees, these companies found work and study opportunities in the First World or in societies that might serve as springboards to the First World, and did the research, paperwork, and other kinds of work necessary to convert these opportunities into visas for those able to pay for them. Fearing illegal immigration, most First World countries severely restricted visas for Chinese people, especially those who were not wealthy or well educated. Obtaining a visa required the expenditure of a great deal of time, energy, and economic and social capital. The financial burden was especially great for parents of students who lived abroad but could not earn enough to pay for their own tuition and living expenses. Even some relatively wealthy Chinese families had to go into debt to support children abroad.

Youth who could not go abroad still aspired to enjoy lifestyles as similar to those of the First World as possible. Government officials have celebrated this aspiration as a powerful force of modernization ever since the early 1980s, when then paramount leader Deng Xiaoping proclaimed that "to get rich is glorious." If an entire generation devoted itself to getting high levels of education and professional work, then surely China would be able to compete with the First World in the capitalist world system. Singletons embraced their role as the generation that would lead China into the First World. Socialized to see First World affluence as their birthright, singletons had much higher expectations than their parents.

In contrast to their less subtle Maoist predecessors, the state-controlled Chinese media of the late 1990s presented images of consumerism that were open to interpretation. On a TV news feature broadcast in December 1999, a reporter conducted an experiment, giving out 100 yuan (US$13) to random passersby on the streets. The reporter and cameramen then followed the recipients around to see how they would spend it. An old woman at first vehemently refused the money, saying, "I don't want what's not mine!" After much persuasion, she finally took the money, used half of it to buy lots of low-quality food and household supplies at cheap markets, and saved the remaining half for her grandson's school fees. A very young, well-dressed office worker, on the other hand, had no qualms about taking the money. The office worker immediately used up all 100 yuan by ordering coffee and snacks for herself, the reporter, and the cameramen at a posh downtown café. The segment provoked a lively debate between Han Dong and his mother.

"That just shows how wasteful young people have become," Han Dong's mother said. "They spend money as if it were just paper."

"No, it shows how free and happy people can be when they have white collar jobs!" Han Dong insisted. "That young lady doesn't have to worry about money, so she realizes that money is only paper, after all!"

I was tutoring He Hong, a college prep high school junior, in 1999, when her father, a factory worker, received a telephone call from his sister. He grew angry as she told him that she had lost her factory job. After he got off the phone, he continued to complain to He Hong and me. "So many people are losing their jobs," he said. "China is doomed!"

"No, China's just becoming more like foreign countries," He Hong replied. "This is just a transition. China's adopting foreign methods, and foreign countries are often like this, with lots of people losing their jobs."

"How do you know all this?" her father asked sarcastically.

"I watch the news," she replied.

"So do I, and all I see is that China is doomed," he said.

"But I see opportunities to learn from foreign countries and get rich," she said. "You're just used to the old way of thinking that the iron rice bowl is the most important thing in the world. I'm young, so I'm more open to new knowledge."

When faced with images of rising socioeconomic inequalities, parents who grew up during the height of Maoist socialism saw themselves losing ground as a globalizing economy rendered them obsolete. Their children, however, focused on how their living standards would rise rapidly once they reaped the economic rewards of their arduous climb up the educational ladder.

Sun Wei was usually excused from chores because her parents wanted her to spend all her time studying to get into a good high school. One winter day in 1998, however, her mother was too ill to do the laundry, and asked Sun Wei to do it instead. Sun Wei obliged, but she rushed through the job, complaining that the cold water was numbing her hands.

"Look at all these stains—it's as if you didn't wash them at all," her mother scolded her after seeing the results. "You have to learn to wash thoroughly. What will you do after I'm dead? Will you wear dirty clothes all the time?"

"As soon as I get a job, I'll get us a washing machine, and we'll never need to hand wash again!" Sun Wei replied.

"Sure, you'll be so rich, why not just go to a laundry service and have others wash your clothes for you?" her mother scoffed.

"I'm glad you thought of that! That's exactly what I'll do!" Sun Wei said with a grin.

## The Inflation of Consumption Standards

In 1998, only a year after he had persuaded his parents to pay for the installation of a telephone line so that he could keep in touch with his friends from primary school after they scattered to different junior high schools, Zhang Yong, my host family's son, started begging his parents for a cellular phone. "All my friends have cellular phones, so it doesn't look good if I don't!" he complained.

Like prices and diplomas, consumption standards inflated rapidly during the final two decades of the twentieth century. Much of this inflation was driven by singletons who enjoyed unprecedented spending power. Parents viewed child-driven consumption as an expression of parental love, as a way to improve or maintain social status, and as a practical investment that could improve their children's academic achievement by giving them comfort and peace of mind. Even those parents and children who wanted to be thrifty were forced by a fear of humiliation to keep up with the spending patterns of friends and neighbors. As the ceilings of job prestige and income rose, so did standards for the minimum consumption levels necessary to gain or maintain respectable status. First televisions, refrigerators, and washing machines, then telephones, machines that provided hot water for bathing, and VCR and VCD (Video Compact Disc) players changed from rare luxuries reserved for the elite to status symbols necessary to the maintenance of a respectable reputation (See Table 2). Computers, air conditioners, and cars seemed next in line.

Gift exchange has long been an integral component of Chinese social

TABLE 2

Consumer Goods Owned by Respondents' Households Compared with Nationwide

| | Respondents whose households owned at least one | Number owned per 100 Chinese urban households (*N* = 36,000) |
|---|---|---|
| Television | 99% (*N* = 2,193) | 112 |
| Refrigerator | 96% (*N* = 2,193) | 78 |
| Washing machine | 91% (*N* = 2,194) | 91 |
| Telephone | 79% (*N* = 2,194) | — |
| Camera | 78% (*N* = 2,179) | 38 |
| Hot water machine for bathing | 77% (*N* = 2,194) | 45 |
| VCD player | 56% (*N* = 2,180) | 25 |
| Stereo | 35% (*N* = 2,181) | 20 |
| Microwave Oven | 30% (*N* = 2,193) | 12 |
| Cellular phone | 33% (*N* = 2,181) | 7 |
| Computer | 13% (*N* = 2,193) | 6 |
| Air conditioner | 13% (*N* = 2,194) | 24 |
| Motorcycle | 9% (*N* = 2,181) | 15 |
| Car (including taxi or business vehicle) | 8% (*N* = 2,181) | — |

SOURCE: Data for all of China are from a sample survey conducted by China's National Bureau of Statistics (Guojia Tongji Ju), *Zhongguo Tongji Nianjian [China Statistical Yearbook], 2000,* Beijing: Zhongguo Tongji Chubanshe (China Statistics Press), 2000, page 318, Table 10-10.

relations.[63] Prior to the 1990s, most gift exchange took place between adults, and the gifts exchanged were primarily consumables such as money, food, alcohol, cigarettes, and clothing. In the 1990s, however, low-income parents were horrified by the rise of a new phenomenon: the exchange of impractical but expensive gifts among teenagers. After learning about Western gift exchange customs through the media, young people started celebrating Christmas, birthdays, and the Western

New Year (January 1) with parties, cakes, restaurant meals, and the exchange of gifts and greeting cards. While elite parents encouraged these practices as yet another way to purchase happiness and social capital for their children, low-income parents were greatly burdened by the expense of enabling their children to participate. Most gifts exchanged by older people were generic enough to be passed on as gifts to others, or practical enough to be used in lieu of household necessities that a family would otherwise have to buy. Teenagers, however, exchanged cards, books, tapes, CDs, jewelry, music boxes, computer games, VCDs (video compact discs), and toys selected to appeal to the unique tastes of the recipient. Some gifts were packaged in wrapping paper that cost as much as the gift itself. Most of a teenager's friends were in the same school-centered social network, so any attempt to pass one friend's highly personalized gift along as a gift to another friend would be prohibitively embarrassing. Therefore, parents had to let their children keep the gifts they received, and buy additional gifts to reciprocate. "When I was small, we didn't even have enough money to buy snacks, much less useless gifts for each other," Chen Yan's mother complained to me in 2000. "But this year I had to spend more on my daughter's New Year's cards for her friends than I spent on a week's groceries!"

Fearing social disgrace, low-income parents felt compelled to allow their children to live beyond their means. When Zhang Yong asked his mother for money to buy snacks, she told him that she could not afford it. He borrowed the money from a friend, and bought the snacks anyway. Afterwards, he told his mother that he needed money to repay his friend. "You should feel ashamed of asking friends for money," she scolded him, but gave him the money to repay his debt.

Parents who did not spend enough on their children risked bringing shame to the whole family. "How can you bear to let your son walk around in such worn clothing!" a neighbor admonished the impoverished mother of Lin Tao, a technical high school tenth grader I tutored. "You only have one child! Surely you can save enough to get him decent clothing."

"My son has nice clothes," Lin Tao's mother lied. "I just don't let him wear them, because he'll get them dirty."

The neighbor offered to give Lin Tao some clothes that her own son had discarded. "He only wore them a few times before saying that he doesn't want them because he doesn't like the style," she said

"My son doesn't like unstylish clothing either," Lin Tao's mother said with barely concealed anger.

Throughout the discussion, Lin Tao stared silently at the textbook I was using to tutor him. The moment the neighbor left, however, he said to his mother, "See, even the neighbor is noticing how bad my clothes are. We lose face whenever I walk down the street!"

After tearfully complaining about her neighbor's arrogance and intrusiveness, his mother took him downtown to buy the stylish, expensive Adidas brand outfit that he had long wanted.

## Singletons as First World Children

Urban Dalian teenagers were used to higher living standards than their parents, who often maintained the thrifty habits they acquired during their own youth. Teenagers desired the luxurious lifestyles they saw in the media, which was full of movies, shows, and news reports that depict the high living standards of the First World. Many managed to persuade their parents that a better standard of living would have a direct, positive effect on their academic achievement. To keep their children healthy and strong, parents provided them with frequent healthcare and food that was not only nutritious but also delicious enough to tempt their finicky appetites. I often observed teenagers telling their parents that they could not concentrate on their schoolwork without snacks, spacious housing, heating in the winter, and air conditioning in the summer. They experienced intense peer pressure to consume, and those who had less spending money and worse clothes than their friends felt ashamed. Refusal to provide a child with expensive clothes and money to spend on leisure, snacks, and gift exchange could result in social and emotional turmoil that distracted the child from the pursuit of academic achievement. Parents invested the bulk of their wealth in their singletons because they believed it was an investment they had to make. Most teenagers were singletons who enjoyed heavy parental investment, so any teenager who lacked such investment was likely to fall behind in the high-stakes competition for academic success, social status, and eventually good jobs and spouses.

Yet children's high consumption standards were not the biggest financial drains their families faced. Parents often saw their investment in children's consumption as just a means to the end of promoting their children's success in the educational system, which demanded fees that usually constituted their households' heaviest financial burdens. Parents were willing to spend all their savings and borrow money from friends and relatives to pay for their children's education. Recognizing the potential of this attitude for promoting economic growth and raising educational levels to First World standards, state officials expanded opportunities for expensive education. These opportunities (and those willing to seize them) contributed to rapid inflation in expectations about the minimum level of education necessary for a respectable job.

CHAPTER 3

# Heavy is the Head of the "Little Emperor"

## *Pressure, Discipline, and Competition in the Stratification System*

IN 1998, NINTH GRADER Guan Ping told me that several students at his top-choice keypoint high school had committed suicide in the past few years. "Let's hope there won't be any more," I said.

"No! I hope even more high school students commit suicide," he replied. "That way, there will be fewer people competing to get into good high schools, colleges, and jobs. And if many students commit suicide, maybe the government will know there's a problem, and change the educational system to make it less stressful."

As a generation of singletons reached adolescence, Chinese officials were indeed alarmed by suicides and mental illnesses caused by overwhelming pressure to succeed in the educational system, which were often reported by the news media.[1] To reduce the frustration caused by unmet demands for higher education, the government created new educational options for those who could afford them. Officials hoped that expanding education would not only diminish the stress produced by competition for educational opportunities, but also hasten modernization by increasing overall education levels, and promote economic growth by encouraging parents to spend large amounts of money on their children's education. The latter two aims have been realized, but the first seems harder to attain.

The root of students' stress lay not in the competition to get into high schools and colleges per se, but rather in the competition to get the kind of education that could qualify one for a "good job." As work in lucrative fields like trade, finance, and technology became available, factory jobs that used to be desirable lost their luster. As the number of job seekers with higher education rose, employers raised the bar of minimum educational qualifications. "Good jobs" became increasingly elusive, as diplomas, expectations, and consumption demands skyrocketed.

In the early 1980s, nearly all urban high school and college graduates were assigned jobs. Most urban residents who had junior high school diplomas could get work, those with secondary education got respectable factory jobs, and those with just a few years of tertiary education—even if it was acquired through junior colleges, adult education, or college equivalency exams—got elite jobs. Even those who were barely literate could easily start their own small businesses, since unemployment was low, the economic reforms were just beginning, and the market was wide open.

By the late 1990s, however, it was difficult for high school graduates to get steady, prestigious, well-compensated work, and nearly impossible for junior high school graduates. Even those with degrees from junior colleges, college equivalency exams, or adult education colleges often had to settle for jobs that would have gone to high school graduates just a decade earlier. Most desirable jobs were reserved for those with four-year degrees from prestigious colleges, and many elite jobs required postgraduate education, special skills, or experience abroad. No one could start a profitable business without considerable social and financial capital, since the market for small businesses was saturated with rural migrants and urban workers who had been laid off or given early retirement. Determined to meet the high expectations that were part of their childhood socialization, many youth who could not get satisfactory work after completing their formal education chose unemployment over underemployment. Rather than resigning themselves to low-paying jobs they felt were unworthy of them, they waited for good opportunities that seldom came, studied for college equivalency exams that few could pass, tried to get further education abroad, or retook the regular and adult education college entrance exams, hoping to qualify for further education.

In response to the singleton generation's demands for education, the Chinese government expanded adult education options, encouraged the establishment of private schools, and allowed state-run schools to increase their enrollment by opening "privately funded" and "expanded enrollment" (*minban, zifei,* and *kuozhao*) programs that admitted students with lower scores if they paid higher fees. By the late 1990s, young people had more educational options than ever before. But these options could only provide temporary relief from competition for elite status. As junior college student Wu Wen told me in 1999, "I used to think I was lucky to have graduated from junior high school just in time to take advantage of the new option for privately funded high school students. Without that option, I would never have been able to attend a college prep high school and get into a junior college. But now that they're expanding college enrollment, the job market will be flooded with college graduates, and my junior college degree will be worthless. So I'll have to go to adult education college to get a four-year degree, and maybe even a master's degree, just to be competitive!" Most people in their 20s continued to seek higher education, or at least certificates of proficiency in subjects like accounting, computer science, and foreign languages, even after they started working. Even those who had jobs feared that they would lose them to younger, better-educated job seekers.

Members of the singleton generation had much more education than their parents and grandparents. Most respondents to my survey surpassed their grandparents' educational attainments after just a few years of primary school, and they were also likely to surpass their parents' educational attainment as soon as they graduated from their high schools (see Tables 3, 4, and5).[2] By 2000, the educational attainment of the singleton generation was much higher than that of the overall Chinese population,[3] among which 4 percent had college degrees, 11 percent had high school degrees, 34 percent had junior high school degrees, 36 percent had primary school degrees, and 15 percent did not even graduate from primary school.[4]

The statistics in Table 5 do not even include students who spent the year after graduation studying abroad, taking private classes to learn skills or earn certificates, studying for college equivalency degrees, attending high schools as auditors instead of regular enrollees, working to save money for further education, or preparing to retake the college or high school entrance exam. Teachers told me that such options were pursued by most urban youth who had not been accepted by regular high schools or colleges.

When I visited adult education college entrance exam sites in 1999 and 2000, I found that most exam-takers were not much older than their counterparts at the regular college entrance exam sites. The adult education college entrance exam and the college equivalency exams were open to everyone, and could be taken as many times as one wanted. Most college prep high school graduates and some graduates of non-

TABLE 3
Literacy Rates of Respondents' Grandparents

| | Deemed literate by respondent |
|---|---|
| Maternal grandmother ($N$ = 1,913) | 61% |
| Paternal grandmother ($N$ = 1,900) | 57% |
| Maternal grandfather ($N$ = 1,898) | 90% |
| Paternal grandfather ($N$ = 1,896) | 88% |

SOURCE: The author's 1999 survey.

college prep high schools could score high enough to gain admittance to adult education colleges, which were less prestigious than regular colleges. Anyone could take the college equivalency exams, but these exams were so difficult that even many regular college students could not pass them.

Driven by intense parental pressure and investment, many singletons ended up with enough skills and education to qualify them for jobs in lucrative, growing fields like tourism, trade, finance, business, and technology. Infused with increasingly educated and ambitious youth, China's economy has developed just as population planners hoped it would. Still, there were not enough elite jobs for all who wanted them. The state's strategy of lowering fertility to accelerate modernization worked all too well. While it increased China's success in the capitalist world system, it also caused the expectations and educational levels of singletons to outpace their country's economic growth.

## The Educational System

Parents saw academic achievement as the main route to wealth, prestige, and power for their children. Parents born in the 1950s had their own education disrupted by the Cultural Revolution (1966–1976), during which many schools closed, no college or high school entrance exams were given, academic instruction was replaced by political struggle in the schools that remained open, and many urban youth were sent to the countryside, where they received no schooling. Those who at-

TABLE 4
Educational Attainment of Respondents' Parents

| | Mother ($N$ = 2,178) | Father ($N$ = 2,171) |
|---|---|---|
| Did not graduate from primary school | 1% | 0% |
| Primary school | 3% | 3% |
| Junior high school | 53% | 46% |
| Technical or vocational high school | 3% | 3% |
| Professional high school | 6% | 6% |
| College prep high school | 23% | 24% |
| Junior college | 8% | 12% |
| Four-year college | 3% | 6% |
| Master's | 0% | 0% |
| Ph.D. | 0% | 0% |

SOURCE: The author's 1999 survey.

tained higher education did so through the college equivalency exams and adult education programs established after the Cultural Revolution ended in 1976. Still, most survey respondents' parents managed to surpass their own parents' educational attainment (see Tables 3 and 4). And even under conditions designed to sever the link between education and elite status, parents' educational attainment still correlated directly with their occupations and consumption patterns[5] (see Tables 6 and 7). Parents had no doubt that educational levels would correlate even more closely with socioeconomic status for their children, who grew up in a system designed to reward educational attainment.

Even the elite realized that their wealth and connections could not sustain their children forever. Ravaged by the inflation that accompanied China's rapid economic growth, parents could not save enough to enable their children to live well on inheritance alone. Parental money and connections could open doors for young people, but further success and promotions depended at least partly on ability and education. Elite parents could help their children only for a limited time, since they gradually lost their wealth and connections after they retired.

TABLE 5

Educational Statistics for Urban Dalian, the Dalian Area, and All of China, 2000

| | Urban Dalian[a] % (*N*) | Dalian Area[b] % (*N*) | All of China % (*N*) |
|---|---|---|---|
| Primary-school-age children attending primary school[c] | — | 100% (455,569) | 99% (124,453,000) |
| Teenagers age 13–15 attending junior high school | — | 100% (231,074) | — |
| Primary school graduates enrolled at junior high schools | — | — | 95% (24,192,000) |
| Junior high school graduates enrolled at high schools | 92% (24,273) | 75% (58,152) | 51% (16,335,000)[d] |
| Enrolled at technical high schools | 5% (24,273) | 6% (58,152) | —[e] |
| Enrolled at vocational high schools | 23% (24,273) | 17% (58,152) | 11% (16,335,000) |
| Enrolled at professional high schools | 13% (24,273) | 9% (58,152) | 8% (16,335,000) |
| Enrolled at college prep high schools | 51% (24,273) | 43% (58,152) | 29% (16,335,000) |
| College prep high school graduates enrolled at regular (not adult education) colleges | 81% (7,976) | 81% (17,835) | 73% (3,015,000) |

SOURCES: Data from Dalian Shi Shi Zhi Bangongshi [Dalian City Archives Office], *Dalian Nianjian [Dalian Yearbook], 2001*, Dalian: Dalian Chubanshe [Dalian Publisher], 2002, pp. 258, 262, 265, 271; Guojia Tongji Ju [National Bureau of Statistics], and *Zhongguo Tongji Nianjian [China Statistical Yearbook], 2001*, Beijing: Zhongguo Tongji Chubanshe [China Statistics Press], 2001, p. 649, Table 20-1; p. 652, Tables 20-6 and 20-7, and p. 656, Table 20-17.

[a] Including only the urban districts of Shahekou, Xigang, and Zhongshan, and the semi-urban districts of Lushunkou and Ganjingzi.

[b] Including all rural and urban areas.

[c] Primary-school-age children are usually defined as children between the ages of 7 and 12. This was stated in the data published by Dalian's Archives Office, but not in the data published by China's National Bureau of Statistics.

[d] The number of students admitted to all high schools was slightly higher than the sum of all students admitted to professional, vocational, and college prep high schools in the data published by China's National Bureau of Statistics. It is possible that the former figure included high school students at specialty schools (such as those for disabled or incarcerated students) that also enrolled junior high school and primary school students.

[e] Unlike Dalian City's Archives Office, China's National Bureau of Statistics did not have a separate category for technical schools (*jigong xuexiao*); Dalian's technical schools are presumably classified as professional or vocational schools in the national data.

TABLE 6
Respondents' Parents Who Ever Did Elite Work

| | Ever Did Elite Work[a] |
|---|---|
| Mother | |
| College diploma ($N = 200$) | 90%*** |
| High school diploma ($N = 644$) | 52%*** |
| No high school or college diploma ($N = 1{,}135$) | 21%*** |
| Father | |
| College diploma ($N = 327$) | 93%*** |
| High school diploma ($N = 637$) | 56%*** |
| No high school or college diploma ($N = 977$) | 28%*** |

SOURCE: The author's 1999 survey.
[a] Elite work is here defined as the work of cadres/managers, professionals, or owners of large businesses.
*** $p < 0.001$

Performance on the citywide high school entrance exam was the main determinant of which kind of high school a student could attend. Dalian's 1999 high school entrance exam tested the students on Chinese, math, a foreign language,[6] physics, and chemistry. The highest possible total exam score was 650. On the high school application form for 1999 graduates, school categories were ranked by selectivity in the following order: (1) keypoint college prep high schools (*zhongdian gaozhong*); (2) ordinary college prep high schools (*putong gaozhong*); (3) private college prep high schools (*minban gaozhong*); (4) professional high schools (*zhongdeng zhuanye xuexiao*); and (5) vocational high schools, adult education professional high schools (*zhiye gaozhong, zhiye zhongzhuan, chengren zhongzhuan*) and technical high schools (*jigong xuexiao*). Though technical, vocational, and adult education professional high schools held the same rank on the registration form, most students considered technical high schools the least desirable option because they trained students for the lowest-paying jobs. Students indicated their school preferences within each category prior to taking the entrance exam, and were admitted on the basis of their exam scores. Parents could also negotiate with school officials to get their children admitted even after initial admissions decisions had been

TABLE 7

Respondents' Ownership of Luxury Goods, by Parents' Education

| | Owned at least 2 of 3 luxury goods[a] |
|---|---|
| Mother | |
| College diploma ($N = 233$) | 22%*** |
| High school diploma ($N = 697$) | 18%*** |
| No high school or college diploma ($N = 1{,}240$) | 8%*** |
| Father | |
| College diploma ($N = 393$) | 25%*** |
| High school diploma ($N = 705$) | 14%*** |
| No high school or college diploma ($N = 1{,}065$) | 8%*** |

SOURCE: The author's 1999 survey.

[a] The three "luxury goods" are the computer, the air conditioner, and the microwave oven. I use ownership of these goods as a measure of family wealth because only 13 percent of survey respondents had at least two of them.

*** $p < 0.001$

made. It was common for elite parents to buy their children enrollment at schools one or two notches higher than their exam scores warranted. Still, most administrators were reluctant to dilute their school's prestige by accepting students who scored too many notches below the school's cutoff, even if their parents offered to pay large bribes as well as extra fees.

Professional high schools trained students for the lower ranks of fields such as accounting, police work, and kindergarten and elementary school education. Vocational high schools and adult education professional high schools trained students for jobs in service fields such as hairdressing, hospitality, tourism, sales, and secretarial work. Technical high schools trained students for jobs as technicians, drivers, and factory workers. Because they did not prepare students for an entrance exam, non-college prep high schools were less demanding than college prep high schools and even junior high schools.

In the late 1990s, Dalian's Bureau of Education began allowing high schools to accept "privately funded" (*zifei*) and "expanded enrollment" (*kuozhao*) students who scored slightly below the cutoff but were willing and able to pay many times the tuition paid by "publicly funded" (*gongfei*) students. In academic year 1999–2000, annual urban Dalian high school tuitions ranged from 500–1,000 yuan (US$63-$125) for "publicly funded" students at college prep high schools, to 1,800–4,500 yuan (US$225-$563) for technical, vocational, and professional high school students, to 2,400–8,000 yuan (US$300-$1,000) for private school students, to 2,500–10,000 yuan (US$313-$1,250) for "privately funded" or "expanded enrollment" students at college prep high schools, to 35,000 yuan (US$4,375) for students at the international private school (which enrolled both Chinese and foreign students). In addition, most students had to pay 1,000–5,000 yuan (US$125-$625) per year for books, supplies, and semi-mandatory classes held at night, on weekends, and during vacations, and some students had to pay one-time fees of 10,000–35,000 yuan (US$1,250-$4,375) for the privilege of being admitted as "privately funded" or "expanded enrollment" at college prep high schools where the demand for this privilege exceeded the supply. Most private, professional, vocational, and technical high schools were established during the 1980s and 1990s in response to rising demands for secondary education. Though non-college prep high schools were supposed to prepare students to enter the workforce, many of their graduates continued to seek higher education because they could not get desirable jobs, or in some cases any jobs at all.

College prep high schools focused on preparing students for the college entrance exam. Keypoint college prep high schools had the best students, teachers, and resources. Private high schools had the same goals and curriculum as state-run college prep high schools, but were less prestigious and selective. Prior to 2001, only graduates of college prep high schools who were unmarried and under age 25 were allowed to take the national college entrance exam, which was administered to all Chinese college applicants each July. These restrictions were removed in 2001 to meet rising demands for opportunities to pursue higher education.

The 1999 college entrance exam tested all exam-takers on math, Chinese, and a foreign language.[7] The exam also tested science majors on physics and chemistry, and humanities / social science majors on politics and history.[8] The highest possible total exam score was 750. For the graduating high school class of 1999, the categories on the application form, in ranked order, were: (1) first-rate four-year colleges (*di yi pi luqü benke yuanxiao*); (2) second-rate four-year colleges (*di er pi luqü benke yuanxiao*); (3) city-level four-year colleges (*shishu benke yuanxiao*); (4) provincial-level junior colleges (*shengshu yishang zhuanke xuexiao*);

(5) provincial-level technical junior colleges (*shengshu gaozhizhuan*); (6) city-level junior colleges (*shishu zhuanke xuexiao*); and (7) city-level junior technical colleges (*shishu gaozhizhuan*). Colleges nationwide selected students on the basis of their scores and geographical locations. Because most Chinese colleges had admissions policies that favored local students, many high school graduates stayed in their own cities or provinces for college. In the late 1990s, the Chinese government began allowing some colleges to accept students who scored slightly below the cutoff if they could pay extra tuition. In academic year 1999–2000, tuition for those who scored above a college's cutoff ranged from 2,500–5,000 yuan (US$313-$625) per year, while tuition for those who scored below the cutoff ranged from 8,000 yuan to 10,000 yuan (US$1,000-$1,250) per year; in addition, a student had to pay 500–2,000 yuan (US$63-$250) per year to stay in a dorm room, and 5,000–8,000 yuan (US$625-$1,000) per year for additional expenses such as books, supplies, food, health insurance, student activities fees, and travel between home and college.

Before they knew their scores on the entrance exam, high school graduates had to submit applications listing several choices in each category, ranked in order of preference. A department or school was likely to give preference to students who ranked it as choice number one. Students, parents, and teachers told me that the process of figuring out which schools and departments to name as one's top choices was "a kind of science" (*yizhong kexue*) that was at least as important as getting a high score on the college entrance exam. This "science" had to take into account a plethora of variables, including the student's likely score, the selectivity levels of various schools and various departments within each school, which departments and schools were more likely to lead to good jobs, which considered interviews or special tests in addition to exam scores, and which might have "back doors" (*houmen*) through which a student might be admitted with the help of bribes and connections.

## The Quest For a Good Job

"I want to have money in the future," Zhang Yong told me in 2000. He ranked at the bottom of his junior high school class, and his parents were low-income workers who had never finished junior high school. Still, he had high ambitions. "In today's society, you need tens of thousands of yuan just to be poor," he told me. "You need hundreds of thousands of yuan just to be comfortable. I'll go to a college prep high school, and then college. I'll learn economics, and then get a good job in a big company. Then I'll use my savings to start my own business, and then I'll have money."

The cultural model of the good job changed as China adopted the modern economy necessary for success in the capitalist world system. Between the 1950s and 1970s, factory jobs were considered decent work. Private enterprise was illegal. There were few jobs in the service sector, and many of those jobs were low paying and not prestigious. Wages were set by a socialist government intent on avoiding large income disparities, so cadres and professionals were paid only slightly more than factory workers.[9] During the turmoil of the Cultural Revolution (1966–1976), factory workers belonged to one of the most politically correct classes, and they were usually not subject to the kind of violence and persecution that devastated cadres and professionals during the Cultural Revolution. Most urban Dalian people were factory workers who enjoyed what they thought would be lifelong job security, medical insurance, and retirement benefits. Many had migrated from rural areas and considered factory work far preferable to farm work.

In the 1990s, however, factory workers' salaries paled in comparison to those available in the service sector, and global competition made it difficult for factories to offer job security or good benefits. Expanding opportunities for lucrative and prestigious work in trade, commerce, finance, and tourism inflated definitions of the "good job." Though they still employed the majority of urban Dalian adults and provided salaries that were close to urban Dalian's average, factories could no longer offer young people the trappings of respectability. Young people who grew up during the 1990s had internalized the same cultural model of "respectability" that motivated First World youth. Such "respectability" was defined in terms of consumption patterns that could only be purchased with incomes far above those of the average Chinese worker. Youth who had to settle for jobs that offered average Chinese salaries were devastated, and many who could not even get those jobs refused to work at all.

By the early 2000s, most urban Dalian secondary school graduates could not get the jobs they wanted without getting some kind of postsecondary education. Throughout the 1990s, each year's graduates found themselves qualified for less desirable jobs than people with similar academic credentials would have qualified for just a few years ago.

These graduates felt unappreciated, frustrated, and dissatisfied with wages, working conditions, and opportunities for advancement, which always seemed less than they thought they were qualified for. As in many societies worldwide,[10] urban Dalian youth found incongruities between the status they expected and the status they attained a major source of stress. Most high school graduates could only get low-level jobs that demanded long hours and hard work in return for meager wages, no job security, and little chance of promotion. Because they could not tolerate such conditions, many high school graduates were fired or quit in tears after just a few weeks or months. Even youth with junior college, college equivalency, or adult education college degrees found themselves working as attendants, salespeople, security guards, and low-level clerks—jobs that high school graduates could have easily gotten a decade earlier, before a generation of intensely competitive and well-educated singletons came of age. Many youth found such underemployment demoralizing. As Song Zhiming, an adult education junior college graduate, told me, "In school, when I worked harder, I got better exam results. But now, no matter how hard I work, there's no way I can be a better security guard. All I do is stand there, and waste my youth."

In the early 1980s, when private business was first legalized, even those with limited education, capital, and connections could start businesses and become wealthy if they had enough luck, skill, and daring. Businesspeople fondly recalled that period as a paradise of little competition, few taxes, and minimal regulations. By the late 1990s, however, most family businesses were not ladders to wealth, but rather a means for low-income people to eke out a living by selling to other low-income people. They could not compete with large, established businesses that had far superior connections, locations, prestige, selection, and product quality. Rising tides of rural migrants and unemployed urban citizens all competed for shrinking small business niches, which catered mainly to low-income people who could not afford to patronize larger businesses. For youth whose parents did not already own large businesses, the main road to affluence outside the educational system was closed.

As their parents' only hope, singletons were socialized to become part of the elite. Work in construction, sanitation, housekeeping, and the bottom rungs of factories and the military could not offer enough income, security, and promotion opportunities to enable urban youth to attain respectable living standards, be competitive on the marriage market, save money to purchase marital housing, provide their own children with expensive education, or support their retired, unemployed, and unemployable parents and grandparents. Therefore, most singletons refused to work at such jobs, even if the alternative was unemployment. Parents were also loath to let their singletons squander their potential by working at bottom-rung jobs. "I didn't pay thousands of yuan to put my son through vocational high school so that he could take a job that any farmer could do," Chen Tianrun's father, who had recently lost his factory job, told me in 2000. "I don't want him to end up like me."

The jobs that urban youth refused to fill drew middle-aged urban parents who had lost their jobs and were desperate for work, as well as rural youth who saw any opportunity to work in urban areas as a means to upward mobility. Even the lowest-paid urban jobs provided wages that were high by rural standards.

Urban high school graduates working at low-level jobs studied part-time, or quit their jobs after saving enough to pay for further education. For those entering the job market at the dawn of the twenty-first century, higher education was a prerequisite for a job that could qualify them for the trappings of respectable adulthood, and four-year degrees or even postgraduate degrees were often necessary for the best jobs. Chinese banks seldom offered educational loans to students from low-income families, but many parents who ran out of money to fund their children's education managed to borrow money from wealthier siblings. Recognizing the singleton generation's demand for education as a powerful force for economic growth and development, the Chinese government made it possible for most urban youth to get some kind of secondary and tertiary education if their parents were willing and able to pay for it.

"I feel sorry for unemployed people, but they deserve some blame as well," Xiao Ying, a neighborhood committee social worker, told her relatives at an extended family gathering I attended in 2000. Her duties included helping unemployed people find work. The manager of a state-run store had asked her to recruit someone to fill a very low-paying salesclerk position. "I offered this job to dozens of supposedly desperate unemployed people, but they all refused!" she complained. "It's been weeks, and we still haven't been able to fill this job! Dalian people are lazy, so they only want jobs that pay a lot but don't require hard work."

Xiao Ying's cousin Shen Xiuli, who had recently lost her factory job, said she would love to take the salesclerk job. "Why didn't you tell me about it earlier? I can start tomorrow!"

"The store only wants young women, not middle-aged people, for its salesclerk positions," Xiao Ying said. "Your daughter could get it if she's interested."

"Of course not!" Shen Xiuli replied indignantly. "I wouldn't let her waste her youth on a low-paying job with no future! If she can't get a good job with her vocational high school degree, I'll send her to adult education college. I'll never let her settle for a job with no future."

Many youth like Wang Song who refused to settle for bottom-rung education and work eventually ended up getting better education and work. By relentlessly pursuing higher education and career opportunities, such youth have made themselves competitive in the capitalist world system. In this way, they have contributed to their nation's quest for core region status, just as population control policy officials hoped they would.

But there were limits to the heights that young people could reach on ambition alone. Not every child could be a winner in the capitalist world system. There were limits to the money parents could earn, save, beg, and borrow to fund further education for their children. There were limits to young people's ability to cultivate enough discipline to succeed at the educational and career opportunities their parents procured for them. Most significantly, there were limits to the number of good jobs available. Having to settle for bottom-rung work was devastating for those who found that not even their burning ambition could carry them past these limits. When young people who failed to achieve the success they expected sank into depression or lashed out in anger at people around them, parents, teachers, and older relatives criticized them for "lacking the ability to adjust to their environment" (*meiyou shiying nengli*). Socialized with the expectation that they would rise to the top of local and global hierarchies, young people like Yu Tao refused to settle for work they considered beneath them, even when they had no other options. Even when they made half-hearted efforts at getting jobs in construction, domestic service, or factory assembly lines, employers were reluctant to hire them. Employers preferred rural migrants for such jobs because they knew that frustrated urban youth were less likely to be humble, obedient, and tolerant of harsh working conditions. Chronically unemployed youth became burdens to their families and society.

## The Cultural Model of Upward Mobility through Academic Achievement

The Chinese cultural model of upward mobility through academic achievement has its roots in the imperial civil service exam system, which began under the Han Dynasty (202 BC to AD 220), became the main path to elite status under the Song Dynasty (960–1279), and lasted until 1905, when it was abolished as part of the Qing Dynasty's last-ditch efforts at reform. Though scholar-officials usually managed to pass their status to their children by providing them with education that was unavailable to the majority of the population, the civil service exam system still produced just enough cases of upward mobility to prevent class boundaries from completely solidifying, defuse tensions between different factions among the elite, and promote a cultural model that promised upward mobility to those who invested heavily in education.[11] To promote destratification, the Maoist government (1949–1976) tried to destroy this cultural model by persecuting intellectuals and severely limiting the socioeconomic rewards of academic achievement.[12] The post-Mao government revived this cultural model, which fit well with the capitalist world system's emphasis on credentialed cultural capital. Yet this revived cultural model was not identical to the one associated with the imperial civil service exam system, which had been salient primarily for the male members of a relatively small number of scholar-official, merchant, and landed gentry families who were already at or close to the top of their society. Rather, a combination of the pre-revolutionary valorization of education, the empowerment of women, the socioeconomic democratization of the Communist revolution, and the meritocratic ideologies of the capitalist world system produced a much more powerful and widespread cultural model that promised upward mobility for all youth, regardless of their gender or socioeconomic backgrounds.

The class system of late twentieth century China was shifting, chaotic, and complex, thanks to Communist destratification policies that culminated with the Cultural Revolution (1966–1976).[13] Some of the elite were descended from countless generations of elite, but they were not the norm. Many of the 1990s elite were descended from impoverished, powerless, illiterate, rural families. Some of these elite had won positions in the Communist government through luck and political loyalty, and eventually turned their political connections into lucrative business networks. Others had become wealthy because they had established businesses right when the economic reforms first began. Some had been assigned or recruited to jobs in industries like shipping and trade, which were not particularly desirable under Maoism but eventually became lucrative due to globalization and the economic reforms. Still others had won professional or managerial positions because they were among the minority of their generation with enough talent, luck, perseverance, or parental investment to have acquired higher education despite the Cultural Revolution. At the same time, some of the poor were descended from elite families that lost everything during the Cultural Revolution, and never managed to gain anything back.

Because they had not seen class statuses passing smoothly from one generation to the next, none of the students I knew in urban Dalian had hopeless attitudes like those of youth whose families had long been trapped at the bottom in societies with entrenched class structures. Even the poorest students were motivated by the cultural model of upward mobility, and had attitudes similar to those of the "Brothers" described by Jay MacLeod,[14] the "voluntary minorities" described by John Ogbu and his colleagues,[15] and the first-generation Mexican and Central American immigrants to the U.S. described by Marcelo Suárez-Orozco[16] and Carola Suárez-Orozco.[17] In MacLeod's study, the "Brothers" were a group of African-American high school students in an impoverished American neighborhood who obeyed school rules because they believed educational attainment would lead to upward mobility. Unlike the white "Hallway Hangers," boys who were cynical about their prospects for upward mobility through education, the Brothers were optimistic partly because their families had recently moved into the neighborhood and considered it a step up from their previous communities.[18] Ogbu and his colleagues have argued that voluntary minorities (who migrate by choice) are more likely to believe in and therefore conform to the educational system instead of trying to resist it as involuntary minorities do. Suárez-Orozco and Suárez-Orozco found that first-generation immigrant teenagers from Mexico and Central America had greater achievement motivation than their counterparts (white or Latino) who had been born in the United States. In all these studies, the key to migrants' and immigrants' greater achievement motivation lay in their belief (misguided or not) that they had new, better opportunities that had been denied to their parents. Most urban Dalian teenagers I knew also held this belief. Many urban Dalian youth were especially receptive to this belief because they were children or grandchildren of migrants who came from less wealthy cities, towns, or villages in search of better opportunities. Moreover, the post-Mao China in which they grew up was almost like a new country, offering new opportunities, when compared with the Maoist China of their parents' youth. They used the cultural model of upward mobility to make sense of their family histories, and poor students saw themselves as ordinary youth unlucky enough to have low-income parents, rather than as members of a "lower class" faced with insurmountable barriers. Even academically unsuccessful children of powerless, low-income parents told me that they intended to attain upward mobility by getting adult education or college equivalency degrees, by starting their own businesses, or by going to wealthier cities or countries to work.

Children of elite parents had obvious advantages in the educational system. Wealthy parents could pay for tutors, private classes, study abroad, extra textbooks and study materials, computers, private schools, educational software and games, and admission to prestigious schools. Well-educated parents could tutor their children, find qualified tutors through their social networks, serve as role models of academic achievement, and provide their children with appropriate guidance about study skills and educational decisions. Yet, when I told students, parents, and teachers about Pierre Bourdieu's theory of how the elite use heritable cultural capital to transmit their status to their children,[19] some told me that "It's just the opposite in China, where poor students are more strongly motivated because they know a good education is the only way to escape their poverty, while rich students are unmotivated because they take it for granted that they can rely on their parents to get them into good schools and good jobs."

In 1998, when I heard this idea from Li Mei, a college prep high school senior whose parents were impoverished factory workers, I countered, "But Bourdieu's theory works very well in America. For instance, most students at Harvard have wealthy parents with white-collar jobs. Not many poor people have scores that are good enough to get them into Harvard, even though Harvard has need-blind admissions, and provides full financial support to students who cannot afford tuition and living expenses. But most students at my high school had parents who were ordinary workers or owners of family businesses, so most of my high school classmates could only qualify for junior colleges, even though they could have gotten full scholarships if their scores had been high enough. Don't you notice the same pattern in China?"

"Certainly not!" Li Mei answered. "In foreign countries, people get rich because of their own high quality, talent, education, and hard work, so of course the rich have high-quality, talented, educated, and hard-working children. But in China, the rich have gotten rich through luck, corruption, or political power. They themselves have no ability, and thus their children have no ability. Poor children don't have any more ability than rich children, but poor children work harder than rich children, so poor children are better students." She pointed out various mutual acquaintances who fit the pattern she proposed rather than the one Bourdieu's theory would predict. I had to admit she was right. In her homeroom, most of the top students were poorer than most of the worst students. On the other hand, I also noticed that, among the families I knew outside the schools I studied, children of the elite tended to have greater academic achievement (whether measured by their educational attainment, by their scores on citywide or nationwide standardized exams, or by the aptitude they seemed to demonstrate when I tutored them) than children of the non-elite. Many junior high school teachers and students told me this was true in their homerooms as well.

Hoping to find broader patterns, I looked for correlations between survey respondents' exam scores and their parents' job statuses and educational levels. The vocational high school students' test scores could not be analyzed because each homeroom was tested on a different set of subjects, but an analysis of the junior high school and college prep high school data produced significant results. At the junior high school, children of the elite tended to score higher than children of the non-elite (see Table 8). At the college prep high school, however, the pattern was reversed, and children of the non-elite tended to score higher than children of the elite.

I was at first puzzled by the patterns I found in my survey data, and by the insistence of many urban Dalian people that poor children tended to be "better students" than wealthier children. Was there something about China, urban Dalian, or the college prep high school students I surveyed that prevented parents from transmitting their elite status to their children? If so, why was this not the case among the junior high school students I surveyed? And why did patterns among the families I knew personally suggest that elite status was being inherited just as Bourdieu's theory would predict? After discussing these issues with many teachers and students, however, I realized why so many people believed that children of the elite were worse students than children of the non-elite. At the junior high school (where enrollment was

TABLE 8

Average Class Ranks of Junior and College Prep High School Students, by Parents' Education and Work Status

| | Junior High School Students | | College Prep High School Students | |
|---|---|---|---|---|
| | Average Percentile Class Rank[a] | *N* | Average Percentile Class Rank[a] | *N* |
| Parents with College Degree | | | | |
| Both parents | 66*** | 29 | 35*** | 46 |
| One parent | 61*** | 81 | 48*** | 103 |
| Neither parent | 49*** | 558 | 54*** | 307 |
| Parents Who Have Done Elite Work[b] | | | | |
| Both parents | 56** | 168 | 45*** | 163 |
| One parent | 54** | 181 | 50*** | 144 |
| Neither parent | 47** | 310 | 58*** | 148 |

SOURCE: The author's 1999 survey.

[a] Percentile ranks are based on students' January 2000 final exam scores. Only the scores of respondents whose homeroom teachers kept complete records of students' scores are included in this ranking. The highest possible percentile rank is 100, and the lowest possible is 1. A percentile rank is the proportion of scores in a distribution that a specific score is greater than or equal to. For instance, a student with a percentile rank of 64 received a score greater than or equal to the scores of 64 percent of the students taking the test.

[b] Elite work is here defined as the work of cadres/managers, professionals, or owners of large businesses.

** $p < 0.01$; *** $p < 0.001$

based on residency rather than on exam scores or ability to pay), students' exam scores correlated directly with their parents' wealth and educational attainment, just as Bourdieu's theory would predict. At the college prep high school, however, 20 percent[20] of students were wealthier, "privately funded" (*zifei*) or "expanded enrollment" (*kuozhao*) students who had scored below the school's regular cutoff but were admitted anyway because they were willing and able to pay about 2,500–5,000 yuan (US$313-$625) per year in tuition. The rest were poorer, "publicly funded" (*gongfei*) students who had scored above the school's regular cutoff, and only had to pay about 600 yuan (US$75) per year in tuition. The school did not have many wealthy students who scored above its regular cutoff, since most such students paid extra fees to become "privately funded" or "expanded enrollment" students at keypoint college prep high schools. Teachers told me that this pattern could be seen at most high schools and colleges throughout China. Any given high school or college was likely to consist of higher-achieving youth who did not have enough money or connections to get into a better school, and lower-achieving youth who would not have qualified for their school without money or connections. This system partially masked the transmission of cultural capital.

While everyone knew that wealthy students had more educational opportunities than poor students did, this knowledge was often less convincing than the observation that most of the best students in one's own high school or college homeroom were poorer than most of the worst students. The fact that high schools and colleges consisted of higher-achieving poor students and lower-achieving wealthy students thus promoted a cultural model which predicted that poor students would be more academically successful than wealthy students. This cultural model buoyed the hopes of the poor and powerless, who dreamed of upward mobility through a child's academic achievement.

Though they complained about corruption and inequality in the educational system, students still saw that system as the most level playing field they would ever have. The idea that "poor children are better students" was not consistent with overall demographic patterns or the majority of individual cases I knew about, but neither was it a completely fictitious myth. On the contrary, it was a self-fulfilling prophecy for some students I knew, just as it was for some of the first-generation immigrants whose unusually strong achievement motivation was documented in the United States.[21] While sheer determination was not powerful enough to overcome the advantages of inherited cultural capital in the majority of cases, it was powerful enough to prevent the solidifying of class barriers, and ensure that the educational system occasionally produced rags-to-riches success stories. Though it was not as likely as they hoped, the dream of gaining upward mobility through academic achievement did have a chance of coming true for students who exercised extraordinary self-discipline. Impoverished students whose self-discipline resulted in top scores on entrance exams could attend elite schools at low cost. Such schools could qualify them for elite jobs, which were denied to wealthy students who scored so low that not even their parents' money and connections could get them into elite schools. Cases of upward and downward mobility were common enough to keep poor families' hopes and wealthy families' fears alive. Regardless of their socioeconomic background, most people I knew in urban Dalian believed that every child could be a winner, and that every child had to work hard to keep from becoming a loser.

## The Complex Relationship Between Gender and Stratification

Prior to the one-child policy, most girls were raised to be losers. Since both the patrilineal family system and the heavy-industry-based economic system favored boys, girls usually lost when they competed with their brothers for family resources, and when they competed with boys for school and job openings. Students I knew in urban Dalian, however, were all raised to be winners, regardless of their gender. Prior to the one-child policy, parents tended to invest more in sons than in daughters.[22] Many parents told me that this was the case in their own natal families. But parents who obeyed the one-child policy had no sons to favor. Like their male counterparts, singleton daughters were their parents' only hope for the future, and received all the encouragement, investment, and pressure their parents could muster. Therefore, daughters' parents were just as likely as sons' parents to have high ambitions for their children.

The post-Mao urban economy provided increasingly favorable conditions for young women. Prior to the 1990s, most jobs available in cities like Dalian were in state-owned factories specializing in heavy industry products such as metals, electricity, coal, petroleum, machines, and construction materials. Heavy industry jobs required stereotypically masculine qualities such as scientific expertise, technical skills, physical strength, and tolerance for harsh, dirty conditions. Most such jobs were reserved for men, while women were relegated to jobs in the light industry and service sectors, which were smaller, less secure, and lower paying.[23] When the Chinese state began exposing its industries to foreign competition, however, Chinese factories specializing in heavy industry could not compete with their more efficient and technologically advanced First World counterparts, and went bankrupt or had to lay off many of their workers. But light industry thrived by producing consumer goods that could be made cheaply, without advanced technology. Meanwhile, the development of fields such as communications, tourism, hospitality, education, commerce, catering, finance, trade, and business led to rapid growth and rising salaries in the urban service sector. Light industry and the service sector needed top-level managers who had the boldness and creativity associated with masculinity, but they also needed mid- and lower-level workers who had the discipline associated with femininity. Therefore, employers in some of the fastest-growing fields preferred to hire women for all but the highest level of work.

The relationship between gender and personhood in Chinese culture is quite different from that in societies that define masculinity as superior to and the opposite of femininity. Unlike the Bedouin autonomy described by Lila Abu-Lughod,[24] the Nicaraguan machismo described by Roger Lancaster,[25] or the Cretan contestation described by Michael Herzfeld,[26] Chinese masculinity (*yang*) was good only in moderation, and only in balance with femininity (*yin*). While they did not prevent brothers, husbands, parents, and parents-in-law from using the patrilineal system to keep sisters, wives, daughters, and daughters-in-law subordinate throughout Chinese history, cultural models that promoted an even balance of yin and yang allowed for the possibility of defining ideal personhood in ways that did not exclude or debase positive traits stereotypically associated with femininity. Even at the height of male dominance, women were considered polluting because their interests often conflicted with those of men who dominated the patrilineal kinship system, and not because of stereotypically feminine traits per se.[27] Among the families I knew in urban Dalian, possession of an even balance of stereotypically masculine and stereotypically feminine positive traits was considered the ideal for boys and girls alike. Girls with no positive masculine traits were seen as fragile, dependent, useless drones doomed to fail in a competitive society. Boys with no positive feminine traits were seen as wild, shameless, dangerous hoodlums doomed to fail in a society that valued discipline and obedience. The rare boy with no positive masculine traits and girl with no positive feminine traits were even worse, since their failure to balance yin and yang could not be blamed on socialization or biological predispositions. But, as in the urban Asante society described by Gracia Clark,[28] comparison to the opposite gender could be a compliment for boys and girls who possessed an admirable balance of positive masculine and feminine traits. Parents and teachers sometimes praised quiet, diligent, studious girls for being as daring, creative, and independent as boys on appropriate occasions, and they sometimes praised daring, creative, and independent boys for being as quiet, diligent, and studious as girls on appropriate occasions.

"My daughter is strong and independent, just like a boy," Zhou Jing's father told me in 1999, as we discussed her role as monitor (*banzhang*) of her college prep high school homeroom. "Her teacher told me that, when her classmates chat during study hall, she stands right up and tells them to stop talking, even if they're her friends."

"My son is studious and obedient, just like a girl," seventh grader Li Ji's mother told me in 1998. "He's not like those bad boys who get into fights."

Most people I knew in urban Dalian subscribed to a cultural model of femininity that portrayed girls as delicate, sensitive, pretty, responsible, obedient, disciplined, domestically oriented, and concerned about saving face. Girls were supposed to be good at the humanities and social sciences because they were patient, meticulous, and good at memorization. Girls were expected to be bad at math and science because they lacked "flexible" (*linghuo*) imaginations. Because of these expectations, women were seen as suitable for jobs as translators, doctors, nurses, teachers, secretaries, flight attendants, public relations representatives, accountants, tour guides, hotel workers, food servers, cashiers, salespeople, beauticians, textile workers, and other light industry workers.[29]

The cultural model of masculinity, on the other hand, portrayed boys as strong, resilient, tough, aggressive, thick-skinned, daring, active, and eager to indulge in leisure activities. Boys were supposed to be good at math and science because they had flexible imaginations. Boys were expected to be bad at the humanities and social sciences because they were impatient, bad at memorization, and unable to sit still. Because of these expectations, men were seen as suitable for jobs as engineers, computer programmers, scientists, sailors, drivers, police officers, technicians, soldiers, repairmen, security guards, manual laborers, and other heavy industry workers.

Cultural models of gender were often self-fulfilling prophecies. As Michael Herzfeld has argued,[30] people often use stereotypes to excuse their own undesirable behavior as normal and inevitable. Boys who fought, disobeyed authority, refused to do housework, scored low on exams in the humanities and social sciences, and played sports and video games instead of studying were criticized less than girls who did the same. When seventh grader Zhang Yong's parents scolded him for not studying one school night in 1998, he rebuffed them with the claim, "It's normal for boys to be unable to sit still and study."

Girls who scored low on science and math exams and showed little ambition, toughness, creativity, boldness, initiative, or leadership ability were criticized less than boys who did the same. Zhou Bo, a female college prep high school senior who frequently cried at school, told me in 1998, "I know I shouldn't be so sensitive, and sometimes I think I should work on improving my psychological quality, but people sympathize with girls who cry, so it's really not so bad that I cry." Gender-appropriate negative traits were often excused by the widespread assumption that "boys will be boys" and "girls will be girls."

While boys and girls alike knew that it was best to have a balance of masculine and feminine positive traits, and no negative traits associated with either gender, most found this ideal too difficult to attain. Therefore, knowing that gender-appropriate negative traits were more likely to be tolerated, teenagers focused primarily on trying to purge themselves of negative traits associated with the opposite gender. Consequently, most ended up exhibiting traits that reinforced dominant cultural models of gender.

Young people were wary about choosing fields dominated by the opposite gender.[31] I often heard successful female science, technology, and computer majors and successful male humanities, social science, and service industry majors talk about how difficult it would be to convince teachers and employers that they were actually good at gender-inappropriate subjects. Many vocational and technical schools in Dalian had openly published gender quotas for each major that excluded most students from occupational training deemed gender-inappropriate. Even schools without openly published quotas unofficially took gender into account when selecting students for particular majors. Fearing that their children might face discrimination in fields dominated by the opposite gender, parents of sons as well as daughters often discouraged their children from choosing gender-inappropriate majors and careers even when their children preferred and excelled at them.

When Guo Da wanted to choose accounting as his major in adult education college after graduating from vocational high school in 1999, he received a stern warning from his father: "Everyone knows women are more meticulous than men, so all the accountants are women. Do you think a company is going to hire you over a woman? You need to major in something more suitable for a man, such as machine repair."

When college prep high school graduate Ding Na chose computer programming as her college major in 1999, her father warned against it. "I know you're good with computers, but employers are just going to take one look at you and not hire you because you're female. Computer knowledge is constantly changing, and once you marry and have a child, you'll start lagging behind, and never catch up with the men. If you really want to work with computers, you should major in computerized accounting. Or better yet, choose medical school instead."

Stereotypically feminine traits were seen as ideal for most jobs in the rapidly expanding light industry and service sectors. Stereotypically masculine traits were seen as ideal for most jobs in the rapidly shrinking heavy industry sector, and for professional careers open only to a tiny elite. This meant that men entering professional careers were more likely to succeed than their female counterparts, but also that women entering the general job market were more likely to get work than their male counterparts, who were more likely to end up unemployed. Daughters were therefore counseled both to conform to cultural models that could give them an advantage in the general job market, and to disregard those that might exclude them from elite professional work. As Ding Na's father told her in 1999, "You'll need a good education so you can get a job in a nice office suitable for a girl. But if you want your career to really develop, remember that a lot of teachers and work units discriminate against girls, so you have to be better than the boys just to be able to stand up."

Young people were sometimes frustrated by parents' contradictory expectations about their gender socialization. "My Ma says I should stay home and study all the time, and never go out," Wang Song complained to me in 1999. "If I were a girl, that would be fine, but I'm a boy! She should understand that she has a son, not a daughter."

High school student Li Ying lamented in an open letter to her mother published in a Dalian newspaper in 1999, "You don't consider my gender and how I want to arrange my life. I'm a quiet, shy girl who doesn't like to exercise, and just likes to stay at home reading novels. But still you buy me clothes that are more suitable for a boy, and ask me to do things that are not suitable for a girl to do. . . . Ma, gender cannot be changed. So please accept the reality that I'm a girl. I want to have my own dreams."[32]

Masculine behaviors gave men an edge in elite professions. If they were not balanced by the discipline associated with femininity, however, masculine behaviors could cause a boy to fail in school and the job market. Recognizing that boys were more likely to fail in school and less likely to get work, many high school administrators set quotas that ensured that their schools would admit more girls than boys. Greater educational opportunities for girls at the mid-ranked and low-ranked schools were reflected in the materials published by Dalian's Bureau of Education and given to the graduating junior high school class of 1999. At the technical school level (sixth-rate), there were 1,346 places open to both boys and girls and 4,492 places reserved for girls, but only 4,301 places reserved for boys. At the vocational school level (fifth-rate), there were 2,949 places open to both boys and girls and 5,189 places reserved for girls, but only 3,849 places reserved for boys. Most professional high schools (fourth-rate) did not publish gender quotas, but teachers told me they tended to enroll boys and girls at roughly the same rate. Among the 18 private schools (third-rate) accepting students in 1999, there were two that only accepted girls, but none that only accepted boys. At the ordinary college prep high school (second-rate) that I studied, 52 percent[33] of students were female, and 48 percent[34] were male. Only the universities and the small minority of high schools classified as "keypoint college prep" (first-rate) had more boys than girls.[35]

Women faced a "glass ceiling" produced by their extra burden of domestic responsibility, by cultural models that favor men in elite professions, and by inequalities between elite husbands and their less elite, hypergamous wives. But women also enjoyed the protection of a "glass floor" created by the hypergamous marriage system, by cultural models that favored women in the educational system, and by the rapidly expanding market for feminine jobs in the service and light industry sectors. This "glass floor" prevented women from sinking to the bottom of society, into poverty, crime, and unemployment. Men had neither the obstacle of the "glass ceiling" nor the protection of the "glass floor." While elite men were more likely than their female counterparts to rise to the top of their society, low-status men were also more likely than their female counterparts to fall to the bottom.

Some aspects of the cultural model of gender actually worked to the advantage of young women and their parents. Girls who conformed to the cultural model of gender were more studious and obedient than boys, and thus more successful in the educational system at all levels besides the very highest. I observed conspicuous differences between classes in male-dominated majors and classes in female-dominated majors. Classes consisting mostly of boys were rowdy, noisy, and difficult for teachers to control; classes consisting mostly of girls were orderly, quiet, and easy to teach. During breaks, boys got together to joke, wrestle, and play soccer or basketball, while girls chatted or even continued to study. Boys and their parents complained that the educational system favored girls by disproportionately rewarding feminine qualities such as patience, diligence, and the ability to memorize large quantities of information. "It makes me sick to see the girls sitting in front of me studying all the time, even during breaks when I'm playing," male college prep high school student Xue Liang told me in 2000. "It's not fair that girls can get such high marks just because they're willing to do a lot of rote memorization, even though their minds are not as sharp as mine." As the exam scores of students at the schools I studied showed, girls were more likely than boys to be good at foreign languages.[36] This gave girls an edge in the competition for desirable jobs in trade, the travel industry, and foreign-funded enterprises. Girls at the college prep high school and the junior high school also tended to have higher overall scores than boys (see Table 9). High school entrance exams tested students on more science and math subjects (which boys favored) than humanities and social science subjects (which girls favored), and four-year colleges accepted more science and math majors than humanities and social science majors. These factors constituted a significant bias against girls at the highest levels of academic achievement, but not at the middle and lower levels where the majority of students found themselves.

One aspect of the cultural model of patrilocality that did not disappear by the late 1990s was the expectation that grooms would provide marital housing. The ability to live up to this expectation remained an important determinant of whether a man could win a bride. Thus, a son and his parents had to try and buy, rent, borrow, inherit, or be assigned marital housing by the time the son reached marriageable age. This became increasingly difficult as more housing became privatized rather than provided by employers. A daughter and her parents could consider the ability to provide or contribute to the purchase of marital housing an extra bonus to enhance the daughter's marriageability and comfort, rather than a requirement. Singleton daughters and their parents considered this an advantage, rather than an indication that daughters were valued less than sons. Singletons of either gender faced no competition for parental investment or inheritance. They and their parents just had to decide what form the wealth transfer would take.

TABLE 9
Average Class Ranks of Respondents, by Gender and School

| | Average Percentile Class Rank[a] |
|---|---|
| Junior High School | |
| Girls ($N = 361$) | 57*** |
| Boys ($N = 325$) | 42*** |
| College Prep High School | |
| Girls ($N = 262$) | 54*** |
| Boys ($N = 201$) | 44*** |

SOURCE: The author's 1999 survey.

[a] Percentile ranks are based on January 2000 final exam scores. Only the scores of respondents whose homeroom teachers kept complete records of students' scores are included in this ranking. The highest possible percentile rank is 100, and the lowest possible is 1. A percentile rank is the proportion of scores in a distribution that a specific score is greater than or equal to. For instance, a student with a percentile rank of 64 received a score greater than or equal to the scores of 64 percent of the students taking the test.

*** $p < 0.001$

Unlike sons' parents, daughters' parents could invest all their savings in their daughters' education, rather than saving part of it for the purchase of marital housing. The need to obtain housing to attract a spouse was thus a disadvantage for sons and their parents.

Cultural models of gender structured Dalian's job market, but not to all women's disadvantage and all men's advantage. Rather, they worked in favor of younger women, low-status women, and elite men, even as they worked against older women, elite women, and low-status men. Middle-aged women in the state sector faced institutionalized discrimination rationalized by the assumption that employment was less important for them because their primary responsibilities were domestic. Thus, they were the first fired and last hired, and their mandatory retirement ages were 5–10 years younger than those of men holding the same positions. Women were rare in the most prestigious and best-paid professions, partly because they were hindered by their "second shift"[37] of domestic work, and partly because many employers believed that women did not have enough daring and creativity to be managers or high-level experts.

Focusing on biases against older women and elite women, many recent studies have argued that post-Mao economic reforms intensified discrimination against women.[38] I found, however, that the consequences of those reforms were more complicated for the majority of youth, who were of average or below-average education and family background. The same economic reforms that encouraged state enterprises to discriminate against middle-aged women also created jobs in light industry and the service industry, both of which favored young women. Like most jobs created after the economic restructuring that began in the 1980s, low-level jobs in these industries came with few or no benefits, and little or no job security. But unlike their mothers and grandmothers, whose premarital earnings sometimes went to fund their brothers' education, weddings, and postmarital housing, brotherless daughters used their savings from low-level service jobs to fund further training and education that could qualify them for more permanent careers. Because the private sector, light industry sector, and service sector were expanding, the skills, experience, savings, and connections these women gained from work were likely to provide at least some of them with a foundation for starting their own businesses or for promotion into more permanent positions. Even jobs that did not provide opportunities for career advancement were preferable to unemployment, which was more likely for boys lacking academic credentials or wealthy, powerful families. Such boys tended to join the emerging youth gangs and fall into lives of poverty, crime, and incarceration.

## The Straight and Narrow Road: Discipline as Means to Success

"Think of yourself as having entered a jail," Xun Jin's father advised her when she enrolled at a college prep high school. "From now on, you must focus entirely on your studies. Like a prisoner, you will not have any freedom to do the things you enjoy. Your only hope is the trial, the college entrance exam, which will determine whether the rest of your life is one of joy or suffering."

Like Michel Foucault, who saw prisons and schools as analogous institutions created to subject all individuals to the discipline of the state,[39] urban Dalian students and parents recognized that discipline was the thread connecting the experiences of incarceration and education. Prisons were for those who had not cultivated enough self-discipline, and therefore had to be disciplined through state coercion. Schools and exam sites, on the other hand, were places where young people could prove that they had enough self-discipline to at least become good workers, and at best become part of the elite willing and able to work toward state goals of modernization. Students, parents, and teachers agreed that discipline was the single most important determinant of educational success. They talked about failure to *guan* (discipline / control / administer / take care of) when discussing reasons for a student's academic failure. Students did poorly on exams if they could not discipline themselves (*guan bu zhu ta ziji*), and if their parents and teachers did not discipline them. As Anne Allison wrote of the Japanese educational system (which bore many similarities to its Chinese counterpart), the key to success was "a willingness to bend to the authority of the school system and an ability to mimetically reproduce its structure of endless surveillance, constant exams, and habitual memorization."[40]

It took great discipline to force oneself to eschew leisure, memorize vast quantities of information, and work through an endless, repetitive series of practice problems modeled after those found on entrance exams. The more time one spent studying, the better one did on exams. Every minute spent on leisure was a minute lost in the race to memorize more information and practice solving more exam questions. Top students had enough discipline to eschew leisure and devote all their time to their studies. Because the college and high school entrance exams tested cumulative knowledge, students were pressured to continue studying during weekends and vacations. For extra fees, schools offered their students extra vacation and weekend classes. While such classes were technically "voluntary," most college prep and junior high school students attended them to avoid falling behind. In addition, many parents arranged to fill their children's scant remaining free time with private classes and tutoring sessions. Among respondents to my survey, 88 percent[41] indicated that they took private classes or were tutored by someone other than their parents at some point in their lives. Tutoring and private classes could start as early as preschool, and continue through college. High-achieving students told me that they could not remember a time when they could indulge in leisure activities without feeling guilty that they were neglecting their studies.

Since the economic reforms began in 1978, Chinese educators have focused on teaching students to perform well on exams that consist primarily of multiple-choice and fill-in-the-blank questions. This was most apparent at junior high schools and college prep high schools, where homework, midterms, and finals were designed to mimic entrance exams. But even elementary schools, colleges, graduate schools, and professional, vocational, and technical high schools based academic assessment largely on exam scores. In addition, many students who did not attend college prep high schools still took extra classes to prepare for the adult education college entrance exam or the college equivalency exams, and some college students focused on preparing for graduate school entrance exams. Some high schools and colleges lowered score cutoffs for a small number of students who displayed extraordinary talent in art, dance, music, or sports, and state-owned work units were somewhat more likely to hire and promote youth with membership in the Communist Youth League or the Communist Party.[42] Entrance exam scores, however, outweighed all other kinds of achievement in determining a student's socioeconomic trajectory.

School-administered tests had no impact on college or high school admissions, but they were important indicators of how well a student was likely to perform on real entrance exams. Class rankings based on test scores were considered more reliable indicators than the scores themselves, which fluctuated because some tests were more difficult than others. Prior to 2000, most schools publicly announced the test scores and class ranks of all their students—even those who ranked at the bottom. In 2000, Dalian's government prohibited this practice as part of its campaign to reduce competitive pressures that might cause "psychological problems" among students. This campaign also encouraged schools to promote "quality education" through extracurricular activities, creative writing, research papers, science experiments, and participation in class discussions. Teachers at college prep and junior high schools, however, continued to de-emphasize such activities because they had little effect on whether students would get into prestigious high schools and colleges.

When I first started teaching English in urban Dalian homes and classrooms, I tried to engage students with games, skits, discussions, and other exercises designed to build their listening, speaking, reading, and writing skills. Students enjoyed my teaching methods, but they stopped taking me seriously when they saw that my efforts did not help them get higher scores on tests modeled after the English sections of the entrance exams. Some students with advanced English conversation skills still scored lower on English grammar, vocabulary, and reading comprehension tests than classmates who were less adept at speaking English but spent more time memorizing English words and doing practice tests. Parents and teachers criticized me for wasting students' time with activities that did not improve their test scores.

In response to these criticisms, I changed my approach. I stopped asking students to read articles, write essays, and play games in English, and started teaching grammar, phonetics, spelling rules, vocabulary word memorization tricks, and strategies for answering exam questions. Though dull and exhausting, this approach produced noticeable improvement in the English test scores of many students I tutored. Like Chinese teachers, I felt responsible for students' academic performance. When their English test score rankings dropped, I blamed myself for failing to teach them the right test-taking skills. When their English test score rankings improved, my heart swelled with pride.

From primary school through secondary school, Chinese students were organized into homerooms, which were divided into orderly rows of assigned seats. Each homeroom consisted of 40–60 students who sat at their desks during the bulk of the school day, while different teachers came in to teach different subjects. The most influential one was the homeroom teacher (*banzhuren*), who not only taught a particular subject, but also supervised study hall periods, met with parents, and was held responsible for the success or failure of all students in the homeroom.

Most students stayed in the same homeroom throughout their time at a given school. Many teachers taught the same students from enrollment through graduation. Because they spent so much time together, students developed warm, close relationships with their classmates and teachers. While academic rivalries sometimes caused tension, such tension was limited by students' understanding that it was not their ranking against their own classmates, but rather their ranking against all exam-takers throughout their city, province, and country, that would ultimately determine their fate. Most of a teenager's friends were current or former homeroom classmates.

Tension between students and teachers was likewise limited by the fact that entrance exam scores would be determined by official exam scorers, and not by a student's own teachers. Many teachers, students, and classmates kept in touch throughout their lives. Students told me that teachers were "like parents," in both good and bad ways. Teachers told me that they felt students were like their own children.

Parents were required to attend "parents' meetings" (*jiazhanghui*), where they sat in their children's seats while teachers and administrators lectured them on how to make their children better students, and told them about their children's behavior and test scores. Teachers also called parents in for special meetings if their children misbehaved. Some parents hired their children's teachers to give their children private lessons during weekends or vacations. Teachers' reputations were based on how well their students performed on the entrance exam. Good reputations could bring teachers respect, praise, promotions, raises, and opportunities to earn high fees as private tutors in their spare time. Students who went on to successful careers constituted a powerful resource for teachers, who could get favors from them and act as brokers of social connections.

In addition to their primary function as gateways to high socioeconomic status, schools were responsible for building students' moral character (*pinde*), which was defined as a combination of self-discipline, agreement with state policies, and being a good person. Ideally, politics classes and propaganda meetings encouraged students to agree with state policies, the benevolent influence of teachers serving as role models and mentors helped students become good people, and the strict enforcement of school prohibitions promoted discipline. In practice, discipline was the main focus of students' moral education, since it was most likely to improve entrance exam scores and the ability to win a good job.

Schools promoted discipline in every aspect of students' lives. Ever since the 1989 protests at Beijing's Tiananmen Square demonstrated the threat students could pose to state discipline, Chinese junior high schools, high schools, and colleges have required their students to undergo at least a few weeks of military training (*junxun*) right after enrollment. Supervised by military personnel, such training taught students to march in formation and obey orders while performing physically exhausting exercises in military uniforms under the hot late summer sun. Some students I knew considered such training a waste of time and energy, but others found it an interesting break from their usual academic routine. Orderly, military-style marches were also an important part of physical education, school assemblies, and weekly flag-raising ceremonies. Administrators selected some teachers and students to be hall monitors who gave demerits to students and homerooms that broke school rules against fighting, eating, or talking in the hallways or during class or study hall. Awards were given to homerooms that had no demerits. Personal demerits could hurt a student's chances at getting homeroom leadership roles, membership in the Communist Youth League and the Communist Party, and other special opportunities or awards. Every homeroom had a student monitor (*banzhang*) responsible for maintaining discipline when teachers were not around.

Students had to adhere to a heavily regimented schedule demarcated by school bells. The lunch period and brief breaks between classes were the only times students were allowed to eat, chat, or use the restroom. Even noontime naps (a tradition in most Chinese schools and workplaces) were strictly enforced. Students were expected to put their heads on their desks and sleep during naptime, which immediately followed lunch and usually lasted less than an hour. Teachers emphasized that naps were necessary to prevent drowsiness during afternoon classes and study halls. While some homeroom teachers allowed their students to study quietly if they could not fall asleep during naptime, most did not allow their students to eat or engage in leisure activities during naptime. From primary school through college, students were kept in school at least eight hours a day, five days a week. Junior high schools and college prep high schools kept students in school 9–14 hours a day, and many held extra classes on weekends and during vacations in order to give students an edge in the entrance exams. Students spent most of the school day, including lunch, naptime, and study hall, in their small wooden chairs, their movement heavily restricted by other students' desks and chairs. Many classrooms were so tightly packed with desks and chairs that one had to walk sideways to get from the back of the classroom to the front.

Romantic relationships between students (*zaolian*, literally "early romance") were prohibited at high schools, junior high schools, and elementary schools. While some teachers declined to enforce this prohibition, others worked hard to keep boyfriends and girlfriends from spending time together during school, and informed parents about their children's forbidden romantic involvements. Most teachers and parents claimed that romantic relationships would distract students from their studies, and top students like Hu Ying, Chen Jun, and Wang Song agreed. Student romances tended to be least common at the most prestigious schools, where discipline was strictest, students were the most obedient, and constant studying left no time for leisure. This pattern reinforced the widespread belief that abstinence from romance could improve academic performance.

Even the student romances that did develop usually did not lead to sex. Most teenagers had little unsupervised time or space in which to be sexually active. They spent the bulk of their time in school. They could not afford cars or hotel rooms. Even youth in their early 20s were unlikely to have private apartments or dorm rooms. Most parents were home during the few hours of the day and week when students were not in school, and only allowed teenagers to go out with friends of the same gender, or large groups that included both genders. Unemployed parents were home almost all the time. Many parents kept careful track of their children's activities by gathering information from their children's teachers, friends, and friends' parents. Teachers informed parents when students were truant. Parents carefully guarded their children's chastity because those known to have had premarital sex were seen as less desirable on the marriage market than those presumed to be virgins. This was especially true for women, but also true for men. Parents and teachers considered the need to find a spouse the only acceptable reason for dating. Spouse seeking was supposed to begin in one's 20s. Women younger than 20 and men younger than 22 were legally prohibited from marrying, and state enterprises gave bonuses to employees who married when they were at least two years older than the legal minimum. Prior to 2001, regular college programs that were not geared toward adult education did not accept married students or allow their students to marry.[43] Young people were expected to enter the marriage market only after finishing their education and finding steady work.

Schools tried to deprive students of everything that might distract them from their studies. From primary school through high school, students had to wear school uniforms, which usually consisted of durable, comfortable unisex sweat suits. Girls were required to either wear short hair or keep long hair tied back, and boys were not allowed to let their hair grow even a little longer than the standard male haircut. Jewelry, makeup, and dyed hair were prohibited for both genders. Alcohol, cigarettes, playing cards, mahjong tiles, checkers, beepers, cellular phones, electronic game devices, portable music players, and other sources of entertainment were prohibited from school grounds. Successful enforcement of school prohibitions enhanced a school's prestige. Failure to enforce these prohibitions was associated with low-ranked schools that enrolled and graduated undisciplined, low-scoring students, who in turn were more likely to defy school rules.

Junior high and college prep high school students had to study not only their official textbooks, but also a vast array of extra materials, including a "sea of practice test questions" (*tihai*), in order to keep up with the competition. These students were assigned large amounts of homework over weekends, vacations, and holidays. Top schools gave so much homework that not even the most diligent student could finish it all. Top students deprived themselves of sleep in order to squeeze more studying into each day. Students, parents, and teachers often asked me to tell them about the specific practices of self-discipline that got me into college. "How did you study?" "How did you manage your time?" and "What time did you sleep and what time did you wake up?" were among their most frequently asked questions.

In the 1990s, education officials began to promote "quality education" (*suzhi jiaoyu*) as opposed to "education for exam preparation" (*yingshi jiaoyu*). Officials called for quality education because they wanted to emulate Western educational methods, because they hoped to reduce the pressure students faced in the educational system, and because they feared that students who learned nothing besides exam-taking skills would be poorly equipped to compete in the capitalist world system. Officials emphasized the importance of providing quality education by trying to spark students' interest in their studies and by providing physical, political, moral, technical, and practical education. They argued that Chinese schools should focus on producing well-rounded citizens rather than physically and psychologically "unhealthy" (*bu jiankang*) bookworms who only knew how to memorize texts and answer exam questions. They wanted education to be seen as a means for producing "high-quality" (*gao suzhi*) people, rather than just as a means of stratification. They exhorted entrance exam writers to design questions that tested students' ability to apply academic knowledge to real-life situations. But their efforts were limited by the difficulty of creating standardized test questions that could fairly and objectively measure this ability. It was hard to get students, parents, and teachers to take quality education seriously when the primary means of measuring academic success continued to reward the students who memorized the most information from their textbooks.

Amorphous, rapidly changing, and widely used, the term "high quality" represented a prestigious, respectable kind of personhood. Though it had multiple and sometimes conflicting meanings, "quality" was generally associated with integrity, cosmopolitanism, and cultural capital. Like their counterparts in the First World, wealthy urban Dalian parents paid for expensive piano, computer, art, foreign language, and sports lessons for their children, hoping to increase their quality. Many employers said they were seeking "high-quality talent," which could be seen in applicants' demeanor and language during interviews. High-quality people had self-discipline, which was vital for success in the capitalist world system. Teachers told me that what separated successful students from unsuccessful ones was the former's high quality, as demonstrated by their ability to force themselves to study all the time instead of indulging in leisure activities. When top students did poorly on the entrance exam because of nervousness, people said that their "psychological quality was not good" (*xinli suzhi buhao*). Urban Dalian people told me that they could tell how much quality people had just by looking at them. They said that people who littered, spat on the ground, or failed to stand at attention during the playing of the national anthem had low quality. In 1998, when I was still trying to get my bearings in urban Dalian, college prep high school student Liu Na told me not to look all around me as I walked. "It makes you look like a rural migrant eagerly feasting her eyes on the splendors of the city," she complained. "You should look straight ahead with a jaded, determined expression that demonstrates your high quality."

Parents, students, and teachers were skeptical of the government's quality education campaign because they knew that a student's performance on the entrance exam was the main determinant of admission to the next level of education, and that educational attainment was the main determinant of what kind of job one could get. While they agreed that education for exam preparation was unhealthy, they feared that socioeconomic failure would be even more hazardous to a teenager's health. Despite the quality education campaign, exam performance was still key to the attainment of high quality. Graduates of college prep high schools, which focused primarily on exam preparation, were widely recognized to have higher quality than graduates of professional, vocational, and technical high schools, which focused more on quality education. The quality education campaign's directives were often disobeyed, especially at keypoint college prep high schools, which were said to produce the highest-quality students of all.

## A Homeroom Meeting to Promote Good Study Habits

Students found the strict discipline enforced by their parents and schools stifling. Boys were especially likely to resist it. At the same time, however, boys and girls alike knew that they needed to cultivate self-discipline if they wanted their dream of high socioeconomic status to come true. Students' ambivalence toward the discipline required for academic success was evident in the mix of serious and lighthearted attitudes expressed at a 1999 meeting (*banhui*) in a senior homeroom at the college prep high school where I taught and conducted participant observation.

After declaring that the homeroom would hold a meeting on "how to study," middle-aged homeroom teacher Wang Aihua gave a pep talk on the importance of discipline, and then turned the meeting over to Zhao Hua, who served as class monitor (*banzhang*), and Zhang Shu, who served as the chair of academics (*xuexi weiyuan*). These two boys ran the homeroom meeting, while Wang Aihua sat at her desk, occasionally chiming in with advice. Like classes and study hall periods, the meeting lasted 45 minutes. Most homerooms had several meetings each semester to celebrate official state holidays, disseminate propaganda, or promote good study habits. Planned by school officials and chaired by student leaders under the supervision of homeroom teachers, these meetings fostered homeroom solidarity while promoting the goals of the school and, ultimately, the state.

"We've all been eating too much in class, even me, the chair of academics!" said Zhang Shu to much laughter. "My main problem is that I can't stop laughing and be serious. I'll try to be more serious, and stop joking around. There's no time for joking around. We have to spend every minute studying." Then, in a solemn deadpan that mocked the Cultural Revolution attitudes he knew only from old movies and stories told by people of his parents' and grandparents' generations, he added, "We must accept the criticisms of the Party and the people. . . ." He was drowned out by his classmates' laughter.

Zhang Shu and Zhao Hua then called on various classmates to stand up and make declarations about their attitudes toward studying. They chose mainly the highest-achieving students, though they also called on some less successful students to fill the time. All of the girls presented earnest declarations of their eagerness to improve their self-discipline, but some of the boys made wisecracks that drew uproarious laughter.

"Often, I've made the mistake of thinking that happiness is the most important thing in my life," confessed Xie Fang, a high-scoring girl. "That attitude is wrong. Studying should be the most important thing in our lives. Now is not the time to be happy. Only after we have careers can we be happy."

"I'll hold on tightly to my time," said her best friend Mei Jing, another high-scoring girl. "I'll spend every minute and every second studying. I have to improve my scores, especially in Chinese and math."

"I've wasted too much time doing useless things, like singing under my breath during study hall!" said Zhu Xi, an above-average-scoring boy. His classmates laughed.

Several boys and girls praised their higher-scoring friends as good role models.

Su Yi, a girl with above-average scores said, "I'm not hardworking, but I'll have to be this semester. I'll try hard to get into college. All my parents' hopes are pinned on me. I don't want to disappoint them."

"We must face our difficulties with strength," said Wang Yong, a boy with above-average scores.

"We'll soon take the college entrance exam, so we must use every minute to study," said Zhou Bo, a high-scoring girl who often burst into tears when she did poorly on tests.

"The next four months are the most critical period of our lives," said Yang Weilai, an average-scoring girl.

"We have only 127 days left till the college entrance exam," said Hang Yu, another average-scoring girl. "We have to hold on tightly to our time."

"I've been too lazy, and wasted too much time," said Chen Lan, a high-scoring girl. "We must remember that a high score on the entrance exam is the only thing that can get us into college. Nothing else will help us get into college, so nothing else matters."

Liu Jifeng, a shy, high-scoring boy, stood up when the chair of academics called on him, but said nothing. He smiled and shrugged sheepishly, while his classmates burst into laughter. Several other boys and girls admitted that they could think of nothing to say.

"I always look forward to the end of class, and I don't pay attention to the teacher," confessed He Xiaowei, an average-scoring boy. "I'm wasting my opportunities. My friends in vocational high schools who visited me during Spring Festival said they wished they had studied more in junior high school. They're working as interns for low pay, and their work is exhausting. I don't want to end up like them, so I have to get into college."

Hao Jinling, a low-scoring girl, said shyly, "We should at least try hard, so that even if we don't do well on the exam, we'll still have no regrets."

"I have no regrets. This is a nice classroom," said Li Chang, an average-scoring boy, to much laughter.

Wang Aihua, who was much loved by her students for her sincerity and compassion, looked on with amusement at her students' performance. She concluded the meeting with a warning that "Even teachers are losing their jobs these days. There's no more iron rice bowl. Society these days is competitive, and you'll depend on your education to eat."

CHAPTER 4

# "Beat Me Now and I'll Beat You When You're Old"

## *Love, Filial Duty, and Parental Investment in an Aging Population*

VIVIANA ZELIZER has argued that, by the end of the twentieth century, American children were "economically worthless but emotionally priceless."[1] While Chinese singletons were likewise emotionally priceless to their parents, they were also economically valuable. Chinese children were more likely than First World children to be their parents' primary source of income and nursing care in old age. While elder care facilities, social security programs, inflation-resistant investment opportunities, elaborate retirement planning industries, and postretirement work opportunities enabled many First World parents to claim that the time and money they spent on their children were nothing more than selfless expressions of unconditional love, most Chinese parents had no such luxury. As the primary source of social security for the elderly, Chinese cultural models of filial duty and parental investment entailed a candid recognition that parents must be repaid in time and money as well as love.

Emotional and economic factors combined to make Chinese singletons achingly precious to their parents. The intensity of this preciousness was a burden for parent and child alike. Singletons like Wang Song felt overwhelmed by pressure to live up to their parents' expectations. Parents felt uneasy at how much power children had over them, and devastated when children were not as filial or successful as they should have been. Many parents and children told me that they envied the less burdensome intergenerational contracts of the First World, where retirement systems had more time to catch up to population aging.

## The Child as Retirement Plan

The cultural model of filial duty remained one of the most salient aspects of China's Confucian legacy. Chinese leaders continued to promote this cultural model because it allowed the state to devote its resources to promoting economic growth instead of social security, on the assumption that most citizens would rely on their children for nursing care, economic support, and the payment of medical expenses in their old age. This assumption also promoted modernization by encouraging parents to invest in their children's education.

By enforcing mandatory retirement while leaving retirees without the means for economic self-sufficiency, the Chinese state practically guaranteed that most people would spend the final decades of their lives dependent on their children. State-owned enterprises enforced mandatory retirement ages of 60 for men, 55 for white-collar women, and 50 for women workers. Only unusually powerful officials and experts with rare skills were allowed to continue working past official retirement ages.

Parents' dependence on their adult children for support in old age steadily increased under economic reforms that dismantled the social safety net in order to make Chinese industries more competitive in the capitalist world system. By the 1990s, many state enterprises were going bankrupt, laying off their workers, reducing or eliminating pensions and medical insurance, and persuading redundant workers to retire as early as age 40 in exchange for promises of small pensions unavailable to those who were laid off.[2] Respondents to my survey indicated that 24 percent of their fathers[3] and 24 percent of their mothers[4] had no insurance or pensions. The government had no social security system to cover those who lacked pensions or healthcare. State and collective enterprises had never paid their employees enough to allow them to amass substantial retirement savings. Even those who became wealthy by taking bribes, starting their own businesses, or working at unusually high-paying jobs had difficulty sheltering their savings from inflation. The Chinese stock market was notoriously risky.[5] Legal and economic barriers made it difficult even for elite Chinese to participate in the less risky mutual funds of the First World. Chinese savings accounts offered interest rates that lagged far behind inflation. The housing market in Chinese cities was partially privatized in the 1990s, but complex, frequently changing property laws made it unlikely for real estate to become a profitable retirement asset. Insurance companies sprang up during the 1990s to sell pension and medical plans, some of which were designed to replace state enterprise pensions and medical benefits. Many parents had to buy labor insurance through their work units to avoid losing the pension benefits they had already accumulated. Some were persuaded to buy life insurance, medical insurance, and old-age insurance by friends and relatives working for insurance companies. Few believed, however, that these plans would offset more than a small fraction of their living expenses and medical care in old age. Most insurance plans offered benefits that seemed only slightly more resistant to inflation than bank savings. Parents also feared that insurance companies would go bankrupt. Since insurance companies must have many young, healthy members to pay for each elderly member's pensions and medical care, they are likely to run into trouble as the population ages. Some parents told me that the terms of their insurance plans were already being revised to reduce benefits and increase restrictions. Meanwhile, the cost of medical care skyrocketed, as new, expensive life-prolonging medications and technologies become increasingly available to those who could afford them, and increasingly demanded by those who could not.

Opportunities for older people to earn incomes after retirement were scarce, as were long-term elder care facilities.[6] Hospitals assumed that patients would rely heavily on their family members. Doctors often did not even tell patients if they had serious illnesses, under the assumption that the anxiety such information caused could worsen illness. Such information was usually reserved for the patient's family members, who took responsibility for deciding the course of treatment, and conspired to keep the patient from learning about the seriousness of the condition. Most hospitals provided little nursing care, and expected that family members would be present all day and sometimes all night to care for the patient.[7] Adult children's duty to provide economic support for their elderly parents was inscribed in article 49 of China's 1982 Constitution, article 15 of the 1980 Marriage Law, article 35 of the 1992 Women's Protection Law, and article 183 of the 1979 Criminal Law (which made failure to support elderly parents an offense punishable by up to five years of criminal detention).[8]

Parents found their duty to provide companionship, economic support, and nursing care for their own parents onerous, even though they had many siblings to help them fulfill their filial duties. Some hired unemployed urban workers or rural migrants to help with nursing care, but many elderly parents bitterly resented this, claiming that their paid nurses were callous and uncaring at best, and abusive at worst. The burdens of elder care are likely to grow heavier as increasing life expectancy combines with fertility decline to produce a rapidly aging population. According to China's 2000 census, people age 65 or older constituted 7 percent[9] of the Chinese population in 2000. According to projections based on China's 1982 and 2000 censuses, those age 65 or older will constitute 22 percent of the Chinese population in 2040.[10] In cities like Dalian, the burden of providing support for this large wave of elderly dependents will fall to a generation that consists primarily of singletons.

## "Daughters and Sons are the Same"

The families I knew in urban Dalian differed significantly from those described in previous studies[11] that attributed much of the male dominance in Chinese societies to parents' preferential treatment of sons. Bias against daughters resulted from cultural models of gender inequality reinforced by the patrilineal descent system, in which daughters could not live with their parents after marriage, provide nursing care or economic support for their elderly parents, inherit their parents' property, or perform annual worship rituals for their deceased parents. In that system, parents had little incentive to invest in their daughters. Though the mothers I knew had grown up under that system, they were able to dismantle much of it by using neolocal living arrangements and income from paid work to maintain strong ties to their parents after marriage.

Female singletons enjoyed unprecedented parental support, both because they had no brothers to compete with, and because they grew up in a socioeconomic system that provided daughters with the means to follow the cultural model of filial duty once reserved for sons.[12] This system began in the 1950s, when the socialist state began providing urban women with opportunities for work, education, neolocal marriages, property ownership, inheritance rights, and legal equality. Heavy childbearing and childrearing duties prevented many women born in the early twentieth century from taking advantage of these opportunities. Women born in the 1950s and 1960s, however, were constrained by fertility limitation policies, and thus had far lighter childbearing and childrearing duties. They could therefore devote more of their time to paid work (see Table 10). It is partly because of urban

TABLE 10

Percentage of Respondents' Parents and Grandparents Who Never Did Paid Work

| | Never Did Paid Work |
|---|---|
| Paternal grandmother (*N* = 1,716) | 36% |
| Maternal grandmother (*N* = 1,493) | 34% |
| Paternal grandfather (*N* = 1,651) | 0% |
| Maternal grandfather (*N* = 1,748) | 0% |
| Mother (*N* = 1,995) | 0% |
| Father (*N* = 1,964) | 0% |

SOURCE: The author's 1999 survey.

women's ability to earn incomes and fulfill their filial obligations that the state has been able to enforce the one-child policy in cities like Dalian without encountering the widespread popular resistance that limited the policy's effectiveness in the countryside.[13] Among respondents to my survey, boys' parents were more likely than girls' parents to have lived in rural areas.[14] Rural girls' parents resisted the one-child policy or made sure their singletons were sons[15] because the patrilocal norms and male-dominated economic system prevalent in rural areas prevented most women from supporting their parents in old age. But urban girls' parents were more likely to obey the policy and avoid sex selection because they knew that urban daughters could be filial and economically productive. The fact that most urban daughters born after 1979 had no brothers in turn increased parents' need to raise daughters to follow the cultural model of filial duty once reserved for sons.

Relationships between married Chinese adults and the parents and parents-in-law who lived with them have long been fraught with tension. Young urban couples were increasingly able to attain neolocality after the 1950s, when the socialist state started instituting policies that empowered women and youth, assigned neolocal apartments to replace large extended family compounds, and confiscated the elder-controlled property that had long been the main reason for several generations to live under one roof. By the 1990s, it was the norm in urban Dalian for couples to live neolocally after the first few years of their married lives.[16] Among respondents to my survey, 86 percent[17] of girls and 73 percent[18] of boys indicated that they wanted to live neolocally after marriage, and only 17 percent[19] of respondents indicated that at least one grandparent lived in their home. While patrilocality was still considered more acceptable than uxorilocality, both were regarded as undesirable conditions to be tolerated only until the couple could live neolocally. Often, patrilocality or uxorilocality were practiced temporarily, during the early years of marriage, while the newlyweds and their parents waited for an opportunity to buy, rent, or borrow a neolocal apartment from their relatives, their employers, or the private market. Even couples living patrilocally often visited the wife's parents, and sent their children to them for childcare, just as couples living uxorilocally often took their children to the husband's parents for visits or childcare. Elderly parents who were widowed or disabled usually moved into an adult child's household, but which child they ended up living with depended less on gender than on interpersonal dynamics and on the amount of time and living space each child's household could spare. In many families, elderly parents rotated between all their children, staying a few weeks to a few months in each child's household. Regardless of their gender, all adult children were expected to contribute as much in care, companionship, money, and gifts to their parents as they could afford.

Conflicts sometimes arose, especially when both spouses' parents needed care at the same time. Still, neolocality absolved couples from the need to declare loyalty to one set of parents over the other, and allowed greater room for negotiation in dealing with such conflicts than either patrilocality or uxorilocality. Living close to their own parents, middle-aged urban women have been able to maintain close ties to their natal families throughout their lives. Because of the socialist campaign for female participation in the urban labor force, most women born after 1949 earned wages, and thus the right and the ability to support their parents financially. The currently low impact of the cultural model of patrilineality on the relationship between elderly parents and their adult children reassures parents that their daughters will be able to follow the same cultural model of filial duty as their male counterparts.

People I knew in urban Dalian claimed that the cultural model of patrilineality was just "baggage from 5,000 years of history" that has been discarded by modern society. Some still invoked this cultural model to support their own interests, as when vocational high school student Gen Tian's mother, a businesswoman who did not want to take her turn caring for her elderly father, grumbled to her siblings at a May 1 (Labor Day) family reunion I attended in 1999 that "it's the sons who are raised as old-age insurance, not the daughters." However, this invocation was quickly rebutted by her brothers as well as her sisters with the retort, "nowadays, daughters and sons are the same," followed by accusations of "feudal thinking" and "looking for self-serving excuses." Gen Tian later told me that his mother did take her turn, though she delegated most of the nursing work to Gen Tian's father, since, as a worker frequently sent home early from his failing state factory, he had more free time.

Most people I knew in urban Dalian accepted that daughters could have the same rights and obligations as sons. Many mothers provided monetary support and nursing care for their own elderly parents (often getting their husbands to help), most who performed annual worship rituals for their husbands' deceased parents also did so for their own deceased parents, and some inherited money, goods, and housing from their parents. In 1989, when researchers in Shanghai asked 173 elderly[20] parents of singletons to name the one person who contributed the most to their care, 15 percent named a son, 27 percent named a daughter, 11 percent named a daughter-in-law, and 1 percent named a son-in-law.[21] In 2000, Zheng Yi's maternal grandmother even told me that, since women were more likely to provide nursing care, "a good daughter-in-law is better than a good son, and a good daughter is best of all." While 12 percent[22] of respondents to my survey were living with at least one paternal grandparent at the time of the survey, 5 percent[23] were living with at least one maternal grandparent. The ubiquity of neolocal couples loyal to both spouses' parents was celebrated by the lyrics of "Return Home Often" (*Chang Huijia Kankan*),[24] a popular song that brought tears to many eyes when it was first introduced in the nationally broadcast Spring Festival variety show of 1999:

Find some time,
Find some time.
Take your child,
And return home often.
Wear a smile,
Bring good wishes.
Together with your spouse,
Return home often.
Mama has prepared some nagging;

Papa has prepared a table of good food.
The troubles of life
Discuss with Mama.
The things at work
Discuss with Papa.

Return home often,
Return home often,
If only to help Mama wash the bowls and chopsticks.
The old people haven't asked their sons and daughters for much;
Their lives have not been easy; they have just wanted the family to be together.
Return home often,
Return home often,
If only to massage Papa's back and shoulders.
The old people haven't asked their sons and daughters for much;
They've worried all their lives, just wanting peace.

Sung by duets portraying young heterosexual couples, the song implied that its exhortation for adult children to visit their parents applied equally to daughters and sons. The song resonated powerfully with the sentiments of many listeners who actually did try to "return home often," rushing from one spouse's parents' home to the other every holiday, every weekend, or even every day.

An old Chinese adage compared daughters to "water spilled on the ground" because their membership in their natal families ended with marriage.[25] By the late 1990s, however, parents in urban Dalian no longer lost their daughters to marriage; rather, they gained sons-in-law and grandchildren. This was true even for many grandparents I knew in urban Dalian, because of the rise in women's power and social status that began with the generation born in the 1950s. It is likely to be true for even more parents as the singleton generation starts getting married. When I attended Wang Xuqun's wedding banquet in October 1999, her mother told me that her own parents had not even attended her wedding banquet[26] in 1972, since back then her family adhered to a traditional ritual in which the bride's parents bid a tearful farewell to the bride as she was taken away to the groom's home (where the wedding banquet was held) by the groom and his party. This ritual symbolized the bride's parents' loss of their daughter to the groom and his parents. In 1999, however, Wang Xuqun's parents, kin, and friends followed her throughout the rituals that culminated in the wedding banquet, where her parents sat onstage next to the groom's parents, and made speeches just as the groom's parents did. Wang Xuqun's mother told me, "This new tradition makes better sense. I have only one child, so I wouldn't be able to stand the pain if I had to miss her wedding."

In 2000, office worker Zhang Zhaohui's parents purchased an expensive apartment for her and her groom, whose parents claimed that they could not afford to buy a new apartment, and expected their son and daughter-in-law to live with them. Zhang Zhaohui's mother told me, "We don't want our daughter to live under poor, cramped conditions, watching her mother-in-law's face. We only have one child, so who else are we going to spend our money on if not her?"

Xu Keyang, a singleton salesclerk, told me in 2000 that she stayed with her husband and his parents on weekdays but stayed in a room of her own at her parents' home on weekends. "I like to relax on weekends, and it's more relaxing to stay in my own home instead of my mother-in-law's home," she said.

The strategy of letting brotherless daughters fill roles traditionally reserved for sons was occasionally practiced even in pre-revolutionary China.[27] As a rare and difficult last resort, the strategy of "raising a daughter as a son" (*guniang dang erzi yang*) had little influence on dominant pre-revolutionary Chinese cultural models or the scholars who studied them. But this strategy became more common after socialist policies made it easier to practice. At the dawn of the twenty-first century, the one-child policy has made it a necessity for half of the families in Chinese cities.

## "A Child Needs Two Parents"

Zhang Zhou's mother told me in 1998 that, though she had won a much-coveted scholarship to study in Japan, she was deferring it for her son's first year in high school, since it would be a less important year than the last year of junior high school (when he would be cramming for the high school entrance exam). Still, she worried about how her absence would affect her son's academic achievement. "To be a good student, a child needs two parents, so that there's always one to keep an eye on him to make sure he's studying, even while the other one is cooking," she said.

Like most mothers worldwide, mothers of respondents to my survey tended to bear primary responsibility for domestic work. Among the generation born in the 1950s, men were still expected to earn more,

TABLE 11

Percentages of Respondents ' Mothers and Fathers Who Usually Did Household Chores

| | Mothers | Fathers |
|---|---|---|
| Cleaned | 94% ($N$ = 2,198)*** | 41% ($N$ = 2,199)*** |
| Did laundry | 94% ($N$ = 2,195)*** | 42% ($N$ = 2,194)*** |
| Shopped for groceries | 94% ($N$ = 2,196)*** | 54% ($N$ = 2,196)*** |
| Cooked | 88% ($N$ = 2,194)*** | 59% ($N$ = 2,194)*** |

SOURCE: The author's 1999 survey.
*** $p < 0.001$

have better jobs, and do less housework than their wives, as Table 11 suggests.

But fathers were also actively involved in their children's lives.[28] The families I knew in urban Dalian were quite different from those common in societies with higher rates of single motherhood[29] or masculine careerism. Few had fathers that followed the cultural model of the Japanese "salaryman"[30] who devotes his life to his career and barely knows his children. Unlike the salarymen commonly found in the middle and upper classes of the First World, most of the fathers I knew did not have satisfying careers with good pay and comfortable pensions. Though state enterprises' efforts to get rid of older workers disproportionately targeted women, they also targeted men. While 25 percent[31] of survey respondents' mothers were laid off or retired, so were 12 percent[32] of their fathers. Most fathers' careers were too unstable and unrewarding to be the sole focus of their lives. They were therefore almost as likely as mothers to pin the bulk of their hopes on their children. Among respondents to my survey, 31 percent[33] indicated that their mothers had tutored them, and 32 percent[34] indicated that their fathers had tutored them. Fathers and mothers usually shared the work of tutoring their children or watching them to make sure they studied. As Zhang Yong's father told me in 1998, "I'll let his Ma deal with the washing and the cooking, but we can't just rely on her alone for important things like my son's education!"

Among respondents to my survey, 91 percent[35] indicated that they were living with both their parents. Childbearing outside of wedlock

TABLE 12

Responses to the Survey Question "Would it be better to have a son or a daughter?"

| | Female respondents ($N$ = 1,241) | Male respondents ($N$ = 872) |
|---|---|---|
| Prefer Son | 8%*** | 28%*** |
| Prefer Daughter | 37%*** | 9%*** |
| No preference | 55%*** | 63%*** |

SOURCE: The author's 1999 survey.
*** $p < 0.001$

was illegal, socially scandalous, and almost nonexistent in urban Dalian. Most unmarried women who became pregnant had abortions, which were readily available and far less stigmatizing than childbirth outside of wedlock. In 1987, less than one percent of Chinese women had remained single through age 50.[36] Even divorced, non-custodial parents like Yang Shu's father tended to maintain their parental roles, especially if they had no other children.[37]

Among the families I observed, daughters seemed more likely to have close relationships with mothers, while sons were more likely to have close relationships with fathers. While fathers could force themselves to see their singleton daughters as their successors, this required a painful ideological leap that was unnecessary with sons. Mothers, however, downplayed the significance of a patrilineal ideology that would not benefit them anyway, and focused on the sentimental bonds of what Margery Wolf called the "uterine family."[38] Daughters tended to be more adept than sons at developing the emotional intimacy that underlies such bonds. Daughters were also more likely to help their mothers with housework and sympathize with their mothers' complaints about gender inequality.

In response to my survey question "would it be better to have a son or a daughter?" (see Table 12), most respondents who expressed a preference selected a child of their own gender. When I asked them to explain their preferences during class discussions in 1999, many students said that they would be more likely to see a child of the same gender as a successor.

"If I have a daughter, I can dress her up in pretty clothes," Tian Xin said. "She'll tell me about the things in her heart, and I'll give her advice based on my own experience. That would be harder with a son."

"If I have a son, I can exercise with him, but a daughter wouldn't be able to keep up with me!" Xu Wang said. "If I teach a son well, he'll grow up to be even better than me, and I'll be proud. That's less likely with a daughter."

## The Child as High-Yield Investment

"Before my daughter was born, I just thought about having fun," seventh grader Han Xue's mother told me in 1998. "But once I had her, I grew up. I realized that if she is successful, I'll follow her to the good life, and if she does poorly, my old age will be bitter. Now my life revolves around her. I have to make her study well so she can get a good job when she grows up."

Scholars have long described the Chinese child as an investment whose value was carefully calculated by parents.[39] As Hill Gates put it, "Young women seem often to approach their need to become mothers much as many people approach the need to earn a living: start early, work hard, get it over with, and hope the investment of effort will suffice for its purpose."[40] Parents I knew in urban Dalian talked openly about the economic costs and benefits of their children, often quoting the old adage, "You raise a child to prepare for old age" (*yang er fang lao*).[41] Though urban Dalian children were at least as emotionally priceless as their First World counterparts, they were also their parents' most valuable economic investments.

Sara Harkness, Charles Super, and Constance Keefer found that Americans created their own cultural models of parenting by drawing on a combination of expert advice, what they liked and disliked about their own childhood experiences, and the advice of other parents.[42] I found that urban Dalian parents used similar methods to craft their own parenting styles.

Parents told me about how their own parents carefully calculated their economic value when deciding how much to invest in them. They applied the same economic rationality to their own children, even as they recognized that economic value was now measured by different standards. "When I was small, my Ma hit my hand with her chopsticks when I tried to take meat, and said 'You're a girl! Leave the meat for your brothers,'" vocational high school student Huang Yan's mother told me in 1999. "My Ma wanted my brothers to eat meat and grow strong so they could do the farm work. Now I save the best food for my daughter so she'll be healthy and get a good job."

Parents who complained about the time and money they spent on their children were told by friends and relatives, "This is an investment in your own future," and those who were perceived as not doing enough to assist their children's education were reminded, "Your fortunes will rise and fall with those of your child." Teachers sometimes advised parents about the economic rationality of investing in children. "Just think about it—if you spend a few thousand extra yuan now, your son will be able to get a good job and earn tens of thousands of yuan more than he could with a junior college degree, and you'll be able to retire with no worries," Teacher Yang Lihua said in 1999, while trying to persuade a factory worker to let his son sign up for an expensive "self-funded" program that would allow him to enroll in a first-rate four-year college rather than a junior college.

A successful child was a poor family's only chance at upward mobility. As the vanguard of modernization, young people had far greater economic potential than their parents, most of whom lacked the education necessary for elite positions in the capitalist world system. Many parents worked for state-owned work units, where salaries were relatively low and unlikely to improve. Unemployed people over age 40 had difficulty getting better jobs. Some tried to start their own businesses, but high taxes and intense competition made it difficult for them to turn a profit. To make matters worse, their customer base was limited to poor people like themselves who bargained for the lowest prices possible. The wealthy preferred to buy from large, often foreign-funded enterprises that exuded prestige and professionalism.

Young people were more likely to be hired by these enterprises and earn salaries many times higher than their parents' salaries. Therefore, it made good economic sense for low-income parents to invest the bulk of family resources in the child. Many of them told me that family resources were wasted on themselves because they had no good work opportunities, and thus no way to convert their time and labor into money. With only one child, parents were painfully aware that their family had only one shot at a good future. Therefore, they did everything they could to make that shot a good one.

## The Beloved Child

While observing Jiang Mei's college prep high school homeroom in 1999, I heard some students ask Jiang Mei why she was unusually sleepy. She responded:

> Late last night, a frantic stranger called our home. "I'm calling all my relatives and friends to warn them that a big earthquake will hit Dalian tonight," the stranger said. "My relative who works for the provincial seismology bureau just called to warn me. I dialed your number by mistake, but since I'm talking to you now, I might as well do a good deed and warn you." My parents didn't know whether to believe him, but they preferred to err on the side of caution, so they woke me up, grabbed all the money in our home, and had all three of us stand under the sturdiest doorway in our apartment. After a few hours, though, nothing had happened and we were sleepy, so my parents decided to go back to bed. But they wouldn't let me go back to bed! They said, "You're the greatest treasure of this family. We're old, so it doesn't matter if we die. But you have to survive." So I had to stay in the doorway all night, holding all my family's money, until it was time for me to go to school!

Parental investment did not just derive from the desire for a comfortable retirement. On the contrary, parents told me that they were willing to sacrifice their own lives for those of their children. Parents saw no contradiction between the cultural model of parental love and the cultural model of parental investment, which itself depended on the assumption that the love between parents and children would last all their lives. Spending money on a child was simultaneously an expression of unconditional love and an investment in parents' own future. When forced to choose between these two motivations, however, parents often found that their love for their children outweighed their concern for themselves. Low-income parents like Sun Wei's mother literally risked their own lives by skimping on their own health care to save money for their children's education.

One of the first things Lin Lin's mother asked me when we met in 1998 was "How many siblings do you have?" When I told her I was a singleton, she immediately sympathized with my parents. "You must be the treasure of your family," she said. "How can your parents stand to have you live so far away from them? Don't they worry about you?"

"If your daughter gets a chance to go abroad, won't you allow it?" I rejoined. "How will you stand it? Won't you worry?"

"I'll cry every day after I send my daughter abroad," she replied. "But my tears are a small price to pay for her happiness."

In pre-revolutionary China, a son was responsible not only for his parents' old-age support, but also for the welfare of his parents' spirits after death, and for the continuation of his patrilineage, which provided his male ancestors with social and symbolic immortality. The Maoist government banned ancestor worship and took away the property that patrilineages depended upon for their very existence as corporate groups. Some families I knew in urban Dalian did not even practice ancestor worship. But parents found new ways to see their children as extensions of themselves, and thus as a means to social and symbolic immortality.

Parents lived vicariously through their children. Poor workers told me that they felt compensation and fulfillment when they saw their children enjoying luxuries they themselves never had. For some parents, children were sources of hope and purpose in otherwise dreary, unfulfilling lives. As college prep high school senior Huang Jie's mother told me in 1999, "Life has not been worth living since I lost my job. I was just a textile worker, but I used to look forward to going to work, and to small pleasures like raises and 'civilized worker' awards at the factory. Now I stay at home all day, and I feel like I might as well be dead. Sometimes I want to kill myself, and the only thing stopping me is the thought of my daughter. When I think of her and her future, I feel a bit of hope."

"My son is a good person," technical high school student Luo Cheng's mother told me in 2002. "After I'm dead, everyone who knows him will say, 'He's a good person. He must have had a good mother who taught him well.' And that will mean my life was not a waste."

"My son is a younger version of me, but with all the opportunities I never had," college prep high school junior Shen Qi's father told me in 2000. "When he's successful, it's as if I'm living my life over again, but getting it right this time."

"When I was small, I dreamed that I would someday be a scientist, and invent new ways to strengthen the motherland," seventh grader Cao Ying's father told me in 1999. "Now I'm 47 years old and an unemployed factory worker, so it seems I haven't accomplished much. But my daughter's smart, so maybe someday she'll be a great scientist. Then she'll be my contribution to the motherland."

Parents were held responsible for their children's successes and failures by friends, relatives, teachers, and even children themselves. Most well-educated parents I knew tutored their children. I also knew many poorly educated parents who sat beside their children for hours every night and weekend to make sure the children studied. Parents sometimes fetched snacks and drinks for their children while they studied, to save them the time it would take to walk to the kitchen. "I didn't know who was more exhausted, me or my son, after I spent all Sunday forcing my son to study!" Ninth grader Bai Bo's father told me in 1999.

The intensity of parents' love was compounded by the fact that they had only one child. Singletons' parents tended to lavish on their children the same intense love expected of First World parents. In the First World, the cultural model of deep, unconditional parental love for each child developed concomitantly with fertility decline.[43] The fewer children one had, the more irreplaceable each child became.

As Caroline H. Bledsoe found in West Africa during the early 1990s, parents with a number of children tended to practice a strategy of "investing heavily in the most promising ones and cultivating different opportunities for the others."[44] Based on evidence collected in 1986–1990 from 15 Third World countries, Sonalde Desai found that children with fewer siblings tended to have better health than children with more siblings.[45] Nancy Scheper-Hughes found that, in an impoverished Brazilian shantytown where she interviewed 36 women between the ages of 40 and 76 and found that they had an average of 12 pregnancies over their reproductive lives,[46] mothers allowed their weaker or less favored children to die in order to conserve resources for their stronger, more favored children.[47] Based on her 1982–1983 research, Nancy E. Levine found that Tibetan parents in Nepal routinely favored children with the right combination of gender, health, disposition, parentage, and sibling position, while allowing other children to suffer higher rates of disease, malnutrition, and neglect-induced mortality.[48] Based on their study of 12,000 people born in northeastern China between 1774 and 1873, James Lee and Cameron Campbell found that girls age 1–5 experienced 20 percent greater mortality than their male counterparts, and estimated that 20–25 percent of all females died from deliberate infanticide.[49] Parents and grandparents I knew in urban Dalian recalled similar instances of triage in their own families during the famine that followed the Great Leap Forward (1959–1961), as well as during other periods of poverty and starvation. Even under the less hungry conditions that prevailed after 1961, siblings received unequal treatment from their parents. Based on the 1988 two-per-thousand survey of Chinese families, Choe Minja, Hao Hongsheng, and Wang Feng found that, between 1965 and 1987, rural Chinese girls between the ages of one and four whose parents already had children of both sexes had 50 percent greater mortality than their male counterparts.[50] Parents' tendency to invest more in favorite sons at the expense of less favored sons and daughters was also documented in rural areas of China in the 1990s by Hong Zhang[51] and by Peng Xizhe and Dai Xingyi.[52]

Many urban Dalian parents told me that, when they were children, they could not take anything for granted, since they had to compete with siblings for their parents' favor. Prior to the one-child policy, parents could invest more in their favorite sons, and less in their daughters and unsuccessful or disobedient sons. Some fathers told me that they were lucky enough to have been raised as favorite sons, with the same kind of high investment they now gave their own singletons. Most parents I knew, however, complained bitterly about how their own parents neglected them because they were female or less healthy, beautiful, obedient, talented, or successful than more-favored siblings. Such favoritism did not exist in single-child families. High-fertility parents had conditioned their love for each child on the extent to which that child met parental expectations, but singleton parents had no choice but to concentrate all their love, hope, needs, and investment on one child, no matter how undeserving.

## The Loving Child

Teenagers reciprocated their parents' love. Students told me that they felt their filial love especially strongly when parental illnesses forced them to stop taking their parents for granted. To pay for their children's needs, many low-income parents skimped on their own food, clothing, and healthcare, and did exhausting work in factories or on the streets, sometimes in harsh heat, cold, rain, snow, or wind. Anxiety about a child's academic performance was also a constant source of stress, or "inflammation" (*shanghuo*),[53] for parents of all socioeconomic levels. When parents came down with arthritis, fatigue, diabetes, chronic pain, heart disease, respiratory ailments, or high blood pressure, they, their children, and their relatives attributed these illnesses at least partly to the physical, emotional, and economic sacrifices parents made for their children. Arthur Kleinman has argued that patients are better able to cope with illness if they can fit their suffering into morally meaningful cultural models.[54] Parents I knew in urban Dalian indeed seemed comforted by the idea that they were suffering so that their children would have a better life. This idea induced guilt and a heightened sense of filial obligation in their children. Confronted with their parents' mortality, teenagers like Sun Wei and Wang Song wept at ill parents' bedsides, and provided clumsy but tender previews of the nursing care they intended for their parents in old age. They told me that they would never put their parents in nursing homes. They dreamed of supporting their parents in luxury. Like the Mexican and Central American students described by Marcelo Suárez-Orozco[55] and the Japanese and Korean students described by George De Vos and his colleagues,[56] students I knew in urban Dalian pointed to the cultural model of filial duty as one of their greatest motivations for pursuing academic achievement and socioeconomic success. Like their parents, teenagers often expressed their love in material terms. They told me detailed fantasies about expensive gifts they would someday buy their parents.

"As soon as I get a job, I'll take out a mortgage to buy my family a new apartment that's heated 24 hours a day," Sun Wei told me in 1999. Her family's apartment had only several hours of coal-powered heat a day, and not enough electricity to power an electric heater. It had no hot water, bathtub, or shower. Her parents could not afford to go to commercial bathhouses, so they bathed every week or two with towels dipped in buckets of boiled water mixed with cold tap water. She also had to do this sometimes, though her parents usually gave her money to go to commercial bathhouses because they feared that she would catch cold if she had to take towel baths in their poorly heated apartment. During the long, cold Dalian winters, her father suffered chronic arthritis pain, which was exacerbated by his work in a poorly heated factory. "I'll buy an apartment with a bathtub, and I'll buy a hot water machine, so we can take warm baths even when it's snowing outside," she said. "My Pa will be able to retire, and we'll all live on my salary. Then my Pa's pain will be gone!"

Though they could not even afford to take taxis, vocational high school student Wang Bin and his father loved reading about cars. They even knew the technical details of luxury cars that were rarely seen in Dalian. "Someday, when I have money, I'll buy a cheap used car for myself, and a new Mercedes Benz for my Pa," Wang Bin told me in 1999, during his first year of vocational high school. "He'll drive all around Dalian just for the pleasure of it. People will see him, and say, 'Is that Old Wang? How did he get a Mercedes Benz?' My Pa will smile, and say, 'My son has never disappointed me.'"

Even while they were fully dependent on their parents for support, children gave their parents gifts as tokens of filial love. Most teenagers

I knew did not get regular allowances from their parents. They had to request money each time they wanted to buy something. Still, many saved small stashes of money by skipping meals, or by buying things at prices lower than the ones they told their parents. Parents usually condoned this practice as long as it was not taken to an extreme. Some parents also allowed their children to keep all or part of the money given to them by relatives during Spring Festival, even though parents had to reciprocate by giving money to those relatives' children. Teenagers spent their personal savings only when their parents refused to pay for certain luxuries, such as expensive snacks, fashionable clothing, or video game sessions. Parents were thus deeply moved when their dependent children bought them gifts from their cherished savings, which were accumulated through personal deprivation, and could have been used to purchase luxuries free of parental supervision.

As a reward for her responsible approach to money management, Hu Ying was usually allowed to keep the Spring Festival money her relatives gave her. She told me that she used these savings to buy gifts for friends and relatives, and extra study materials for herself. On the first day of vacation after she took the college entrance exam of 1999, Hu Ying took me along on her quest to buy a birthday gift for her mother. At an expensive department store, Hu Ying used her savings to buy a pearl necklace that cost 72 yuan (US$9), a fortune by the standards of her factory worker parents. Hu Ying at first wanted to hide the necklace until her mother's birthday. She was so eager to see her mother's reaction, however, that she ended up giving it to her several weeks before her birthday. Though Hu Ying's mother made token protests about the necklace being too extravagant, she was moved to tears by her daughter's gift.

Zhang Yong, my host family's son, was not allowed to keep the Spring Festival money his relatives gave him. He told me that he frequently skipped lunch and saved his lunch money to buy toys, clothing, or snacks that his parents refused to buy for him. One day, I saw him drive his mother to tears during a fight over his homework. Her hearing was temporarily impaired by an ear infection, and he made fun of her partial deafness. The next day, however, he apologized and gave her an issue of *Zhiyin* (*Bosom Friend*), a popular women's magazine that she loved but seldom bought because it was too expensive for her tight budget. The title of the magazine literally means "one who understands my sound," a phrase derived from a classic Chinese story about the friendship between a brilliant lute player and a woodcutter who could understand his music better than anyone else. She wept once again, but this time because she was touched by his willingness to spend his carefully hoarded money on a luxury for her, and by the significance of the magazine's title in light of the misunderstandings that had caused the fight between them.

After they started working, many teenagers and young adults I knew in urban Dalian still handed their wages to their parents, who continued to give them spending money on an as-needed basis. It was understood that parents would try to save a child's earnings for the child's expenses, education, weddings, or marital housing, and only spend it on regular household expenses as a last resort. By letting their parents manage their money, children demonstrated their love and trust.

## The Unfilial Child

Children did not always follow the cultural model of filial duty. In the heat of argument, even ordinarily devoted children made unkind comments that caused their parents anguish. Worse yet was the singleton who did this on a regular basis. Parents of such a singleton grieved about being stuck with an unfilial child as their only object of devotion, and their only hope for the future.

The father of eighth grader Sun Jian sat next to him during my English lesson one Sunday afternoon in 1999, to make sure Sun Jian paid attention. Sun Jian had wanted to go out with his friends, but his parents made him stay home so that I could tutor him.

I explained some of the grammatical rules in his English textbook. He paid no attention. His father pushed his head toward the textbook whenever he looked away.

"Did you hear what she said?" his mother yelled from the kitchen, where she was cooking dinner.

"Test him to see if he was listening to you!" his father told me.

"How do you say 'I like apples' in English?" I asked.

"I don't know," Sun Jian replied in Chinese.

I told him the answer, and asked, "How do you say 'I don't know' in English?"

"I don't know," Sun Jian replied in Chinese. "I don't want to study anymore." He got up to go to his room.

His father shoved him back in his seat. "How can you be so impolite to your teacher after all the trouble I went through to get her here?" he demanded.

"How can you be so ungrateful after all your parents have done for you?" Sun Jian's mother yelled.

Sun Jian slumped in his seat, his eyes downcast and sullen, while his parents scolded him. I tried to go on with the lesson. Sun Jian paid no attention. "I'm sleepy," he complained. "I can't get anything into my mind."

"You slept till 8:00 this morning! How can you be sleepy now?" His mother demanded.

"I'm tired because I don't like to study," Sun Jian replied.

"What do you know about being tired? When I was small, I couldn't study because I had to work on the farm all day. That's what it takes to get tired! We don't ask anything of you. We don't make you work. We work hard all day so that you can eat well and dress well, and all we ask is that you study. How can you be tired?"

I continued my lesson, but Sun Jian looked away and refused to listen. "I can't stand it!" he said, and got up to leave. His father shoved him into his seat and hit him hard on his arms and back.

"Stop beating me!" Sun Jian said.

"I'll beat you as long as you don't study!" his father said, and slapped his face.

"Beat me now and I'll beat you when you're old! When you're old and weak, I'll beat you till you can't move!" Sun Jian said defiantly, with tears streaming down his face.

"You won't live that long! I'll beat you to death!" his father yelled furiously, raining blows on Sun Jian until he ran into his room, slammed the door, and held it shut. Sun Jian's father tried to force the door open, but gave up after a few minutes, cursing his son all the time.

"Why did you give birth to such an unfilial son?" Sun Jian's father asked his wife. "He should die!"

Declaring that he could not stand to be in the same apartment as his son, Sun Jian's father went out to visit friends. Sun Jian's mother sat with me, crying. "When Sun Jian was a baby, I always looked forward to when he would grow up," she sobbed. "I imagined that he would study well and be filial. Now I wish he had never been born!"

"It's all right, things will be better once he's old enough to understand things," I said, though I had my doubts.

Sun Jian's mother put the meat and vegetable dishes she had prepared on the table, and brought out two bowls of rice, one for herself and one for me. Upon hearing the clatter of chopsticks, Sun Jian came out of his room and sat at the table, waiting to be handed his bowl of rice.

"If you want to eat, go fill the bowl yourself," Sun Jian's mother said coldly. "If I fill your bowl, I'll put poison in it. I would have choked you to death as an infant if I had known you would turn out like this. Maybe one of these days, I'll poison your food. I gave you life. I can take it away."

"You wouldn't dare!" Sun Jian said. "I'm your only child, and you're too old to have another."

## Elder Life in the 1990s

Parents were afraid about what would happen to them in old age. Their fear did not just derive from doubts about the filiality of their children. Parents only had to look at their own elderly parents to see the indignities that awaited them.

Since the socialist state began its policies of rapid modernization, each generation of Chinese youth has had more power than the previous one. Most of the grandparents I knew in urban Dalian grew up in rural or semi-rural areas, or had parents who grew up in such areas. They were socialized in the patriarchal system often described in the literature on Chinese societies of the early twentieth century.[57] In that system, elders enjoyed authority, control of household property, and deference from children and daughters-in-law. Powerless and downtrodden, young people of that system were buoyed by Confucian cultural models, which promised that if they invested all their time, energy, and resources in the bearing and rearing of many sons, they, too, would one day enjoy the high status of the elders who oppressed them. So they entered arranged marriages as teenagers and worked hard to bear, rear, and support large numbers of children.

Yet, when they finally reached old age, they were nothing like the powerful elders of their own youth. Urbanization and socialist policies deprived them of the control over housing, property, and ritual power that had once reinforced the cultural model of filial duty. One by one, their children married and moved out into neolocal housing provided by their employers or their spouses' employers. In the end, many old people were left alone in the tiny apartments where they had raised all their children.

Most grandparents had not accumulated significant assets, and those fortunate enough to have retired from state enterprises that had not gone bankrupt found that their pensions lagged far behind inflation. Even cadres gradually lost most of their connections, power, and prestige after retirement. The end of arranged marriages, the rise of neolocality, and the emancipation of women deprived elders of control over their children and daughters-in-law. It became common for grandparents to live precariously, at the mercy of their children's filial sentiments. Those who lived alone complained of loneliness and boredom. Those who needed nursing care were often shuffled from one adult child's household to another every few months. Even those who lived permanently in stem families found that they were powerless dependents rather than household heads.[58]

Several grandparents living with teenagers I tutored habitually took the worst and least food for themselves, and skipped meals or ate leftovers when no one else was at home. They told me that they did this voluntarily. They were used to paltry diets because they grew up with a much lower standard of living and higher standard of thrift than their children and grandchildren. Some also said that good food was wasted on their aging bodies. As Zheng Bohua's maternal grandmother told me in 2000, "I've lost most of my teeth and everything tastes the same to me now. I don't need good food."

But grandparents had more difficulty accepting that they had to take responsibility for household chores. In their own youth, they were taught to expect rest, freedom from chores, and the high status of honored elders in their old age. Once they reached old age, however, they found that they were expected to do housework to free up time for adult children who could still earn money. Some did this willingly. Others fought with their adult children over their respective housework responsibilities, and complained that "children these days are so unfilial, and daughters-in-law are so lazy."

The most agonizing dilemmas came when elderly parents fell ill. Even with many siblings to help with elder care, middle-aged parents had difficulty satisfying the needs of their own elderly, bedridden parents.

Office worker Chen Wei's maternal grandfather started developing dementia in the late 1980s, several years after his wife died of cancer. "In the end, he was bedridden, and we had to turn him to prevent bedsores," Chen Wei's mother told me in 1999. "But he didn't recognize us, so he hit us and struggled with us." Though all his children helped with his medical costs and nursing care, the greatest burden fell on his youngest son, who lived with him until he died. "No woman wanted to care for a senile father-in-law, so my brother never married," Chen Wei's mother told me. "My Pa died last year, but now my brother's too old to find a wife."

"We tried to hire nurses to take care of my Ma when she was hospitalized with bronchitis, but she kept fighting with them!" professional high school junior Li Bo's mother told me in 1999. "She accused this one of stealing her money, and that one of eating her food. She said no one could care for her like her own children. So my sister and I had to take turns going to the hospital to bring her food and keep her company. Sometimes she didn't even let me leave after my sister had come to take over. I had to take so many days off, everyone at work was getting annoyed at me. I love my Ma, but it would have hurt all of us if I had lost my job because of her!"

Li Jian's widowed paternal grandmother needed constant care because of her blindness and diabetes. She had spent the early years of her own marriage living with her husband and in-laws in a rural village near urban Dalian. Though she eventually bore and raised eight children, none had enough time or patience to allow her to live with them on a permanent basis in her own old age. Therefore, every few months, she had to move to a different child's home. "Up to the day she died, my mother-in-law was treated like an empress," she told me bitterly in 1999, on the night before she had to move from Li Jian's home to Li Jian's paternal aunt's home. "My sisters-in-law and I had to serve her, or our husbands would beat us. But now that I'm old, I don't have any filial children. I'm homeless, and handed from child to child like a piece of garbage. I have nothing but the clothes on my back."

Like the elderly parents and adult children of Baoding City who participated in Martin Whyte's 1994 attitudinal survey[59] and the adult children whose harrowing dilemmas were described in Lawrence Cohen's study of aging and dementia in India and the United States,[60] people I knew in urban Dalian believed in the cultural model of filial duty. Teenagers as well as middle-aged parents insisted that they were, and would continue to be, as filial as they could possibly be. Yet their other responsibilities often prevented them from providing the kind of social, physical, and economic support their parents and parents-in-law expected. The agony caused by their inability to live up to the powerful and widespread cultural model of filial duty was exacerbated by elderly parents' frequent complaints. Even grandparents who usually praised the filial devotion of their adult children complained about their lack of filial devotion when they had trouble dealing with escalating demands for medical payments and nursing care. As Michael Herzfeld has argued, elders of every generation tend to use "structural nostalgia" as a "moral ploy" to cast themselves as victims of a ruptured reciprocity.[61] The complaints grandparents made about the decline of filiality were strategically intended to shame their adult children into providing better care. At the same time, such complaints also reflected the widespread understanding that elders have been continuously losing power since China began its quest for modernization during the early twentieth century.[62] This understanding led parents to anticipate even worse conditions in their own old age.

## Imagined Futures

"I don't want to ask my son for money," ninth grader Guo Zhan's mother told me in 2000. "I'd rather die as soon as I've lost the ability to earn money and take care of myself. Besides, my son isn't going to be filial anyway. I can just see it now. After my son has a wife and his Pa and I have stopped working, they'll shunt us both into the smaller room, and at every meal they'll look at us with disgust and say 'are you still eating? Why aren't you dead yet?'"

Singletons' parents feared that the cultural model of filial duty would have even less motivational force for their singletons than for themselves. They dreaded the day when they would be at the mercy of the questionable filiality of their singletons. They were alarmed that, in their own old age, four elderly parents and possibly eight grandparents and two children would depend on each working couple. Knowing how hard it was for their own generation to provide monetary support and nursing care for elderly parents even when these duties were spread out among large numbers of siblings, parents shuddered to think of how their singletons would be able to carry out these duties. They joked bitterly that they would simply have to die before they reached old age, because a singleton would not have the time, energy, money, or filiality to take care of elderly parents.

At a Spring Festival family reunion in 2000, I sat with vocational high school student Li Hui, her mother's siblings, and their spouses and children as they lingered over the dinner table, talking about the future.

Fourth Uncle said to his son, "I don't expect you to take care of me. The most I can expect is for you not to be a burden on me. I'll rely on my insurance when I'm old."

"Whatever I earn will also be yours, Pa! You know that!" said Fourth Uncle's son.

"We can't depend on this generation for old-age support," said Third Aunt. "They're all singletons, so they're too selfish to do for us what we do for our parents. And even if they're not selfish, they won't be able to take care of so many parents and parents-in-law all by themselves."

"That's not right!" Third Aunt's daughter protested. "I owe everything to my parents. I'll always take care of my parents, no matter what it takes."

"It won't be so bad in a nursing home," said Second Uncle. "We could all go to the same nursing home, and play poker all day. It'll be like Spring Festival every day!"

"I would never put you in a nursing home!" Second Uncle's daughter protested.

"What we have to do is exercise so that we'll always be healthy, and never need our children to take care of us!" Third Aunt's husband said.

"But everyone gets old, no matter how much you exercise," Fifth Aunt said. "The best we can hope for is an early death, so that we never get to the point where we're a burden on our children."

Many parents told me that they hoped to be financially and physically independent in old age. Yet they also fretted about how insurance policies were unlikely to provide enough money to cover all their expenses in old age, layoffs and company bankruptcies had ravaged the pension and medical insurance system, personal savings were unlikely to survive inflation and low interest rates, the costs of medical care were rising, and professional nursing care was likely to be both expensive and inadequate. Despite their desire for independence in old age, parents feared that they would have no choice but to depend on their singletons as their primary source of income, medical payments, and nursing care.

## The Powerful Child

Singletons were empowered by the expectation of parents' future dependence. Parents told me that, in their own natal families, parents had much more power over their children, who had to compete with each other for their parents' favor. If a child was unfilial, disobedient, or unsuccessful, parents could invest less in that child, and more in the children they favored. Singletons, however, faced no competition for family resources. As the sole focus of all their parents' love, investment, and hope, singletons had tremendous power. Sometimes, parents even competed for a singleton's favor.

I was tutoring Chen Nan in 1999 when her father came home from his factory job. "Why haven't you made dinner? Are you pretending to be sick again?" he scolded his wife when he saw her lying on the bed.

"I have a cold," replied Chen Nan's mother, a retired factory worker who usually stayed home but sometimes worked as a street peddler.

"You always have a cold these days! That's just an excuse. You never take care of me anymore!" Chen Nan's father grumbled.

"You're an adult!" Chen Nan's mother replied. "Why do you need me to take care of you? You have hands too! Why don't you cook?"

"Because you're my wife!" Chen Nan's father exclaimed. "Why do I give my salary to you and not someone else? Why should I support you if you don't take care of me?"

"Why don't you cook dinner for once, Pa?" Chen Nan interjected. "Ma isn't feeling well. Let her rest. She does all the work around here. Can't you let her rest for once?"

"My daughter takes her Ma's side, as always!" Chen Nan's father complained to me. "Why can't she take my side for once?"

"She's not taking my side. She's just being fair," Chen Nan's mother said smugly from the bed where she still lay.

"You think she's good to you now, but wait till she marries," Chen Nan's father snapped at his wife. "A daughter is water spilled on the ground. Once she's married, she'll forget all about us."

"That's not true!" Chen Nan protested. "I'll be filial even after I'm married, just like Ma is to Grandma!"

"That's what you say now, but I know what you'll do once you marry out!" Chen Nan's father replied.

"Well then, I'll never marry! I'll stay with Ma forever!" Chen Nan said. Then, with a mischievous grin at her mother, she added, "But we'll have to kick Pa out."

"Fine! See how you do without me!" Chen Nan's father growled. He then went to the kitchen to make dinner. "I'm only doing this because Teacher Fong is here, and I can't let your teacher go hungry!" he yelled from the kitchen.

CHAPTER 5

# "Spoiled"

## *First World Youth in the Third World*

IN THIS CHAPTER, I discuss some attitudes regarding private space, food, chores, social relations, and achievement that adults I knew in urban Dalian saw as evidence that singletons were spoiled. Not all singletons had these attitudes, but they were common enough to cause adults to cite them as distinguishing characteristics of the singleton generation. These attitudes did not seem unusual when I compared them with attitudes prevalent among the First World youth and children I had known or read about, but they were horrifying to adults in urban Dalian.

Chinese leaders promulgated the one-child policy in order to produce a generation of citizens with First World levels of health, consumption, and education. Growing up in the small sibsets characteristic of the First World, urban Dalian teenagers exhibited behaviors, attitudes, and expectations similar to those of their First World counterparts. But First World cultural models were more problematic in China than in the First World. Though they wanted the rising generation of singletons to bring China closer to the First World, parents, teachers, and older relatives were also alarmed by the poor fit between these singletons' First World cultural models and their Third World families and society.

Low fertility has been commonplace in the First World for several generations. In 1970, when China had a total fertility rate of six births per woman, Canada, Japan, the United States, and most European countries had total fertility rates close to two births per woman.[1] The intense parental investment and great expectations lavished on singletons did not seem extreme to First World parents who themselves grew up under similar conditions. But they did seem extreme to Third World parents who grew up under radically different conditions.

Almost all late twentieth century studies of singletons in First World societies have concluded that there were no statistically significant differences between singletons and non-singletons other than some minor associations between small sibsets and greater academic achievement and educational opportunities.[2] Some studies of Chinese singletons have drawn similar conclusions.[3] But many other studies (particularly those conducted during the 1980s, the first decade after the one-child policy began) have focused on Chinese singletons' social and psychological problems. A late 1970s study comparing 120 Shanghai children (evenly divided between singletons and non-singletons) between the ages of 5–6 concluded that, while they were more likely to have greater knowledge and understanding than non-singletons, singletons were also more likely to be timid, uncooperative, careless about others' property, hostile to others, unable to care for themselves, disrespectful to elders, and full of bad eating habits.[4] Between 1984 and 1991, researchers comparing 248 Nanjing singletons aged 3–5 with 174 peers who had at least one sibling concluded that singletons were more likely than children with siblings to be characterized by their parents as exhibiting behaviors such as short attention span, obstinacy, demand for immediate gratification, bossiness, disrespect for elders, timidity, moodiness, temper, self-aggrandizement, delinquency, neuroticism, and emotionalism.[5] An early 1980s study of 1,148 Beijing children (aged 4–12) concluded that singletons were more likely to exhibit eccentricity, offensiveness, selfishness, dependence, willfulness, delicacy, weak will, laziness, dishonesty, and timidity.[6] An early 1980s study of 180 pairs of Beijing singletons and siblings matched by age and background factors concluded that singletons were more likely to be rated by their classmates as egocentric and less likely to be rated as cooperative, competent, and popular.[7] Bian Yanjie's mid-1980s Tianjin area study (which compared 375 single-child families with 425 non-single-child families) found that the average singleton consumed more parental time and money than the average non-singleton.[8] Bian argued that heavy parental investment spoiled singletons, and observed that "The undesirable psychological characteristics of single children noticed by most people include willfulness, finicality [sic], selfishness, jealousy, complacency, timidity, pettiness, obstinacy, vanity, aloofness, conceitedness and unscrupulousness."[9] A study based on a 1997–1999 survey of over

20,000 Beijing high school students reported that 4 percent had moderate psychological difficulties and 28 percent were psychologically disturbed, showing signs of depression, anxiety or hostility.[10] Based on a review of the Chinese literature on singletons published in the 1980s and 1990s, Wang Yuru has argued that, though better educated, more creative, and more interested in developing their talents than non-singletons, singletons also were more likely than non-singletons to have difficulty getting along with others, dealing with problems in the workplace, and cultivating a sense of social responsibility.[11]

None of these studies found large statistical differences between the singletons and non-singletons they compared. Still, they focused on analyzing the small correlations they did find between singleton status and various undesirable traits.[12] This focus echoed concerns about "maladjusted singletons" expressed by Chinese parents, teachers, and older relatives. It also resonated with the concerns that framed American studies of singletons conducted during the early twentieth century.[13] American adults used to large families were also alarmed when families started shrinking. After several generations of low fertility, however, this alarm faded. By the 1970s, most scholarly work about First World singletons focused on the neutral or desirable aspects of singleton status.[14] As small families became the norm rather than the exception, First World societies got used to the heavy parental investment and high expectations common in single-child families. First World children did not seem so alarming to parents who themselves grew up under First World conditions.

Chinese adults' disapproval of singletons often resembled the disapproval that each generation of adults expressed toward the next generation during processes of modernization and fertility transition that occurred over the course of several hundred years in the First World. In China, however, such discomfort was magnified by an especially rapid process of modernization and fertility transition. Parents, teachers, and older relatives told me that most singletons were spoiled (*guan huai le*) and unable to adjust to their environment (*meiyou shiying nengli*). They complained that singletons tended to be noticeably more spoiled and less able to adjust than non-singletons just a few years older, or even the same age. They said that a singleton was used to being the most important member of the family, and by analogy the most important person in the world. They lamented the sharp contrast between singletons' unrealistically high expectations and the thrift, humility, self-abnegation, and communalism inculcated in previous generations.

But the students I knew in urban Dalian only seemed spoiled in comparison with their parents, and not in comparison with First World youth worldwide. The heavy parental investment enjoyed by singletons may have seemed natural to First World adults who themselves grew up in small families, and had the resources to provide themselves as well as their children with First World living standards. Chinese singletons, however, were considered "spoiled" and "unable to adjust" because they had First World expectations even though they were living in a Third World society. Used to heavy parental investment, teenagers felt entitled to privileges that older generations never had. What many in First World societies that experienced more gradual fertility transitions might have considered typical youth behavior seemed excessive by the standards of Chinese adults who grew up with the harsh triage of resources and attention common in high-fertility Third World families.

Many parents I knew in urban Dalian still lived in Third World conditions, even as they provided First World conditions for their children. Used to living under better conditions than their parents, teenagers often took their parents' sacrifices for granted. Parents found this attitude disconcerting, even though it resulted from their own strategy of using First World living standards to help their children to stake their place in the First World. Parents saw the good life they provided for their singletons as a means to an end. Heavy parental investment was meant to enable singletons to achieve the academic and career success necessary for the fulfillment of their filial duties. Children, however, saw the First World living conditions their parents provided them as a lifestyle to which they were entitled. This sense of entitlement was deeply disturbing to older generations.

## A Room of One's Own

When Guo Da started attending adult education college in 1999, he was dismayed that he had to share a tiny dorm room with seven other boys. After just a few weeks, he vacated his dormitory and went home, where he had his own room. "I can't live in such a crowded room!" he complained to his parents. "Some of my roommates smoke all the time, and it makes me nauseous!"

Though his parents grudgingly allowed him to commute to his college despite their concern that the twice-daily hour-long bus rides would waste time that could be used for studying, many of their relatives were appalled when they heard about this. "What he should have done was avoid going to his dorm room except at night, when everyone was asleep and no one was smoking, and spend the rest of the time in a classroom reserved for study hall," said his older cousin Zhao Lili, who had shared a room with her brother until the day she married.

Many of the singletons I knew in urban Dalian had rooms of their own by the time they started junior high school. Their parents believed that they would spend more time on their studies if they were isolated from entertainment and social activities, which were reserved for adults who had more free time. While this strategy worked, it also created an expectation of privacy that seemed unreasonable to older people who had grown up sharing space and belongings with siblings. Parents feared that singletons would be unable to adjust to the more crowded conditions they would face in adulthood. Most Chinese college dormitories housed 4–12 students in each room. Chinese offices tended to have multiple employees in each room. Few married couples could afford a private study for each spouse. Despite their First World expectations of private space, singletons still had to deal with Third World space shortages.

Though they were low-income factory workers, Pan Na's parents spared no expense when it came to providing for Pan Na. Their apartment had no bathing facilities or hot running water. Like Sun Wei's parents, Pan Na's parents bathed with towels dipped in buckets containing a mixture of cold tap water and hot boiled water, but gave their daughter money to shower at a commercial bathhouse every weekend. When I first started tutoring her in 1999, the summer after she graduated from primary school, Pan Na and her parents all slept on the same old, worn bed in their apartment's only bedroom, which also contained the family's television and telephone. When Pan Na entered junior high school, however, her parents moved into the living room, taking the television and telephone with them. "We don't want her to be distracted from her studies when we watch TV or talk on the phone," Pan Na's father told me. "She needs a room of her own so that she can spend every minute studying."

Pan Na's parents continued to sleep on their dilapidated bed, but purchased a new bed and new blankets for Pan Na. "We want you to sleep comfortably so you'll be well rested and alert in class," Pan Na's mother told her.

Though she missed easy access to the television, Pan Na enjoyed having a room of her own. She kept it neat and clean, and filled it with posters of movie stars she admired.

Pan Na's maternal grandmother had poor eyesight and severe osteoporosis, so she could not cook or shop on her own. Therefore, she rotated between the homes of her four children, each of whom spent a few months a year taking care of her. When staying at Pan Na's home, she slept with Pan Na's mother on the bed in the living room, while Pan Na's father slept on a cot beside them.

I was tutoring Pan Na in her room one Saturday when her mother and grandmother came in. Her grandmother started to get into her bed.

"What are you doing?" Pan Na cried in dismay.

"Your Pa wants to watch TV, but your Grandma wants to sleep, so I told her to sleep in your bed," Pan Na's mother said.

"Don't let her lie on my bed!" Pan Na cried. "She's dirty, and she smells!"

"How can you say that?" Pan Na's grandmother demanded. "I'm your Grandma!"

"Ungrateful wretch!" Pan Na's mother scolded. "Don't you remember when your Grandma took care of you when you were a toddler? If you're so clean, it's only because we give you money to pay for showers! Your Grandma never goes to the commercial showers, because she wants to save us money so we can buy good food and nice clothes for you. None of us get to bathe as much as you do, because we're trying to save money for your education, and you dare complain that your Grandma's dirty?"

"Fine, you can sleep on my bed," Pan Na told her grandmother. "But don't take off your clothes or use my blanket!"

Pan Na's grandmother lay on Pan Na's bed for about an hour, but then declared that sleeping to the sound of me tutoring Pan Na was more difficult than sleeping to the sound of the television, and went back into the living room.

"I'm not unfilial," Pan Na told me guiltily. "Of course I'm grateful to my Grandma. But I just washed my blanket covers, and she really does smell bad. You notice the smell, don't you?" I nodded uneasily, and went back to explaining the rules of English grammar.

"I've spoiled my daughter to the point where she doesn't care about other people," Pan Na's mother told me later. "All the singletons are like that. They're used to getting the best of everything, and never stop to think about others."

## First World Diets

Many parents limited themselves to Third World diets in order to provide their children with First World diets. Most families I knew in urban Dalian had tight budgets. The poorest could not afford to provide all household members with three meals a day. Even middle-class families could not afford to buy as much of the most desirable foods as they wanted. All but the wealthiest parents had diets that cost less than those of their children.

After a factory worker lost her job in 1999, she told her daughter Xun Jin that she could no longer afford to give her money to buy snacks during school. "If you don't give me money to buy snacks to eat during breaks, I'll be hungry and unable to concentrate during class!" Xun Jin replied.

"Give her the money!" Xun Jin's father said. "It's a small price to pay if it helps her get into college." Xun Jin continued to get her snack allowance, while her parents skipped lunch on weekdays in order to save money.

Because their attitudes toward food contrasted sharply with those of their parents, teenagers seldom ate as much as their parents wanted them to eat. Most parents had Third World attitudes toward food. Having lived through the famine that followed the Great Leap Forward (1959–1961), parents equated thinness with bad health, and felt they had a duty to feed their children as much as possible. Teenagers, however, had First World attitudes toward food. Even the poorest teenagers I knew in urban Dalian had never starved, so they did not value food as much as their parents did. Unlike their parents, they accepted a globalized cultural model of beauty defined by thinness. Girls were especially likely to limit their food intake for fear of getting fat. When presented with food that was not to their liking, some students refused to eat. They had no qualms about throwing food away. Because their educational schedules left them with little leisure time, they valued their time more than they valued opportunities to eat. They often ate small, quick meals in order to save time for leisure, studying, sleeping, and socializing. They then supplemented their diets with ready-to-eat snacks, which were much more expensive than the meals their parents cooked. Parents were alarmed by their children's finicky eating habits. Yet they continued to indulge these habits, because the only way to get teenagers to eat as much as parents wanted them to eat was by tempting their appetites with delicious, expensive foods.

Some low-income parents told me that they often let their children eat first, and then ate the leftovers after their children were done, and that they usually ate leftovers, and sometimes skipped meals entirely, when their children were not home, because it would be "a waste of time and money" to prepare meals for themselves. When they ate with their children, they picked out less desirable tidbits for themselves, leaving the unbroken dumplings, the freshest vegetables, and the meatiest pork chops for their children, who took for granted that the choicest morsels were reserved for them. When they received gifts of expensive food from guests, they ate just a little bit and saved the bulk for their children. They told me that they felt guilty about buying bowls of noodles from restaurants for lunch, but often bought expensive candy, cookies, and soft drinks to reward their children for good scores, provide them with the energy and good mood necessary for concentrating in class, or lift their spirits when they were upset. When they rewarded their children's high scores by taking them to expensive fast food restaurants like McDonald's or Kentucky Fried Chicken, they made no purchases for themselves.[15] Instead, they ate cheap food that they brought from home. "It's all right if I die early; then I'll be less of a burden to my son," said technical high school student Chen Xudong's frequently ill mother, who often skipped lunch to save money while she was unemployed in 1999.

Schools had giant steamers that could warm students' metal lunchboxes right before lunchtime. These lunchboxes usually contained leftovers from the previous night's dinner. But some students refused to eat such lunches because they tasted stale. When their parents packed lunchboxes for them anyway, these students threw the entire contents of their lunchboxes away, and then told their parents that hunger prevented them from concentrating in class. While parents disapproved of such tactics, they usually gave in to their children's demands for better lunches because they did not want to risk diminishing their children's ability to study. Fearing that cheap restaurants and street stalls were unsanitary, parents gave their children enough money to eat at cleaner, more expensive restaurants.

"Have you seen all the food our students throw in the trash?" Song Aimin lamented to her colleagues in the teachers' office in 1999. "They throw away more food than they eat! We who lived through the Three Years of Natural Disasters[16] would never be so wasteful. These students don't realize that they're throwing away money earned with their parents' blood and sweat. Their parents spoil them so much that they'll be dissatisfied when they're older, because they don't know how to be poor."

## "What If I Fail to Get into College Because of The Time I Waste Taking Out the Garbage?"

"I have two sisters and three brothers, and by the time I was 12, I was like a mother to them," college student Li Meng's mother told me in 1999. "I was the oldest, so the cooking, cleaning, sewing, and laundry was often done by me. Now look at my daughter—she's already 18, and she doesn't even know how to do any of these things!"

Before industrialization made education the primary determinant of socioeconomic status, most children worldwide were full participants in household labor.[17] In societies where education was unlikely to lead to wealth, it made sense for children to spend most of their time on work rather than education. Only the elite let their children spend time on education instead of work. After industrialization, however, First World children became consumers of education rather than producers of labor. By the mid-twentieth century, First World children's housework contribution was so low that most studies of the division of household labor in North America and Europe barely discussed it.[18] Third World children, on the other hand, continued to serve as labor resources for their families.

The cultural model of children as household laborers was exemplified by a famous song from *The Red Lantern* (*Hong Deng Ji*), one of only five "model operas" allowed during the Cultural Revolution (1966–1976). Set during the Sino-Japanese war (1937–1945), the opera began with an impoverished, illiterate Communist hero singing proudly about his adopted 17-year-old daughter Li Tiemei, whose martyred birth parents had also been impoverished workers:

> She's a good girl!
> She peddles goods, collects cinders.
> Carries water and chops wood.
> Competent in all she does, a poor man's child
> Soon learns to manage the house.
> Different trees bear different fruits,
> Different seeds grow different flowers.[19]

Sometimes quoted by parents in reference to their own youth, this song was meant to praise Li Tiemei and poor children in general for being precociously ready to take charge of household chores, a noble quality lacking in the spoiled, well-educated children of the pre-Communist elite. Like some grandparents I knew in urban Dalian, Li Tiemei, her adoptive father, and her adoptive grandmother were illiterate.

Many parents told me that they could empathize with Li Tiemei when they were teenagers listening to *The Red Lantern* on the radio. They told me that they spent many hours each day doing chores, working on the farm, or taking care of their younger siblings. Occasionally, an unusually talented son would be allowed to focus on his studies rather than on household duties. For the rest, however, schoolwork was no excuse for shirking household work. A junior high school education was enough to get them work. Higher education was neither valued nor available during the Cultural Revolution. Elite work was reserved for those with higher education before and after the Cultural Revolution, but even then parents with many children did not desperately need each child to get an elite job. Daughters and less-talented sons were not encouraged to study when there was work to be done at home. Even those who were encouraged to study considered chores to be compatible with education. Because most students spent part of their time doing chores, academic competition was not so fierce that every student had to spend every minute studying to avoid falling behind.

Teenagers I knew in urban Dalian, however, were socialized in a system where education served as the primary determinant of socioeconomic status, and no parents could afford to neglect their child's education. In a system where most parents hoped that their children would win elite status through academic achievement, even poor children did not "soon learn to manage the house." I found no significant correlations between survey respondents' tendency to do chores and their parents' educational levels, consumption patterns, or occupational statuses. Like wealthy parents, low-income parents wanted to give their children every possible chance at academic success. A student's time was too precious to waste on chores. Most parents had dinner waiting for their children to eat when they came home from school, and woke up before dawn to prepare breakfast so that their children could simply jump out of bed, spend a few minutes gulping down breakfast, and rush out the door to get to school.

Among those who had spare time, girls were more likely to be pressured to do housework, while boys were more likely to be allowed to indulge in leisure. When overwhelming academic burdens prevented boys and girls alike from having spare time, however, there was little correlation between gender and housework burdens. Thus, girls at the vocational high school did considerably more housework than their male counterparts, girls at the junior high school did somewhat more housework than their male counterparts, and girls at the college prep high school did about the same amount of housework as their male counterparts (see Table 13).

Students I knew in urban Dalian felt entitled to freedom from the most time-consuming household duties. This sense of entitlement may seem unremarkable in the First World, where children's household duties have been light for generations. But it was more problematic for parents I knew in urban Dalian, who had spent much of their time on chores during their own childhood. Though they granted their own children freedom from housework, they did not feel their children were entitled to it. Rather, they saw it merely as a means to free up time for studying. Therefore, while studying should take priority over housework, housework should still take priority over leisure. Parents were distressed when their children refused to do housework even when they were not studying.

While Wang Song was in high school, his parents seldom asked him to do chores. His father told me that he sometimes brought Wang Song fruit and drinks while he was studying so that he would not waste time walking to the refrigerator. His mother told me that she put toothpaste on his toothbrush every morning before waking him up, to save him a few precious seconds as he prepared to go to school. In 1999, the summer after he failed to get into college, however, his mother tried to get him to help with chores.

"Turn the TV off and come help me make dinner!" Wang Song's mother told him while he was watching a television drama with me in the living room.

He refused because he did not want to miss the show. "Stop talking!" he told his mother. "I can't hear the TV!"

"Don't you feel sorry for your Ma, who works all day to earn money to send you abroad, and then comes home just in time to make dinner? I wouldn't ask you to help if you were actually studying English with Teacher Fong, but right now you're just watching TV! You're not doing anything important!"

"This show is important to me!" Wang Song insisted.

"My son is too lazy," his mother lamented to me. "I've spoiled him to the point where he takes me for granted."

TABLE 13

Percentages of Respondents Who Usually Did Household Chores

| | "I usually cook" | "I usually clean" | "I usually do laundry" |
|---|---|---|---|
| College Prep High School | | | |
| Girls | 6% ($N$ = 393) | 34% ($N$ = 394) | 26% ($N$ = 394) |
| Boys | 8% ($N$ = 366) | 33% ($N$ = 366) | 21% ($N$ = 364) |
| Junior High School | | | |
| Girls | 14% ($N$ = 362) | 56% ($N$ = 362)* | 47% ($N$ = 363)*** |
| Boys | 19% ($N$ = 323) | 44% ($N$ = 362)* | 33% ($N$ = 321)*** |
| Vocational High School | | | |
| Girls | 18% ($N$ = 528) | 59% ($N$ = 529)*** | 56% ($N$ = 529)*** |
| Boys | 16% ($N$ = 220) | 44% ($N$ = 221)*** | 36% ($N$ = 221)*** |

SOURCE: The author's 1999 survey.
* $p < 0.05$; *** $p < 0.001$

In 1999, while Lu Jing was in her final year of junior high school, her mother invited me to their home to tutor her. When Lu Jing tried to help with dinner, her mother shoved her away. "Every minute should be spent on your studies," her mother told her. "Don't waste your time in the kitchen."

"Why won't you teach me to cook?" Lu Jing protested. "What'll I do when I have a family of my own?"

"If you study hard and get into college, you'll get a good job and be able to buy prepared food and hire a housekeeper, so you won't need to cook!" her mother replied.

After Lu Jing failed to get into a college prep high school, however, her mother's attitude changed. "My Ma was telling me, 'You have a lot more time now that you're in a vocational high school, so you might as well learn what it takes to be a good wife and mother,'" Lu Jing told me.

At first Lu Jing was eager to learn how to cook. After awhile, however, she grew tired of it, and tried to avoid it whenever possible.

"Don't you want to learn to cook, to prepare for when you have a family of your own?" her mother asked her while I was visiting them in 2000.

"Yes, but I've already learned!" Lu Jing said. "I don't need to cook every day!" she said.

Most urban Dalian schools did not have enough money to pay for janitors to do all the cleaning. Therefore, they required students to take turns doing janitorial work. Teachers lamented to me that the singleton generation was much more reluctant and incompetent than previous generations when it came to doing school chores. "When I was in school, everyone did chores without complaining, and some of us even fought for the chance to do chores to demonstrate our collectivist spirit," Ren Jun, a middle-aged female college prep high school teacher told me in 1999. "But nowadays, all the students are singletons whose parents never let them work, so they're lazy and expect to be spoiled at school just like they are at home!"

Singletons admitted that they were "lazy" when it came to doing chores, but insisted that it was only because they had more important priorities. As Xu Xueying, a college prep high school student, complained to her classmates in 1998, when it was her turn to take out her homeroom's garbage, "What if I fail to get into college because of the time I waste taking out the garbage?"

## "Singletons Don't Know How to Defer to Others"

"Harvard students must be completely carefree," said Liu Yang, a vocational high school student I was tutoring in 1999. "They've succeeded, and all doors are open to them."

"Not necessarily," I replied. "Even Harvard students can't get everything they want. I know many who are unhappy and worried about failure in their classes, relationships, extracurriculars, and job searches. Someone at Harvard commits suicide just about every year."

"Why would they do that?" Liu Yang asked. "If I got into Harvard, I wouldn't worry about anything! Even if they fail at one thing, there are still so many other opportunities for students at name-brand schools!"

"It's true that they have more opportunities than most people in the world, but they also have higher expectations, so even a small setback can be devastating," I said.

"This is going to be more common in China as well, now that there are so many singletons," said Liu Yang's cousin Tang Hairong, a 26-year-old-wife and mother. "We're hearing more and more reports of Chinese students committing suicide. Singletons are spoiled and don't know how to deal with failure. They have unrealistic expectations, and can't handle it when their expectations are not met. They're used to being the most important people in their families, so they can't adjust to being unimportant in society."

"Not all singletons are like that!" Liu Yang protested. "I'm not. It all depends on individual personalities and abilities. Some of my friends couldn't stand the scoldings they got when they first started working, but I won't be like that!"

"You're relatively good, for a singleton," Tang Hairong said diplomatically. "But most singletons I know are terribly spoiled."

"But you're from a small family, too," I said to Tang Hairong. "You just have one brother. How does that make you so different from singletons?"

"Just having one brother taught me that I wasn't the most important person in the world," Tang Hairong said. "If there's anything good in the home, singletons immediately assume that it belongs to them. They assume that they have top priority for the best of everything. They are used to thinking that they will achieve great things. They are not used to caring about others or looking after others. But it's different if you have a sibling. For instance, if someone gave my Ma a nice leather wallet, I didn't naturally assume that it would be mine, because it might have been more suitable for my brother. I always looked out for my brother. Sometimes I washed his dishes. He also looked out for me. He didn't eat all the good food. He made sure to leave some for me. Siblings are used to living and sharing with others, and are willing to eat bitterness for the greater good of the family. But singletons aren't."

"Does this make a difference once singletons are out in society?" I asked.

"Of course it does!" Tang Hairong replied. "Singletons don't know how to defer to others. At home, everyone defers to them, and at school they can fight with someone and not worry. They can just be friends with those they like. But in society you have to be nice to those in power even if you hate them. In school, if you offend a friend or make the friend lose face, you can still be friends again soon afterwards. Children forgive easily and there's not much at stake. But in society there's a lot more at stake, and if you make someone lose face once, that person will hold it against you forever. Two of the recently hired clerks at my office are singletons, and it's very obvious that they're different from everyone else. Once, after everyone ate, the boss left his lunchbox unwashed, and one of these clerks refused to wash it, even though it was right next to hers. She complained that he should wash it himself! Eventually, another employee washed it."

"Do such small mistakes really matter?" I asked.

"Small mistakes add up!" Tang Hairong said. "Singletons don't know how to hide their ability so as not to arouse the anger of their superiors, and they don't know how to flatter their superiors and refrain from criticizing them. Young people everywhere have to start out at the bottom because they have a lot to learn, but singletons don't realize this. They just want to get ahead fast and demonstrate their ability. But they'll be fired if they do this. The smart thing to do is to only use one's ability in critical moments, and at all other times to give one's superiors face by not showing that you're better than them, even if you really are. Social relations are hard for everyone, but especially hard for singletons because they have not had experience with the give and take of sibling relations. Social relations take a lifetime to learn, and no one will truly learn all of it, but singletons are way behind. Singletons are likely to criticize the boss when the boss is wrong, instead of keeping their criticisms to themselves no matter how uncomfortable it is, as they should. The boss is likely to fire them even if they are right in their criticism, because the boss cares about face."

"But that's not the singletons' fault!" Liu Yang protested. "That just shows the low quality of the boss! When people of my generation become the bosses, this will no longer be a problem, because we have high quality."

"You're wrong," Tang Hairong said. "This will never change. This is not a matter of quality but a matter of Chinese culture. Chinese people will always care about saving face. It's just like in ancient China, when the emperor would execute a minister even if the minister was correct in his criticism, just because the emperor was angry that the minister made him lose face. Then the emperor would implement the executed minister's suggestion, because the emperor knew that his own idea was wrong and the executed minister was right."

## "Singletons Have No Ability to Adjust to Their Environment"

When observing homerooms, I noticed that students frequently burst into tears in response to academic or social failure. Though boys and older students were generally less prone to tears than girls and younger students, even male 18-year-olds cried sometimes. In one homeroom of college prep high school seniors, there were several incidents of crying every week. Tears usually elicited sympathy rather than derision from classmates. Teachers, however, were more likely to chide students for being unable to adjust to their environment. Teachers complained that the singletons they taught in the late 1990s were more high-strung and oversensitive than the non-singletons they had taught in earlier years. "Nowadays, all the students are singletons whose parents expect them to be the best, so they can't stand failure, and cry whenever they get low scores," Peng Fengchun, a middle-aged college prep high school teacher, told me in 1999. "But of course some students are going to get lower scores than others. There's not a homeroom in the country where every student gets a perfect score all the time. Singletons have no ability to adjust to their environment. When I first started teaching in the 1980s, students would feel bad when they scored low, but they would still be able to endure it."

One of the lessons in the college prep high school seniors' English textbook included a simplified and condensed version of the climactic courtroom scene from William Shakespeare's play *The Merchant of Venice*. In 1999, Liu Hongyan, an innovative 25-year-old English teacher who often expressed dissatisfaction with "education for exam preparation," decided that this lesson would provide a good opportunity to try out some "quality education" methods by having several groups of students volunteer to perform the scene. Excited about this rare opportunity to participate in a novel activity, students who liked English eagerly organized themselves into small groups. I helped coach them. Liu Hongyan said that, at the end of the week, each group would get to perform before the homeroom, and the best groups would get to perform during a parents' meeting. The performers spent many hours during lunch and after school memorizing their lines, rehearsing, and preparing props and movements to enliven their performances.

The homeroom performances took place during a 45-minute English class period. The class thoroughly enjoyed the performances, responding to serious moments with appreciative attention, and to humorously exaggerated moments with uproarious laughter. By the end of the class period, all but one group had performed. The members of that group were upset when they realized that there was not enough time left for their performance. Liu Na (the girl who played the Narrator) and Zhou Bo (the girl who played Shylock) burst into tears, and were inconsolable for the rest of the day.

"I spent so much time memorizing my lines, I was reciting them in my sleep!" Zhou Bo sobbed. "We had such good rehearsals, and I so much wanted the homeroom to see what we prepared. It's not fair that we didn't get to perform when everyone else did!"

"My parents will be disappointed when they don't see me perform at the parents' meeting, especially since I'm the English class representative," Liu Na told me.

Liu Hongyan offered to let the group perform at the parents' meeting. Some members were interested, but others said they were so upset at not being allowed to perform before their classmates that they had lost all interest in performing. "I never want to look at those lines again," Zhang Yabei said.

"I feel bad that we ran out of time before this group could perform, but I think these students are overreacting," Liu Hongyan told me. "They should see this as a learning experience, to help them practice their ability to adjust to their environment. There will be many times in life when they will work hard for something and still not get it. But they're all singletons, used to their parents giving them every opportunity to show off, so they can't stand it when that doesn't happen at school as well."

During a meeting at the college prep high school in 1999, administrator Jiang Fenglai warned teachers to be careful not to push their students too far. "Nowadays, all the students are singletons, so they're psychologically unhealthy," he said. "Students across the country have killed themselves over things as small as being told by a teacher to stand outside the classroom as punishment."

"I'm worried about my daughter," He Hong's mother told me a few months before the college entrance exam of 2000. "I know I'm lucky to have a daughter who devotes herself wholeheartedly to her studies, and a lot of people envy me because of that. But I'm worried that she won't be able to adjust to her environment if she encounters a setback. My co-worker's daughter went insane after getting a low score on the college entrance exam. Now she just stays in her room, mumbling, 'I want to go to college.'"

## A World of Spoiled Elite

In the context of the deprivation experienced by their parents, the singletons I observed in urban Dalian seemed spoiled indeed. Yet there was nothing unusual, unreasonable, or excessive about their demands and expectations when compared with those of the First World elite they were trying to join. In 2002, after writing a draft of this chapter, I read translated descriptions of some First World childrearing practices to some of the urban Dalian singletons and parents mentioned in this chapter. I learned that First World adults as well as children could seem spoiled by Chinese standards.

With a 1998 total fertility rate of 1.2, Italy had one of the lowest fertility rates in the world.[20] Elizabeth Krause, Jane Schneider, and Peter Schneider found that the rising costs of childrearing among those who aspired to join the urban middle class helped produce Italy's steep fertility decline.[21] After describing the burdens Carlotta, an Italian singleton's mother, felt that an additional child would place on her, Krause quoted from her 1997 fieldnotes:[22]

> "Everything has to be a name brand. Last year Alice (then gearing up to enter third grade) had a backpack that cost Lit30,000 (US$18.00). All the kids looked at her, so this year I spent Lit130,000 (US$78.00) and got her a Sailor Moon backpack, the type used in middle school. Otherwise you're looked upon as *genterella*," a low-class or disrespectable person.
>
> "Ah," her mother-in-law chimed in, "they're all really *genterella*."
>
> "Of course they are," said Carlotta. "But everybody wants to cover it up, to show the next person up."

"It's like this in China, too," Lu Jing's mother told me. "Wealthy parents will buy their children name brand things, not because these things are especially good, but just to show off. Some children are always complaining to their parents that their things are not as good as their classmates' things, and parents will give them whatever they want. But it's wrong for classmates to look down on someone just because her backpack is cheap."

"If everyone else had a name brand, I'd want it too," Lu Jing told me. "Spending more for a name brand is worthwhile because name brands are sturdier and last longer. But I wouldn't ask for a backpack that costs 624 yuan [US$78]! That's too much."

In 2002, Italy's highest appeals court ruled in favor of a 30-year-old man who sued his father, a prominent 70-year-old medical professor, for cutting off his monthly child support payment. The son owned property, had a law degree, was in good health, and had access to a trust fund, but remained unemployed because he could not find a job that matched his high aspirations. The court ruled that the son had a right to parental support when "labor conditions do not satisfy his specific qualifications, his attitudes and his real interests, so long as there is a reasonable possibility of satisfying his aspirations within a limited time, and support is compatible with the economic possibilities of the family."[23]

"It's shameful for a son to sue his Pa for money," Guo Da's father told me. "But in China, they don't have to sue, because parents are willing to support their children all their lives. If I were wealthy, I would support Guo Da as long as he needed me to. But my factory is so close to going bankrupt, I don't even know if I'll have a pension. So Guo Da can only rely on himself."

"In China, parents voluntarily give money to their children," Guo Da agreed. "My cousin's parents paid for his wedding and bought an apartment for him when he was almost 30. But I don't want to be a burden on my parents when I'm 30. By that time, I should be supporting my parents, and not the other way around!"

Though they resented Japan for its role as a former colonizer of their city and nation, many urban Dalian people saw Japan as a model of how a once-poor Asian society could rapidly adopt a modern economy and launch itself into the First World. Despite its core region status, Japan was haunted by a sense of being "behind" the United States, and needing to "copy" American methods in order to improve or at least maintain its place in the global hierarchy.[24] As in China, the rapid adoption of the cultural model of modernization in Japan has led to low fertility, high parental investment, and an extremely competitive educational system that demands constant studying. Building on Lois Peak's observations about the transition from home to preschool in Japan,[25] Anne Allison wrote that Japanese mothers indulged their children despite their recognition that "children's position as center in a family and the willingness of mothers to indulge them in a relation of spoiled dependent (this behavior of acting spoiled is called *amae* in Japanese) is inimical to the behavior expected of students."[26] Based on her late 1980s fieldwork, Allison observed that mothers of students at her son's preschool spent 25–45 minutes each morning to prepare an exquisitely beautiful lunchbox meal (*obento*) for each preschool child to take to school.[27] Based on her 1988–1991 research in Japan, Merry White[28] found that parents invested heavily in their teenaged children. White wrote that "many middle-class mothers are forced to take part-time jobs at low wages to pay for the luxuries their children 'need'—lessons in elegant table manners; resort trips; and large water, electricity, and telephone bills as their children shower profligately, keep their lights burning late, and spend hours on the telephone. Many parents are in debt, making term payments on a piano, computer, or motorcycle, all items creating status for their teens."[29]

Xun Jin and her parents told me that Japanese practices described above reminded them of Chinese practices, but were even more "extreme."

"It's good of those mothers to spend so much time preparing lunchboxes for their children," said Xun Jin. "My Ma would never have spent so much time doing that for me. But I didn't need her to, either. What a waste of time that would be!"

Xun Jin's mother laughed and said, "If I were rich and idle like those Japanese mothers, maybe I'd do the same. I know some rich mothers in China who don't have to work, and they have nothing better to do than fuss over their children's food, and buy them all kinds of things."

"Xun Jin asked us to buy her a computer, and we will if we can save enough money, because it'll help her learn and get a good job," Xun Jin's father said. "But who would borrow money to buy their children pianos and motorcycles? That's too much."

Living in the pinnacle of the capitalist world system, American parents could indulge their children and themselves even more than Japanese and Chinese parents could. Teenagers' demands for private space, snack foods, freedom from chores, and recognition at school and work were seldom the focus of concern of American scholars, who were more likely to concentrate on factors that prevented some youth from attaining the socioeconomic success that every American presumably deserved. In their study of why many teenagers who were considered "talented" by their teachers at the start of high school failed to live up to their potential, Mihaly Csikszentmihaly and his co-authors asked 249 students at two prestigious suburban American high schools to write diary entries when paged at random times over the course of a week during academic year 1985–1986. The authors quoted the following diary entry that Sandy, an academically talented 14-year-old girl, wrote at 8:35 AM on a Friday morning:[30]

> I hate my mom so much. I was leaving for school, where I should be now. My little brother wanted to take his bike to school, so my mom made me give him

my lock. I thought that meant she was going to give me a ride to school, when it came time to go I went upstairs to say 'let's go.' She started yelling at me saying, 'Why didn't you take the bus? Why do you hate me so much? Why do you try as hard as you can to ruin my life?' We got into a big fight and then she started to cry. Then she said to walk to school which is about 2 miles; there is no way I could make it on time. So I am still at home and late to school.

Later that day, Sandy wrote that her mother "packed up and left," causing Sandy to worry that she was not coming back (though she did return that evening). Sandy called her father, who came home from work and drove her to school, where she hid in bathroom stalls and cried instead of going to class. Csikszentmihaly and his co-authors presented Sandy's diary entries as evidence of how her pursuit of academic success was hindered by the fact that "a great deal of her attention, or psychic energy, is taken up by the problems of surviving among family and peers."[31]

Liu Na and her parents, however, focused on how unreasonable both Sandy and her mother seemed.

"The girl should have walked or taken the bus," said Liu Na's father. "And once she was at school, she should have gone to class instead of crying in the bathroom. But her Ma wasn't reasonable either. Why did she have to yell and cry? She's a mother, but she acted like a child. And why did she give her daughter's bike lock to her son? Maybe she favored sons over daughters."

"This girl is really spoiled," said Liu Na. "Her Ma told her to ride the bus or walk, and that's reasonable. If I were her Ma, I'd be angry too. But her Ma shouldn't have yelled or cried or left, and she should have just explained that she just wanted her daughter to be more self-reliant."

"It's terrible that the mother would yell at her daughter for something so small," said Liu Na. "I might have acted just like this girl if I were angry. In China, parents are more generous to their children. A child might run away in anger, but not the mother!"

Csikszentmihaly and his co-authors found that teenagers in their sample spent the bulk of their time on leisure rather than on chores, studying, or paid work (see Table 14). Urban Dalian singletons and their parents told me that Chinese high school students spent about the same percentage of their time on chores as the talented teenagers in the American sample, but added that not even the most spoiled Chinese teenagers would spend as much time on leisure as these American teenagers did. They told me that they would prefer to live in a less com-

TABLE 14

Percentage of Waking Hours During a School Week in 1985–86 That Students at Two American High Schools Spent on Different Activities

| | "Talented" students ($N = 208$) | "Average" students ($N = 41$) |
|---|---|---|
| Productive | | |
| Classwork | 16.32%*** | 10.38%*** |
| Studying | 12.19% | 10.90% |
| Job | 1.60%** | 4.94%** |
| Leisure | | |
| Socializing | 13.43%** | 18.08%** |
| Sports and Games | 2.70% | 3.96% |
| Television | 11.67%*** | 6.17%*** |
| Listening to music | 1.70% | 1.76% |
| Art and hobbies | 4.25%*** | 1.22%*** |
| Reading | 3.43% | 3.22% |
| Thinking | 3.51% | 2.52% |
| Other | 1.11%*** | 3.08%*** |
| Maintenance | | |
| Eating | 5.05% | 5.88% |
| Personal care | 7.06% | 7.18% |
| Chores and errands | 4.73%*** | 11.86%*** |
| Rest and napping | 3.23% | 3.05% |
| Other activities | 3.15% | 2.19% |

SOURCE: Mihaly Csikszentmihalyi, Kevin Rathunde, and Samuel Whalen, *Talented Teenagers: The Roots of Success and Failure* (New York: Cambridge University Press, 1993), p. 37, Table 5.1. Reprinted with the permission of Cambridge University Press.

** $p < 0.01$; *** $p < 0.001$

petitive system, where even students who spent more time on leisure than on studying could still be considered talented.

Wang Song's mother disapproved of how parents of "average" students in Table 14 presumably made their children spend more time on work and less time on studying. "Stupid birds have to start flying earlier," said Wang Song's mother, quoting an old adage. "If a child is not talented, the parents should make their child spend even less time on chores, and more on studying. They should get tutors and private classes for their children. Housework and jobs should be for practicing independence, and not for disrupting learning."

"The American method is better, because it lets children learn that knowledge is multi-faceted," said Wang Song's father. "But it's unimaginable for Chinese students to spend so much time on leisure. Parents and teachers won't allow it, because there's too much competition. Chinese students have to spend all their time studying."

"It's not fair that American students can spend so much time on leisure and still be successful," said Wang Song. "I wish China were like that. Then we'd be happier, and cultivate our abilities by listening to music, watching TV, and playing around with friends, rather than spending so much time studying useless things in school."

Barbara Schneider and David Stevenson found that American teenagers of the 1990s had far less realistic ambitions about gaining high socioeconomic status than their 1950s counterparts.[32] Researchers who analyzed results from the Sloan Study of Youth and Social Development found that 17 percent of 3,891 American teenagers[33] surveyed in 1992–1993 expected to become doctors or lawyers, even though doctors and lawyers constituted less than 1 percent of the United States labor force (according to the 1990 U.S. census).[34] In the 1990s, when Sherry Ortner conducted a study of the alumni from her high school class of 1958, she found that the "Generation X" children of these low-fertility, "Baby Bust" families were raised with high expectations. Several fathers told Ortner "that they spoiled their kids by design, that they wanted them to become attached to the good things of life, so that they would want to work hard to get them."[35]

"Those fathers have a good reason, but will their children really work hard?" asked He Hong when I told her about Ortner's article and the work of Schneider, Stevenson, and the Sloan Study researchers. "Or will they be like those private school students in China, whose parents drive them to school every day, causing them to think they're better than everyone else?" He Hong added that she, along with classmates at her non-keypoint college prep high school, also expected to get high-paying, professional jobs. "No one wants to work in a factory," she said. "Even the ones who don't study well say they'll think of a way to get rich."

"It's like this in China, too," He Hong's mother said. "Most parents in China don't want their children to suffer. We suffered too much when we were small. But if children who have never suffered run into difficulties, how will they endure?"

"In China, our children also want to be doctors or lawyers, or do other white-collar work," He Hong's father said. "We were satisfied with factory jobs when we were young, but we want our children to always move up, so they can be in the white-collar class, and not work in factories or do other low-level work. As soon as a couple marries, they scrimp and save money for their children to have good conditions, so they can study well. Children are used to living well, and they want white-collar work so they can live even better."

Many of the expectations common among First World youth were considered unrealistic in China, where private space, leisure time, elite jobs, and the money to buy expensive luxuries were scarcer than in the First World. Parents I knew in urban Dalian considered their children spoiled for demanding such luxuries, but did not want their children to lower their ambitions; rather, they wanted their children to have high ambitions but remain humble, feel grateful for the heavy parental investment they received, recognize that they would eventually have to rely on themselves rather than their parents to attain the good living conditions they desired, and avoid getting upset when such conditions were denied. Schneider and Stevenson likewise refrained from recommending that American youth lower their ambitions. Rather, they recommended that parents and the state help teenagers attain their high ambitions by intensifying the very elements that produced competitive pressures in the stratification system: Parents should invest even more in children's education, teenagers should start preparing for college admissions at an even earlier age, and the higher education system should make it even easier for students to get bachelor's degrees.[36] Implicit in this recommendation was the assumption (shared by many Chinese students, parents, and officials) that opportunities for elite work would expand to absorb the increasingly disciplined and well-prepared youth who desired them. While such opportunities were limited by the inequalities built into the capitalist world system, this system depended on the sacrifices made by people worldwide in the hope that they, or at least their children, could eventually join the global elite.

# Conclusion

*Making a Road to the First World*

"HOPE CANNOT be said to exist, nor can it be said not to exist," the renowned Chinese writer Lu Hsun wrote in 1921.[1] "It is just like roads across the earth. For actually the earth had no roads to begin with, but when many people pass one way, a road is made."

Lu Hsun was a leader of the 1919 May Fourth Movement that laid much of the intellectual foundation for China's cultural model of modernization. Lu Hsun's evocative statement about roads created through sheer force of will by those trying to go somewhere was often quoted in reference to the strengthening of China's ties to the capitalist world system. Jiang Zemin, then President and paramount leader of China, quoted it during an Asia-Pacific Economic Cooperation meeting in 1996, when he talked about his desire to "go forward, constantly enriching and supplementing our experience of cooperation, so as to blaze a new trail towards even closer Asia-Pacific economic cooperation."[2]

Al Gore, then U.S. Vice-President, also quoted Lu Hsun's statement in 1997 when he made a speech at China's prestigious Qinghua University. But Al Gore's emphasis was less on the transformative power of individual agency than on the transformative power of the capitalist world system. In the same speech where he quoted Lu Hsun, Al Gore also declared that "it is impossible to come here without realizing that China is in the process of profound change; that it is on its way to becoming something very different from what it has been. As I said at the beginning of these remarks, the American people are primarily interested not in what was, but in what can be. We believe that the only constant in life is change. We must accept change because it is inevitable. And we believe that only those human arrangements that are flexible and adaptable can best endure."[3]

Children of China's one-child policy were born and bred to adapt to the changes demanded by the cultural model of modernization. Indeed, like Lu Hsun, Jiang Zemin, and Al Gore, the singletons I knew in urban Dalian often used the metaphor of the road to describe their hopes. But their talk was more about how, in the quest for elite education and work, "there's just one road that everyone is trying to squeeze onto."

They are still struggling to move forward on that road. Though their experiences were shaped by their own unique circumstances, their hopes and fears also resonated with those of their counterparts in other societies that have adopted the cultural model of modernization and its concomitant pattern of low fertility.

In societies where low fertility has been the norm for several generations, the heavy investment and great expectations commonly experienced by children of low-fertility families may appear to be natural. In Chinese cities like Dalian, however, the stark contrast between those who grew up in the 1960s and those who grew up in the 1990s demonstrates that such investment and expectations are part of the cultural model of modernization, of which low fertility is both a symptom and a cause. As more and more societies worldwide have modernized, global fertility rates have declined, and increasing proportions of young people worldwide have been raised with dreams of joining the global elite. These young people have been spared from having to compete with large numbers of siblings for family resources, only to find themselves in an even fiercer and more risky competition for elite status in a capitalist world system structured by steep inequalities.

Chinese officials established the one-child policy in order to create a generation of "high quality" people with the resources and ambition to make China competitive in the capitalist world system. Born and bred to become part of the First World, teenagers I knew in urban Dalian were frustrated by their parents' low incomes and the scarcity of educational and professional opportunities that could enable them to attain First World lifestyles. Though it accelerated modernization, China's state-mandated fertility transition also produced diploma inflation, unrealistic expectations for children's success, fear that parents will not have enough support in old age, and widespread complaints about a rising generation of "spoiled" singletons. While these problems have accompanied the development of a modern economy in many societies worldwide,[4] they were especially severe in Chinese cities because of the unusual rapidity and extremeness of the fertility decline hastened by the one-child policy.

Demands for First World conditions do not seem unusual by First World standards. But they seem extreme by the standards of parents who grew up under Third World conditions. The desire to gain elite status against all odds can be problematic in a world where opportunities to attain elite status are far outnumbered by those who aspire to attain it. Though singletons were constantly pressured to push themselves forward on the straight and narrow road to First World careers, they were also criticized for being "unable to adjust to their environment" when they cracked under that pressure.

Parents told me that competition for elite status was far less intense during their own youth. The low fertility and high parental investment common among all socioeconomic levels during the 1980s and 1990s had been confined to a tiny elite during the 1950s and 1960s. Prior to 1970, most parents had large numbers of children but concentrated their limited resources on just a few (usually the most talented sons), while providing daughters and less favored sons with little investment or pressure to succeed. Thus, most parents born in the 1950s were raised with neither the expectation that they would aim for elite status, nor the resources that would help them win it. With many siblings who could help support their parents in old age and provide loans and other assistance in times of need, children of that era did not need high-paying jobs as desperately as singletons do. In addition, egalitarian socialist policies kept the socioeconomic gap between the elite and the non-elite so small that many youth felt that winning elite status through academic achievement was not worth the effort. There were few elite jobs, but also few who aspired to them.

Things were quite different for the generation of singletons coming of age at the dawn of the twenty-first century. Every singleton needed a job that paid enough to provide for the needs of many dependents. So every singleton, male or female, talented or not, aspired to elite status, even though only a small minority could attain it. As the state-appointed vanguard of modernization, singletons were charged with the duty of dragging themselves, their families, and their country to the top of a class structure that looked increasingly like a pyramid as China adopted capitalist practices in order to raise its position in the capitalist world system, which itself was shaped like a pyramid. Allowed to live beyond their means by parents who hoped that heavy investment would propel them to the top of the pyramid, students believed they were entitled to First World affluence. Though parents encouraged this belief, they were also disturbed by the incongruence between singletons' sense of entitlement and the limited resources of their families and society. Older people lamented that singletons were spoiled because they felt entitled to elite status in a world where most people could not be elite. By that definition, urban Dalian singletons were spoiled, but no more so than the First World youth they were born and bred to emulate.

Because of parents' willingness to go into debt to pay for their singletons' education, an unprecedented proportion of Chinese youth coming of age at the dawn of the twenty-first century had the means to compete in the capitalist world system. The availability of such a pool of what the Chinese government calls "high-quality talent" (*gao suzhi rencai*) is likely to hasten China's modernization, both by developing domestic industries and by attracting foreign investment. Some students managed to go abroad for education or work. Those who return to China may bring with them skills, credentials, and connections that will aid in China's quest to become part of the First World. Those who stay abroad may send money to their parents and provide connections and information to friends and relatives who want to do business with foreigners. At the same time, however, there are likely to be many singletons who will fall short of their parents' and their own expectations. Even those who have "high-quality talent" are not likely to get jobs as prestigious and high paying as they believe they deserve. The adoption of a modern economy does not necessarily make a society part of the First World. Even after adopting the cultural model of modernization, latecomers on the road to the First World may still remain disadvantaged in the competition for dominance in the capitalist world system.

Unlike their Maoist predecessors, Chinese leaders at the end of the twentieth century no longer justified the sacrifices they asked of their people as the price of building a communist utopia. Instead, they promised that policies of rapid modernization would propel China to the top of the capitalist world system. Like Japan, Taiwan, Hong Kong, and Singapore, mainland China will eventually become a center of capital rather than a purveyor of cheap labor. Highly educated and ambitious urban singletons will lead the way on the road to the First World, and their rural counterparts will follow, until there is no cheap labor left in China. The capitalist world system will remain intact, but with China at the core rather than the periphery.

To Immanuel Wallerstein, however, the rapid economic growth China has experienced since the 1980s was merely a windfall from First World capitalists' latest attempt to find a new source of cheap labor.[5] Once a region's labor is no longer cheap, core regions will relocate their capital to a cheaper region. Wallerstein predicted that, even if China does manage to become a core region by the time this happens, it will merely find itself in the first-class quarters of a sinking ship. After the First World runs out of cheap labor and natural resources to exploit, conflict between capitalist demands for profit and workers' rising, unmet expectations of affluence will result in a global cataclysm that will dismantle the capitalist world system and replace it with something quite different.

Though students I knew in urban Dalian diligently memorized information from textbooks on Marxist theory to prepare for the history and politics portions of their entrance exams, I seldom heard them say anything that evoked Wallerstein's neo-Marxist vision. Born and raised in an era of local and global disillusionment with the promises of socialism, they saw little relationship between the Marxist approaches to history they learned in school and their own hopes, fears, and everyday experiences. They were convinced of the solidity and permanence of the capitalist world system, and they believed that they had the potential to succeed in this system. They and their parents had a lot invested in the hope that modernization would propel them and their society to the top of the global hierarchy. As they waited for the elite careers they expected, however, they grew increasingly fearful that the sacrifices they made were too great, or that the payoff would never come.

Will a generation of Chinese singletons with unprecedented education and ambition make a road that will lead them, their families, and their country to a dominant position in the capitalist world system? Will the road they make be wide enough to accommodate all of them? If not, what will become of those who fall by the wayside? Lu Hsun feared that there would not be enough people willing and able to make a road that would lead China to modernization. Students in urban Dalian, however, fear that too many people are trying to squeeze onto a road that is not widening fast enough.

APPENDIX

# Biographical Details of People Quoted or Mentioned in this Book

BELOW IS AN alphabetical list of the pseudonyms of people quoted or mentioned in this book, along with a brief snapshot of how I met them and what I knew about their biographical details at the time I met them. In the interest of conciseness and consistency, I have not included information about work and schooling that occurred before or after the first time I met them. Nor have I listed people I knew in Dalian who were not quoted or mentioned in this book.

Not everyone gave me information about their ages, school levels, singleton / non-singleton status, or parents' occupations, so this information is not included in every listing. Data culled from my survey or school records describe occupational statuses with general categories rather than specific job titles. These general categories are: "worker" (*gongren*, which includes salesclerks, food servers, and factory workers); "small business owner" (*maimai/getihu*, which includes peddlers, vendors, and owners of businesses with no more than two employees); "professional" (*gongwuyuan/bailing*, which includes doctors, teachers, lawyers, researchers, office staff, and other white-collar workers); "mid-level managers" (*guanli renyuan*, which includes mid-level cadres and company managers); and "high-level managers" (*gao ganbu/jingli/laoban*, which includes upper-level cadres and company managers, and owners of large businesses). My survey asked students to indicate which of these categories best described their parents' occupations, and many students and parents also used such categories to describe themselves on school forms and during conversations. I use the term "not working" to describe parents who were either "retired" (*tuixiu*) or "laid off" (*xiagang*) and had not found new work.

Throughout this book and my fieldwork interactions, I referred to many people not by name but by their relationship to the family member I knew best. In keeping with this practice, this appendix lists most parents and other relatives under the name of a student I knew.

Bai Bo, 15, was a singleton ninth grader. His mother was not working, and his father was an office worker. I was invited to their home.

Cao Ying, 13, was a singleton seventh grader. Her mother was a factory worker, and her father was not working. I was invited to their home.

Chen Jun, 18, was a singleton senior at a regular college prep high school. His parents were factory workers. I was invited to their home.

Chen Lan, 17, was a singleton senior at a regular college prep high school. Her mother was not working, and her father was a worker. I observed Chen Lan's homeroom.

Chen Nan, 17, was a singleton junior at a regular college prep high school. Her mother was a street peddler, and her father was a factory worker. I was invited to their home.

Chen Yan, 14, was a female singleton eighth grader. Her parents were both factory workers. I met them at a Spring Festival family feast held at Chen Yan's paternal grandparents' home.

Chen Xin, 12, was a male singleton sixth grader. Chen Xin's mother was an office worker, and his father was not working. I met them at a Spring Festival family feast held at Chen Xin's paternal grandparents' home.

Chen Tianrun, 20, was a singleton who had graduated from vocational high school and was not working. His mother was an office worker, and his father was not working. I was invited to their home.

Chen Wei, 24, was a singleton office worker who graduated from an adult education junior college. His mother was an office worker, and his father was a factory worker. I was invited to their home.

Chen Xudong, 17, was a singleton technical high school student. His mother was not working, and his father was a factory worker. I was invited to their home.

Ding Na, 18, was a singleton senior at a regular college prep high school. Her parents were factory workers. I was invited to their home.

Guan Ping, 15, was a singleton ninth grader. His mother was a mid-level cadre, and his father was a sailor. I was invited to their home.

Guo Da, 17, was a singleton senior at a vocational high school. His parents were factory workers. Guo Da's paternal cousin Zhao Lili, 25, was an office worker with a younger brother who was also an office worker. Their parents were both office workers. I met them at a gathering of extended family at the home of Guo Da's paternal uncle.

Feng Yongqin, 18, was a singleton senior at a regular college prep high school. Her parents were not working. I observed Feng Yongqin's homeroom.

Gen Tian, 16, was a singleton tenth grader at a vocational high school. His mother owned a clothing store, and his father was a factory worker. I was invited to their home.

Guo Zhan, 15, was a singleton ninth grader. His mother was a clothing vendor, and his father was a factory worker. I was invited to their home.

Han Dong, 20, was a singleton freshman at an adult education junior college. His parents were food vendors. I was invited to their home.

Han Xue, 13, was a singleton seventh grader. Her mother was a hair stylist, and her father was a factory worker. I was invited to their home.

Hao Jinling, 18, was a singleton senior at a regular college prep high school. Her mother was a driver, and her father was a mid-level manager. I observed Hao Jinling's homeroom.

Hang Yu, 18, was a senior at a regular college prep high school. She had a younger brother. Her mother was a small business owner, and her father was a mid-level manager. I observed Hang Yu's homeroom.

He Hong, 17, was a singleton junior at a regular college prep high school. Her parents were factory workers. I was invited to their home.

He Xiaowei, 17, was a singleton senior at a regular college prep high school. His parents were professionals. I observed He Xiaowei's homeroom.

Hu Ying, 19, was a singleton senior at a regular college prep high school. Her mother was a clothing vendor in an outdoor market, and her father was a factory worker. I was invited to her home.

Huang Jie, 17, was a singleton senior at a regular college prep high school. Her mother was not working, and her father was a factory worker. I was invited to their home.

Huang Yan, 16, was a singleton tenth grader at a vocational high school. Her parents were factory workers. I was invited to their home.

Jiang Fenglai was a middle-aged administrator at a college prep high school. I met him at a teachers' meeting at that school.

Jiang Mei, 18, was a singleton senior at a regular college prep high school. I observed her homeroom.

Li Bo, 17, was a singleton junior at a professional high school. His parents were office workers. I was invited to their home.

Li Chang, 17, was a singleton senior at a regular college prep high school. His mother was an office worker, and his father was a doctor. I observed Li Chang's homeroom.

Li Ji, 14, was a singleton seventh grader. His mother was a factory worker and his father was a clerk. I was invited to their home.

Li Jian, 14, was a singleton eighth grader. His parents were factory workers. I was invited to their home.

Li Hui, 15, was a singleton tenth grader at a vocational high school. Her mother was a clothing vendor, and her father was a factory worker. Li Hui's Fourth Uncle and his wife were both office workers, and their son was a singleton eighth grader. Li Hui's Third Aunt and her husband were both factory workers, and their daughter was a singleton ninth grader. Li Hui's Second Uncle was not working, his wife was a factory worker, and their daughter was a singleton ninth grader. Li Hui's Fifth Aunt was a food vendor, her husband was a factory worker, and their son was a singleton sixth grader. I was invited to a Spring Festival family reunion at Li Hui's home.

Li Mei, 18, was a singleton senior at a regular college prep high school. Her parents were factory workers. I observed Li Mei's homeroom.

Li Meng, 18, was a singleton freshman at a four-year college. Her mother was a doctor, and her father was not working. I was invited to their home.

Li Yue, 18, was a singleton senior at a regular college prep high school. Her parents were professionals. I observed Li Yue's homeroom.

Lin Lin, 17, was a singleton senior at a keypoint college prep high school. Her parents were high-level company managers. I was invited to their home.

Lin Tao, 17, was a singleton junior at a technical high school. His mother was a factory worker, and his father was not working. I was invited to their home.

Liu Hongyan, 25, was a college prep high school teacher. She had an older brother and a younger sister. Their mother was a teacher. I met Liu Hongyan in the teachers' office of her school, where I was teaching English.

Liu Jifeng, 17, was a singleton senior at a regular college prep high school. I observed his homeroom.

Liu Na, 18, was a singleton senior at a regular college prep high school. Her mother was not working, and her father was a factory worker. I was invited to their home.

Liu Yang, 17, was a singleton junior at a vocational high school. His mother was a mid-level manager, and his father was a high-level manager. I was invited to their home.

Lu Jie, 18, was a singleton senior at a regular college prep high school. His mother was not working, and his father was a small business owner. I observed Lu Jie's homeroom.

Lu Jing, 15, was a singleton ninth grader. Her parents were factory workers. I was invited to their home.

Luo Cheng, 16, was a singleton tenth grader at a technical high school. His parents were factory workers. I was invited to their home.

Luo Jun, 18, was a singleton senior at a regular college prep high school. His parents were workers. I observed Luo Jun's homeroom.

Mei Jing, 18, was a singleton senior at a regular college prep high school. Her mother was not working, and her father was a worker. I observed Mei Jing's homeroom.

Pan Na, 12, was a singleton sixth grader. Her mother was a worker, and her father was not working. I was invited to their home.

Peng Fengchun was a middle-aged college prep high school teacher. I met him in the teachers' office at the college prep high school where I taught.

Ren Jun was a middle-aged junior high school teacher. I met her in the teacher's office of her school, where I was teaching English.

Shen Na, 17, was a singleton senior at a regular college prep high school. I observed her homeroom.

Shen Qi, 17, was a singleton junior at a regular college prep high school. His parents were factory workers. I was invited to their home.

Song Aimin was a middle-aged college prep high school teacher. I met her in the teacher's office of her school, where I was teaching English.

Song Zhiming, 23, was a singleton security guard who graduated from an adult education junior college. His parents were not working. I met Song Zhiming while we were waiting for a bus at a bus stop.

Su Yi, 17, was a singleton senior at a regular college prep high school. Her mother was not working, and her father was a worker. I observed Su Yi's homeroom.

Sun Jian, 14, was a singleton eighth grader. His parents were factory workers. I was invited to their home.

Sun Pei, 18, was a singleton senior at a regular college prep high school. Her parents were workers. I observed her homeroom.

Sun Wei, 14, was a singleton seventh grader. Her mother was not working, and her father was a factory worker. I was invited to their home.

Tan Gang, 17, was a singleton senior at a regular college prep high school. His parents were professionals. I observed his homeroom.

Tang Hairong, 26, was an accountant who had graduated from a professional high school. She was married to an office worker, and she had a younger brother who was also an office worker. Their mother was a doctor, and their father was an engineer. I was invited to Tang Hairong's natal home.

Teng Fei, 15, was a singleton ninth grader. His parents were restaurant owners. I was invited to their home.

Tian Xin, 17, was a singleton senior at a regular college prep high school. Her parents were workers. I observed Tian Xin's homeroom.

Wang Aihua was a teacher in her 40s. Her husband was a worker, and their singleton daughter, 13, was a seventh grader. I observed Wang Aihua's homeroom.

Wang Bin, 16, was a singleton tenth grader at a vocational high school. His mother was not working, and his father was a factory worker. I was invited to their home.

Wang Song, 17, was a singleton senior at a keypoint college prep high school. His mother was an accountant, and his father was an engineer. I was invited to their home.

Wang Xuqun, 24, was a singleton office worker who had graduated from a four-year college. Her parents were mid-level cadres. I was invited to Wang Xuqun's wedding.

Wang Yong, 18, was a singleton senior at a regular college prep high school. His mother was not working, and his father was a worker. I observed Wang Yong's homeroom.

Wu Wen, 21, was a junior college senior. She had an older sister. Their mother was an office worker, and their father was a mid-level cadre. I met her while eating at a restaurant.

Xue Liang, 17, was a singleton junior at a regular college prep high school. His parents were workers. I observed Xue Liang's homeroom.

Xiao Ying was a middle-aged neighborhood committee social worker. Her husband was a mid-level cadre. Xiao Ying's cousin Shen Xiuli was a former factory worker who was not working, and Shen Xiuli's husband was an office worker. Shen Xiuli's daughter was a 19-year-old singleton who had graduated from vocational high school and was not working. I met them at a dinner party at Xiao Ying's brother's home.

Xie Fang, 18, was a singleton senior at a regular college prep high school. I observed her homeroom.

Xu Keyang, 28, was a singleton salesclerk who had a college equivalency junior college degree. Her father was a factory worker and her mother was not working. I met Xu Keyang when she visited the home of her younger cousin, whom I was tutoring.

Xu Wang, 18, was a singleton senior at a regular college prep high school. I observed his homeroom.

Xu Xueying, 17, was a singleton senior at a regular college prep high school. I observed her homeroom.

Xun Jin, 15, was a singleton tenth grader at a regular college prep high school. Her parents were factory workers. I was invited to their home.

Yang Lihua was a teacher in her 30s. I met her in the teachers' office at the regular college prep high school where I taught.

Yang Weilai, 17, was a singleton senior at a regular college prep high school. Her parents were office workers. I observed her homeroom.

Yang Shu, 14, was a singleton seventh grader. Her mother was a small business owner, and her father was a high-level manager. I was invited to their home.

Yu Tao, 17, was a singleton student who had dropped out from a technical high school and was not working. His parents were peddlers. I was invited to their home.

Yu Xu, 17, was a singleton senior at a regular college prep high school. Her parents were workers. I observed her homeroom.

Zhang Shu, 18, was a singleton senior at a regular college prep high school. His mother was a cadre and his father was a sailor. I observed Zhang Shu's homeroom.

Zhang Yabei, 18, was a singleton senior at a regular college prep high school. I observed her homeroom.

Zhang Yong, 14, was a singleton eighth grader. His mother was a salesclerk at a small, privately owned shop, and her father was a factory worker. Zhang Yong's mother invited me to live with her family.

Zhang Zhaohui, 23, was a singleton office worker who had graduated from a junior college. Her mother was an accountant and her father was a high-level manager. I was invited to their home.

Zhang Zhou, 14, was a singleton ninth grader. His parents were college professors. I was invited to their home.

Zhao Hua, 18, was a singleton senior at a regular college prep high school. He had an older sister. Their parents were not working. I observed his homeroom.

Zheng Bohua, 19, was a singleton freshman at a junior college. Her mother was a worker, and her father was not working. I was invited to their home.

Zhou Bo, 17, was a singleton senior at a regular college prep high school. Her father was a mid-level manager, and her mother was a professional. I observed Zhou Bo's homeroom.

Zhou Fei, 18, was a singleton senior at a regular college prep high school. His mother was a worker, and his father was not working. I observed Zhou Fei's homeroom.

Zhou Jing, 17, was a singleton junior at a regular college prep high school. Her parents were office workers. I was invited to their home.

Zheng Yi, 16, was a singleton tenth grader at a vocational high school. His parents were factory workers. I was invited to their home.

Zhu Xi, 17, was a singleton senior at a regular college prep high school. I observed his homeroom.

# Notes

## INTRODUCTION

1. I use the term "singleton" because it is more concise and grammatically graceful than terms like "only child" or "person without siblings."

2. I spent June–August, 1997, August 1998–May 2000, and June–July, 2002 in China. I lived in urban Dalian during most of this time, though I also made brief visits to Beijing, Guangzhou, Hong Kong, Shanghai, Shenyang, Tianjin, and several rural villages near urban Dalian. Since 2000, I have also kept in regular contact with 31 urban Dalian families by phone and e-mail.

3. Becker 1981; Bongaarts and Watkins 1996; Caldwell 1982; Easterlin 1978; Easterlin and Crimmins 1985; Hirschman 1994.

4. As of 1998, fertility rates at or below replacement level (2.1 births per woman) were documented in all societies commonly considered part of the First World, including Australia, Austria, Belgium, Canada, Denmark, Finland, France, Germany, Greece, Hong Kong, Iceland, Ireland, Italy, Japan, Luxembourg, Macao, the Netherlands, New Zealand, Norway, Portugal, Singapore, South Korea, Spain, Sweden, Switzerland, Taiwan, the United Kingdom, and the United States (U.S. Bureau of the Census 1999).

5. The fertility transition seems to be a necessary but not sufficient condition for membership in the First World; while all First World societies have fertility rates at or below replacement level, there are many societies (such as those of Eastern Europe and the former Soviet Union) with similarly low fertility rates that are not part of the First World.

6. The total fertility rate for a given year and population is an estimate of the average number of births per woman's reproductive lifetime, assuming that all women in that population will experience that year's age-specific fertility rates as they move through their reproductive lives.

7. Coale and Chen 1987; United Nations Department of Economic and Social Affairs 1998; Whyte and Gu 1987:473.

8. Greenhalgh 1990, 1993, 1994a; Greenhalgh, Nan, and Chuzhu 1994; White 1987b, 2000.

9. According to a survey of a representative sample of the Chinese population conducted in 1999, women who were between the ages of 15 and 49 that year had an average of 1.33 live births and 1.31 surviving children over their lifetimes (Guojia Tongji Ju [National Bureau of Statistics] 2000:109). In 1986 (when Dalian's government first started collecting population statistics for publication), 82 percent of births (*N* = 68,057) in the Dalian area (including the rural counties and small towns near urban Dalian) were born to mothers with no other children, and 18 percent were born to mothers with one other child (Dalian Shi Shi Zhi Bangongshi [Dalian City Archives Office] 1990:153). In 1999, 86 percent of births (*N* = 38,287) in the Dalian area were born to mothers with no other children, and 13 percent were born to mothers with one other child (Dalian Shi Shi Zhi Bangongshi [Dalian City Archives Office] 2001:273). Singleton status was higher among respondents to my survey than in the Dalian area as a whole, because the schools where I conducted my survey did not enroll students from the rural counties and small towns that were counted as part of the Dalian area in government publications. These publications did not break down the number of Dalian area births per year by district, though they did provide information about the percentage of births in each district that were born to mothers with no other children. Shahekou, Xigang, and Zhongshan are the three completely urban districts of urban Dalian. In 1986, 99 percent of Shahekou, Xigang, and Zhongshan births were born to mothers with no other children (Dalian Shi Shi Zhi Bangongshi [Dalian City Archives Office] 1990:153–154). In 1999, 98 percent of Shahekou births and 97 percent of Xigang and Zhongshan births were born to mothers with no other children (Dalian Shi Shi Zhi Bangongshi [Dalian City Archives Office] 2001:274).

10. *N* = 2,167.

11. *N* = 1,998.

12. *N* = 2,006.

13. Arnold and Liu Zhaoxiang 1986; Banister 1987; Cooney and Li 1994; Croll, Davin, and Kane 1985; Feeney and Wang 1993; Feeney and Yuan 1994; Goldstein and Wang 1996; Greenhalgh 1986, 1988, 1993, 1994a; Li Jiali 1995.

14. Davin 1985; Davis-Friedmann 1985; Wasserstrom 1984; Anagnost 1988, 1995, 1997a, 1997b; Gates 1993; Greenhalgh 1990, 1993, 1994a; Greenhalgh, Nan, and Chuzhu 1994; White 1987b.

15. Bian 1987; Chen Kewen 1988; Falbo and Poston 1993; Feng Xiaotian 1992; Jiao, Ji, and Jing 1986; Meredith, Abbott, and Zheng Fu 1992; Poston and Falbo 1990; Shanghaishi Youerjiaoyu Yanjiushi [Shanghai Preschool Education Study Group] 1980, 1988; Tang Yuankai 2001; Tao and Chiu 1985; Tao et al. 1995; Tseng et al. 1988; Wan 1996; Wang Yuru 1999:325; Wu Naitao 1986; Yang et al. 1995.

16. Chee 2000; Davis and Sensenbrenner 2000; Gillette 2000b; Jing 2000b; Lozada 2000.

17. *N* = 2,489.

18. *N* = 2,167.

19. $N = 2{,}167$.

20. Some respondents' parents had more than one child because they gave birth to all their children before the one-child policy began in 1979, because they had multiple births from one pregnancy, because they violated the one-child policy, or because they qualified for exemptions. A couple was allowed to have two children if both husband and wife were singletons or ethnic minorities, or if their first child was disabled. Students were also likely to have siblings if they were born in rural areas where officials started enforcing the one-child policy later or more laxly than urban Dalian officials did.

21. $N = 2{,}171$.

22. $N = 1{,}265{,}830{,}000$; Guojia Tongji Ju [National Bureau of Statistics] 2001:93, 100.

23. $N = 42{,}380{,}000$; Guojia Tongji Ju [National Bureau of Statistics] 2001:100.

24. $N = 2{,}253$.

25. $N = 2{,}125$.

26. $N = 2{,}128$.

27. Of the 2,273 respondents, 738 (33 percent) were from the junior high school, 753 (33 percent) were from the vocational high school, and 782 (34 percent) were from the college prep high school.

28. $N = 752$.

29. $N = 2{,}267$.

30. Chu 1984; Guldin 1994; Litzinger 2000; Pasternak 1983; Wong Siu-lun 1979; Ye 2001.

31. I modeled my approach after a similar strategy used by Mayfair Yang during her study of social relationships in late 1980s Beijing (Yang 1994).

32. I have translated all Chinese speakers' words into fluent English because such translations tend to be more faithful to the speaker's original tone and meaning than more verbatim translations would be. Chinese syntax differs so greatly from English syntax that word-for-word English translations of Chinese dialogue and direct reproductions of the broken English or mix of Chinese and English some students used to speak with me would be easily misunderstood at best, and unintelligible at worst.

33. This figure includes the populations of Zhongshan District, Xigang District, Shahekou District, Ganjingzi District, and Lushunkou District (Dalian Shi Shi Zhi Bangongshi [Dalian City Archives Office] 1990:17; Dalian Shi Shi Zhi Bangongshi [Dalian City Archives Office] 2000:281).

34. In 1949, the largely rural areas of Dalian were called Wafangdian City, Jin County, Xinjin County, Zhuanghe County, and Changhai County. Some of these names have since changed.

35. Dalian Shi Shi Zhi Bangongshi [Dalian City Archives Office] 1990:17; Dalian Shi Shi Zhi Bangongshi [Dalian City Archives Office] 2000:281.

36. Dalian Shi Shi Zhi Bangongshi [Dalian City Archives Office] 1990:15; Dalian Shi Shi Zhi Bangongshi [Dalian City Archives Office] 2002:35.

37. China's National Bureau of Statistics only counted the people living in the urban area of each city when it ranked cities by population size, even

though the governments of Chinese cities sometimes counted large rural and semi-rural areas as part of their total population. According to China's National Bureau of Statistics, urban Dalian's 1999 population size ranking was based on a population estimate of 2,624,000 people (Guojia Tongji Ju Chengshi Shehui Jingji Diaocha Zongdui [National Bureau of Statistics Urban Society and Economy Research Team] 2000:38, 389). Because China's National Bureau of Statistics and Dalian City's Archives Office used different criteria for determining which parts of the Dalian area were urban, the former's estimate of urban Dalian's population differed slightly from that provided by Dalian City's Archives Office (Dalian Shi Shi Zhi Bangongshi [Dalian City Archives Office] 1990:17; Dalian Shi Shi Zhi Bangongshi [Dalian City Archives Office] 2000:281).

38. $N = 2{,}169$.

39. See Lisa Hoffman's dissertation (2000) for an analysis of Dalian's transformation.

40. $N = 2{,}123$.

41. $N = 2{,}138$.

42. $N = 1{,}769$.

43. According to survey respondents, 28 percent ($N = 1{,}862$) of their paternal grandfathers, 22 percent of their paternal grandmothers ($N = 1{,}871$), 19 percent of their maternal grandfathers ($N = 1{,}870$), and 19 percent of their maternal grandmothers ($N = 1{,}876$) had been or were still farmers.

44. $N = 2{,}165$.

45. Horowitz 1991; Mandler 1984; Tomkins and Izard 1965.

46. Casson 1983; D'Andrade 1995; D'Andrade and Strauss 1992; Garro 2000; Holland and Quinn 1987; Holland and Cole 1995; Schwartz, White, and Lutz 1992; Strauss and Quinn 1997.

47. Strauss and Quinn 1997.

48. Bourdieu defined "habitus" as "systems of durable, transposable *dispositions*, structured structures predisposed to function as structuring structures, that is, as principles of the generation and structuring of practices and representations which can be objectively 'regulated' and 'regular' without in any way being the product of obedience to rules, objectively adapted to their goals without presupposing a conscious aiming at ends or an express mastery of the operations necessary to attain them and, being all this, collectively orchestrated without being the product of the orchestrating action of a conductor" (1977:72).

49. Wallerstein 1974; 1979; 1998; 1992.

50. Sassen 2000.

51. Harvey 1990, 2000; Marx 1977; Marx and Engels 1967 [1848]; Sassen 1991, 2000; Sassen and Appiah 2000.

52. Weber 1958:60.

53. Sahlins 1972:39.

54. Core regions' efforts to incorporate China into the lower rungs of the global capitalist hierarchy ranged from the Opium War (1839–1842), to the Boxer Protocol (1901), to the Japanese invasion of China (1941–1945), to the negotiation of economic relationships with China in the post-Mao era (1978–pres-

ent) (Esherick 1987; Sahlins 1994; Spence 1990; Spence 1980; Teng and Fairbank 1979). These efforts succeeded in forcing China to pursue modernization in order to avoid being colonized and humiliated. Chinese efforts at modernization range from Qing dynasty's Self-Strengthening Movement (1874–1894), to the 1905 formation of Sun Yat-sen's Revolutionary Alliance (which became the Nationalist Party in 1912), to the anti-imperial Revolution of 1911, to the iconoclastic May Fourth Movement that began in 1919, to the formation of the Communist Party in 1921, to the Maoist transformation of China (1949–1976), to the economic reforms and fertility limitation policies that began in 1978 and have continued through the dawn of the twenty-first century (Chow 1960; Lieberthal 1995; Shirk 1993; Spence 1990; Teng and Fairbank 1979; Yeh 1990).

55. Orlove and Bauer 1997:28.

56. The fetishization of First World currency has also been documented in other societies outside the First World, including Russia (Lemon 1998) and Nicaragua (Lancaster 1992).

57. The Chinese category *waiguo* has analogies in other Third World societies, such as Zambia, where the First World societies were conflated into categories such as "outside," the "well-developed countries," or "the donor countries" (Hansen 2000:252).

58. Keyfitz 1990:729; Sauvy 1952; Tabah 1991:357; Wolf-Phillips 1987.

59. Escobar 1995.

60. Appadurai 1996; Bhabha 1991:207; Brenner 1998; Coronil 1997; Gewertz and Errington 1996; Mankekar 1999:99; Piot 1999, 2001; Robbins 2001; Robertson 1998:214; Rofel 1999.

61. Hansen 1997; Kirsch 2001; Leonard, Keenleyside, and Ivakine 1997; Scheper-Hughes 1992; Weismantel 2001.

62. Liu 2000; Mueggler 2001.

63. Gregory C. Chow estimated that China's Gross Domestic Product grew an average of 6 percent annually from 1952 to 1978, an average of 9.7 percent annually from 1978 to 1998, and an average of 7.6 annually from 1952 to 1998 (2002:93). Thomas G. Moore estimated that, from 1978 and 2000, the annual growth rate of China's economic output and foreign trade averaged nearly 10 percent and 16 percent, respectively (2002:1). Mark Selden estimated that China's national income grew about 8 percent annually from 1952 through 1989 (1993:4). Though economists acknowledge that it is possible that actual growth figures were several percentage points lower than their estimates (which were based largely on official Chinese government records), they do not doubt that the Chinese economy experienced tremendous growth during the second half of the twentieth century (Holz 2003; Lardy 1999; Moore 2002:1).

64. Arturo Escobar's analysis of development programs (1995) and Katherine Verdery's analysis of postsocialist "shock therapy" programs (1991) have shown how modernization schemes can produce increased suffering and inequality rather than prosperity.

65. Friedman 2000; Fukuyama 1992; Goode 1970; Inkeles 1974, 1983; Lerner 1958; Parsons 1971; Rostow 1990.

66. Comaroff and Comaroff 1993; Coronil 1996, 1997; di Leonardo 1998; Es-

cobar 1995; Ferguson 1999; Herzfeld 1987; Lowe and Lloyd 1997; Lutz and Collins 1993; Scheper-Hughes 1997; Verdery 1991.

67. Harvey 2000:154.

68. Bourdieu 1977:166.

69. Though many researchers (Attane and Sun Minglei 1999; Chan and Xu 1985; Feeney et al. 1989; Lardy 1999; Luther, Feeney, and Zhang 1990; Moore 2002:1; Phillips, Li, and Zhang 2002; Travers 1982) have criticized biases, inaccuracies, and incompleteness in statistics published by Chinese governmental bureaus, they have also continued to draw on those statistics, recognizing that, while small inaccuracies are likely, large ones are likely to be caught by scrutiny from competing Chinese governmental bureaus, as well by Chinese and foreign journalists and scholars. I take a similar approach in my use of statistical archives published by China's governmental bureaus. These archives often failed to include key information about how survey samples were collected, and how many respondents actually responded to each question. While I suspect that there inaccuracies in statistics from these archives (and indeed in all statistics), I still use them as evidence of general patterns, on the assumption that the inaccuracies they contain are not large enough to render them completely meaningless.

70. Dalian Shi Jiaoyu Weiyuanhui [Dalian City Educational Committee] 1999; Dalian Shi Jiaoyu Zhi Bian Zuan Bangongshi [Dalian City Education Records Compilation Office] 1999; Dalian Shi Shi Zhi Bangongshi [Dalian City Archives Office] 2001.

71. Unlike high schools and colleges, junior high schools and primary schools in urban Dalian were not given official prestige ranks by Dalian's government. Some junior high schools and primary schools had especially good reputations that drew children whose parents could afford the high fees and bribes required of students from outside the school's neighborhood, and others had especially bad reputations that caused many students to flee to other schools. But most (including the junior high school where I conducted research) were not good or bad enough to attract or repel a large proportion of the children residing in their neighborhoods.

72. $N = 2,192$.

73. $N = 2,193$.

74. An elite job was defined as one which provided power, prestige, high remuneration, and opportunities for advancement, and required special expertise (usually in the form of high educational attainment). Doctors, lawyers, bankers, sailors, accountants, engineers, computer programmers, flight attendants, airplane pilots, technical and scientific experts, high school and college teachers, government officials, company managers, celebrity performers and athletes, professionals working in multinational companies, high-ranking army and police officers, and owners of large businesses were generally considered to have elite jobs. Because the decline of Maoism blurred the lines between social, economic, academic, and political capital, teenagers' cultural models of elite status often conflated these kinds of capital. Rampant corruption meant that political

power and social connections could lead to significant academic and economic opportunities. At the same time, the revival of imperial China's cultural model of meritocracy, combined with the capitalist world system's demands for meritocracy, made academic credentials vital to the attainment of wealth and managerial or official positions. Wealth, in turn, could be used to buy considerable social connections, political power, and academic credentials.

75. Ong 1999.

76. Davin 1999; Murphy 2002; Solinger 1999; Zhang 2001.

77. Cheng and Selden 1994; Davin 1999; Selden 1993; Solinger 1999; Tang and Parish 2000; Zhang 2001:25.

78. Solinger 1999:43–44; Tang and Parish 2000:24–26.

79. Mallee 2000; Solinger 1999:16.

80. Quanguo Renkou Chouyang Diaocha Bangongshi [National Census Office] 1997:538–543; Solinger 1999:17–20; Tang and Parish 2000:30.

81. $N$ = 1,265,830,000; Guojia Tongji Ju [National Bureau of Statistics] 2001:91.

82. $N$ = 2,181.

83. $N$ = 2,193.

84. Anthropologists have argued that ethnography (Clifford and Marcus 1986; Dwyer 1982; Fabian 1995; Rabinow 1977) as well as statistical analysis (Appadurai 1993; Douglas and Ney 1998; Kertzer and Arel 2002; Scheper-Hughes 1997) are biased by the interests of the researcher, likely to distort or ignore key aspects of human experience, and historically associated with oppressive forces of colonialism, imperialism, capitalism, neoliberalism, and governmentality.

85. The political economy and cultural models I observed in urban Dalian were similar to those described by others who have conducted research in other large Chinese cities during the 1990s (Chen et al. 2001; Davis 2000; Dutton 1998; Farquhar 2002; Farrer 1998; Gillette 2000a; Gold, Guthrie, and Wank 2002; Jing 2000b; Hertz, 1998; Link, Madsen, and Pickowicz 2002; Liu 2002; Perry and Selden 2000). Many of my survey findings about demographic and socioeconomic patterns were also similar to those found by censuses and surveys conducted by government bureaus in urban Dalian and other Chinese cities (Dalian Shi Shi Zhi Bangongshi [Dalian City Archives Office], 2001; Guojia Tongji Ju [National Bureau of Statistics] 1999, 2000, 2001; Guojia Tongji Ju Chengshi Shehui Jingji Diaocha Zongdui [National Bureau of Statistics Urban Society and Economy Research Team] 2000).

86. Harvey 2000:115.

87. Gramsci 1992.

88. Bourdieu 1977, 1998.

89. Comaroff and Comaroff 1991a, 1991b.

90. Such resistance bore some resemblance to the "weapons of the weak" described by James C. Scott (Scott 1985). Unlike the "weak" Malaysian villagers described by Scott, however, the "weak" urban Dalian residents I knew seem to have fully internalized the hegemony of the cultural model of modernization.

91. $N$ = 2,190.

92. $N$ = 2,190.

## CHAPTER 1

1. (Office of the Federal Register 1999: 13428–13430). Throughout this book, I convert Chinese yuan to U.S. dollars at the rate of 8 yuan = 1 U.S. dollar when discussing incomes and expenses. This was the approximate currency conversion rate prevalent between 1995 and 2000, rounded off to the nearest whole yuan (Guojia Tongji Ju [National Bureau of Statistics] 1998:940; Guojia Tongji Ju [National Bureau of Statistics] 2000:885; Guojia Tongji Ju [National Bureau of Statistics] 2001:895). The conversions I present are rough estimates that do not account for inflation or daily fluctuations in exchange rates. All monetary figures have been rounded off to the nearest whole dollar or yuan.
2. Guojia Tongji Ju [National Bureau of Statistics] 2001:135.
3. Dalian Shi Shi Zhi Bangongshi [Dalian City Archives Office] 2001:223.
4. $N = 36{,}000$.
5. Guojia Tongji Ju [National Bureau of Statistics] 2001:313, 315, 319.
6. Survey respondents included the members of 500 households (the total number of people in these households was not published) (Dalian Shi Shi Zhi Bangongshi [Dalian City Archives Office] 2001:271).
7. Behar 1995:150.
8. Abu-Lughod 1993:27.
9. Abu-Lughod 1993:25–36.

## CHAPTER 2

1. Malthus 1809.
2. Mao Zedong 1958, 1961a, 1961b, 1961c.
3. The "four modernizations" refer to the modernizations of agriculture, industry, science / technology, and national defense (Chen Muhua 1979:729).
4. White 1994.
5. White 2000.
6. Banister 1987; Kane 1987; Liu Zheng 1981; Peng Xizhe 1991; Peng Xizhe and Guo Zhigang 2000.
7. Guojia Tongji Ju [National Bureau of Statistics] 2001:93.
8. Though this census may have undercounted China's population due to the difficulty of tracking down migrants and getting people to report illegal residents, Chinese and international experts doubt that the inaccuracies are large (Chu 2001; Kennedy 2001).
9. Greenhalgh 2001b; T. White 1987, 1994.
10. Chinese State Council Information Office 2000.
11. Anagnost 1995, 1997a, 1997b.
12. Orleans 1979:58–60.
13. Renmin Ribao [People's Daily] 1979:205.
14. Tien 1980:29–30.
15. Institute of Population Research 1980:42.
16. Anagnost 1988, 1995; Greenhalgh and Li 1995; Kaufman 1993; Liu 2000; Mueggler 2001; Wasserstrom 1984; Wolf 1985; Yan 2003:190–196.

17. Aird 1990; Mosher 1993.

18. Arnold and Liu Zhaoxiang 1986; Coale and Banister 1994; Croll 2000; Johnson 1996; Lee and Wang Feng 1999; Li Yongping and Peng Xizhe 2000; Zeng Yi et al. 1993.

19. Susan Greenhalgh found critical stances toward the one-child policy in the work and comments of five prominent Chinese intellectuals she interviewed. The five intellectuals were Zhu Chuzhu, Professor and Director of the Population Research Institute at Xi'an Jiaotong University; Liu Bohong, Assistant Director of the Women's Studies Institute in the Women's Federation; Qiu Renzong, a philosopher and ethicist in the Institute of Philosophy at the Chinese Academy of Social Sciences; Li Xiaojiang, a famous independent feminist who used to be a professor of Western Literature and Director of Women's Studies Center at Zhengzhou University in Henan; and Xie Lihua, the head of a nongovernmental women's organization and editor of several periodicals about women's issues. Greenhalgh (2001a) found that these scholars were sometimes critical of the problems the one-child policy has caused for women, but still muted in their criticism, partly because they did not dare to challenge the state too overtly, and partly because they agreed with the rationale behind the one-child policy.

20. Greenhalgh 1990, 1993, 1994a; Greenhalgh, Nan, and Chuzhu 1994; Liu 2000; Mueggler 2001; Short and Zhai Fengying 1998; Zhang Weiguo 1999.

21. Neighborhood committee cadres responsible for enforcing the one-child policy and parents who had violated the policy told me that the fine for having a second child in urban Dalian was around 1,000 yuan (US$125) during the early 1980s, and 10,000–50,000 yuan (US$1,250–6,250) by the late 1990s. Though these fines were burdensome, they were often far less than the cost of providing a child with schooling from primary school through college. See chapter 3 for estimates of educational expenses.

22. $N = 1{,}215$.

23. $N = 853$.

24. Gates 1993.

25. Milwertz 1997.

26. Bledsoe et al. 1998; Coale and Watkins 1986; Inhorn 1996; LeVine and White 2003.

27. Notestein 1953.

28. Bledsoe, Banja, and Hill 1998; Bledsoe 2001; Bledsoe and Banja 2002.

29. Leslie 2002; Winterhalder and Leslie 2002.

30. Winterhalder and Leslie 2002.

31. $N = 4{,}952$.

32. Frisancho, Klayman, and Matos 1976.

33. $N = 72$. These women ranged in age from 19 to 76, with a median age of 39.

34. Scheper-Hughes 1992:307.

35. $N = 23$. These women ranged in age from 24 to 48, with a median age of 38.

36. Scheper-Hughes 1992:287, 331.

37. Becker 1981; Caldwell 1982; Easterlin 1978; Easterlin and Crimmins 1985.
38. LeVine 2003; LeVine et al. 1994.
39. Fricke 1994.
40. Ariès 1996:413.
41. Knodel, Havanon, and Pramualratana 1984.
42. Oshima 1983.
43. Handwerker 1986:3.
44. Blake 1981, 1989; Claudy 1984; Downey 1995; Hernandez 1986; Knodel, Havanon, and Sittitrai 1990; Polit and Falbo 1988; Xiao Fulan and Zhang Qibao 1985.
45. Hollos and Larsen 1992; Renne 1993.
46. Caldwell, Orubuloye, and Caldwell 1992.
47. LeVine et al. 1991.
48. LeVine, LeVine, and Schnell 2001.
49. Felmlee 1993.
50. Burggraf 1997.
51. Gates 1993.
52. Gerson 1985.
53. Hochschild and Machung 1989.
54. Sander 1990.
55. Essock-Vitale and McGuire 1988:229, 233.
56. Weinberg 1976.
57. Stafford 1995.
58. Kishor 1993.
59. Rosenweig and Schultz 1982.
60. Murthi, Guio, and Dreze 1995.
61. Cohen 1995:138–144; Guojia Tongji Ju [National Bureau of Statistics] 2000:109; Peng 1994; United Nations 1997b; United Nations Department of Economic and Social Affairs 1998.
62. Banister 1987; Lavely and Freedman 1990; Lee and Wang Feng 1999; Whyte and Parish 1984:164.
63. Yan 1996; Yang 1994.

## CHAPTER 3

1. Michael Phillips and his colleagues found that suicide was the leading cause of death for Chinese people between the ages of 15 and 34, accounting for 19 percent of all deaths in this age group (Phillips, Li, and Zhang 2002:1). Despite the discourses on suicides caused by the competitive pressures of the Chinese educational system, these pressures did not seem to be the main cause of the suicides Phillips and his colleagues investigated, which were more likely to be attributed to mental or physical illness, financial problems, and social or familial conflicts (Phillips, Liu, and Zhang 1999; Phillips et al. 2002). Yet Chinese journalists often wrote about the suffering, mental illnesses, and suicides caused by overwhelming pressure to succeed in the educational system (Chu

Jun 1999; Han Yan 1999; Liu Ying 1999; Yu Jingquan 1999). As Sing Lee and Arthur Kleinman have argued (Lee and Kleinman 2000), suicide has long been seen as an idiom of protest and resistance in China, and it is likely that fears, threats, and sensational reports of suicides caused by educational stress were used by the media as well as parents, teachers, and students to critique the overwhelming competitiveness of the stratification system.

2. My finding that survey respondents' parents (who grew up during the Cultural Revolution) had more education than their own parents fits with larger demographic studies of urban Chinese populations (Bian 1994; Tang and Parish 2000:60–62), even though it seems to contradict dominant discourses produced by Chinese intellectuals (Chang 1991; Cheng 1986; Gao Yuan 1987; Yue Daiyun and Wakeman 1985) about the downward mobility caused by the Cultural Revolution. Though the Cultural Revolution caused children of intellectual families to get less education than their parents (Davis 1992), such families were just a small proportion of the Chinese population, which experienced an increase in educational attainment even during the Cultural Revolution (Pepper 1996).

3. $N$ = 1,265,830,000; Guojia Tongji Ju [National Bureau of Statistics] 2001:93.

4. Guojia Tongji Ju [National Bureau of Statistics] 2001:96.

5. Based on 1988 statistics from cities throughout China, Wenfang Tang and William L. Parish estimated that, for each extra year of education, an urban Chinese person's income increased by three percent (Tang and Parish 2000:85–87).

6. Students could choose to be tested on English or Japanese; most students chose English, since few junior high schools offered Japanese instruction.

7. Students could choose to be tested on English, Japanese, or Russian; most students chose English, since few high schools offered instruction in Japanese or Russian.

8. The combination of subjects covered by the college entrance exam changed every few years in response to curricular reforms.

9. Howe 1973; Korzec and Whyte 1981.

10. Thomas W. McDade (2001; 2002) found that incongruities between one's status as defined by local traditions and one's status as defined by Western standards caused stress among Samoan adolescents, and William W. Dressler and his co-authors found that status incongruities caused stress in Brazil (Dressler et al. 1987a), Mexico (Dressler et al. 1987b), the West Indies (Dressler 1982), and an African American community in Alabama (Dressler 1990; Dressler and Bindon 2000).

11. Elman 1990, 1991; Esherick and Rankin 1990; Fei 1953; Hymes 1987; Waltner 1983.

12. Pepper 1996.

13. Davis 1992; Pepper 1996; Shirk 1982; J. L. Watson 1984; Whyte and Parish 1984:27–56.

14. MacLeod 1995.

15. Ogbu 1983, 1987; Ogbu and Gibson 1991; Ogbu and Simons 1998.

16. Suárez-Orozco and Suárez-Orozco 1995; Suárez-Orozco 1989.

17. Suárez-Orozco and Suárez-Orozco 1995.
18. MacLeod 1995:130–131.
19. Bourdieu 1977, 1984; Bourdieu and Passeron 1977.
20. $N = 782$.
21. MacLeod 1995; Ogbu 1983, 1987; Ogbu and Gibson 1991; Ogbu and Simons 1998; Suárez-Orozco and Suárez-Orozco 1995; Suárez-Orozco 1989.
22. Greenhalgh 1994b; Salaff 1995; Wolf 1972, 1985.
23. Guojia Tongji Ju [National Bureau of Statistics] 1981:121–128; Robinson 1985:356–357.
24. Abu-Lughod 1986.
25. Lancaster 1992.
26. Herzfeld 1985.
27. Ahern 1973; Sangren 1983.
28. Clark 1999.
29. See Wang Zheng (2000) and Zhang Zhen (2001) for further discussions of young women's advantages in the service industry.
30. Herzfeld 1997:156–164.
31. See Lisa Hoffman's dissertation (2000) for an analysis of gender roles and employment options in urban Dalian.
32. Li Ying 1999.
33. $N = 2{,}266$.
34. $N = 2{,}266$.
35. C. Montgomery Broaded and Chongsheng Liu's 1992 study of educational stratification among relatively elite urban junior high school graduates in Wuhan (1996) found that boys had slightly higher scores than girls and were considerably more likely than girls of the same academic levels to aim for and attend better schools. According to a survey of a representative sample of the Chinese population conducted in 1999, girls constituted only 47 percent of the children ($N = 443{,}999$) who had ever been born alive to women who were between the ages of 15 and 49 that year (Guojia Tongji Ju [National Bureau of Statistics] 2000:109). According to population statistics for all Chinese students in the year 2000, girls constituted 48 percent of primary school students ($N = 130{,}133{,}000$), 47 percent of vocational high school students ($N = 5{,}032{,}000$), 46 percent of junior high school and college prep high school students ($N = 73{,}689{,}000$), 57 percent of professional high school students ($N = 4{,}895{,}000$), and 41 percent of college students ($N = 5{,}561{,}000$) (Guojia Tongji Ju [National Bureau of Statistics] 2001:649, 658). This suggests that the glass floor and glass ceiling may be relevant for girls throughout China, though for rural girls the glass floor may be less evident, and the glass ceiling may be higher.
36. Among respondents to my survey, girls in grades 8–12 ($N = 624$) scored an average of 82 on the foreign language sections of their final exams of January 2000, while boys in grades 8–12 ($N = 527$) scored an average of 66 (significance of differences between girls' and boys' scores: $p < 0.001$). The highest possible score was 150.
37. Hochschild and Machung 1989.

38. Croll 1995; Honig and Hershatter 1988; Hooper 1998; Kerr, Delahanty, and Humpage 1996; Summerfield 1994.

39. Foucault 1977.

40. Allison 1996a:xiv.

41. $N = 2{,}193$.

42. Most high-achieving, well-behaved teenagers qualified for the Communist Youth League, but very few qualified for Communist Party membership, which was only available to unusually well-connected, socially adept, well-behaved, high-achieving, and politically savvy people age 18 or older.

43. College prohibitions against marriage declined after 2001, when a new policy allowed people of all ages and marital statuses to take the college entrance exam.

## CHAPTER 4

1. Zelizer 1994.

2. Bauer et al. 1992:353; Davis 1983:2–3, 24–25; Davis 1988, 1989; Davis 1993; Ikels 1996; Wolf 1985.

3. $N = 1{,}899$.

4. $N = 1{,}919$.

5. Hertz 1998.

6. Davis 1983; Ikels 1983, 1990a, 1990b, 1990c, 1996; Liang and Gu Shengzu 1989.

7. Pearson 1995.

8. Palmer 1995:116.

9. $N = 1{,}265{,}830{,}000$; Guojia Tongji Ju [National Bureau of Statistics] 2001:93.

10. The projection based on China's 1982 census was made by the United States Bureau of the Census (Banister 1990:272).The projection based on China's 2000 census was made by the China Population Information and Research Center, an official Chinese think-tank (China Population Information and Research Center 2001).

11. Cohen 1976; Greenhalgh 1985a; 1994b; Harrell 1982; Salaff 1995; Watson 1980; Watson and Ebrey 1986; R. Watson 1984; Watson 1986, 1996; Whyte 1979; Wolf 1968; Wolf 1972.

12. Fong 2002.

13. Greenhalgh 1990, 1993; Milwertz 1997; White 2000.

14. In response to my survey questions, 38 percent of female respondents ($N = 1{,}254$) and 29 percent of male respondents ($N = 852$) indicated that they had at least one parent who had not lived in the countryside, while 62 percent of female respondents and 71 percent of male respondents indicated that both parents had lived in the countryside. Significance of differences between male and female respondents' likelihood of having parents who had lived in the countryside: $p = 0.017$.

15. China's skewed gender ratio may result from female infanticide, parents' refusal to register daughters, parents' abandonment or lethal neglect of daugh-

ters, sex selective abortions, or some combination of these factors (Arnold and Liu Zhaoxiang 1986; Coale and Banister 1994; Croll 2000; Johnson 1996; Lee and Wang Feng 1999; Li Yongping and Peng Xizhe 2000; Zeng Yi et al. 1993).

16. Yunxiang Yan also found that neolocality became widespread during the 1990s in the rural northeastern Chinese village where he conducted fieldwork (1997b; Yan 2003).

17. $N = 1{,}144$.

18. $N = 834$.

19. $N = 2{,}188$. Most grandparents lived with just one adult child at a time; only 2 percent of respondents ($N = 2{,}002$) lived with a relative who was not a sibling, parent, or grandparent.

20. The survey defined the "elderly" as people age 65 or older.

21. Gui Shixun and Li Jieping 1996:25.

22. $N = 2{,}187$.

23. $N = 2{,}188$.

24. Che Xing 1999.

25. Greenhalgh 1985b:271.

26. Wang Xuqun's mother's wedding occurred during the Cultural Revolution, so the wedding "banquet" was actually a home-cooked meal made from staples acquired with donated or borrowed food rationing coupons.

27. Pre-revolutionary traditions of women maintaining strong social and economic ties to their natal families throughout their lives have been documented in areas of China where women's labor had unusually high economic value (Gates 1997; Siu 1990, 1993; Stockard 1989; Topley 1978). Scattered instances of uxorilocal marriage, high investment in daughters, reliance on daughters for old-age support, and the designation of daughters or daughters' sons as heirs have also been documented even in times and places that were dominated by strong patrilineal, patrilocal, and patriarchal cultural models (Pasternak 1985; Rofel 1999:80–94; Wolf 1972:191–204).

28. William Jankowiak has documented similar findings about strong father-child bonds in Hohhot, an Inner Mongolian city (Jankowiak 1992, 2002; Jankowiak 1993).

29. Borneman 1992:57–73; Coontz 1997; Lancaster 1992; Scheper-Hughes 1992; Wilson 1987.

30. Allison 1994, 1996b; M. White 1987.

31. $N = 2{,}190$.

32. $N = 2{,}190$.

33. $N = 2{,}193$.

34. $N = 2{,}193$.

35. $N = 2{,}188$.

36. Zeng Yi 2000:93.

37. A divorced person who already had a child was allowed to have a second child only if he or she married a childless person.

38. Wolf 1972.

39. Gates 1991, 1993, 1996; Greenhalgh 1985b, 1994b.

40. Gates 1993:262.

41. While the adage traditionally referred to sons, parents I knew in urban Dalian also quoted it in reference to their expectations that their daughters would support them in old age.

42. Harkness et al. 1992:171.

43. Badinter and Gray 1981; DeMause 1974; Fox and Quitt 1980; Laslett 1965; Lewis 1980; Ross 1993; Shorter 1977; Stone 1977; Walvin 1982.

44. Bledsoe and Banja 2002:46.

45. The data was collected from Bolivia, northeastern Brazil, Colombia, the Dominican Republic, Guatemala, Trinidad and Tobago, Egypt, Morocco, Sri Lanka, Thailand, Burundi, Ghana, Mali, Senegal, and Zimbabwe (Desai 1995:198).

46. Scheper-Hughes 1992:311.

47. As a shantytown mother told Scheper-Hughes about her sick baby, "But I can't afford to treat him special. I couldn't breast-feed him because I am not in good health. It wouldn't help him or me, would it? I can't make him special foods. He's no better than the others! So he gets the same inferior quality of milk in bulk that they do. I know it is too weak for him, and that's why he is so witless. But if he dies, so be it. He is *not* the only one I have" (Scheper-Hughes 1992:370).

48. Levine 1987.

49. Lee and Campbell 1997:64; Lee and Wang Feng 1999:51.

50. Choe Minja, Hao Hongsheng, and Wang Feng 1995:61.

51. Zhang 1998.

52. Peng Xizhe and Dai Xingyi 1996.

53. The term *shanghuo* literally means "rising fire," and is used to refer to both emotional stress (particularly that caused by frustration) and the physical infection, inflammation, blisters, and sores that emotional stress is said to cause. The conflation of physical and psychological symptoms derives from traditional Chinese medical ideas about the need to balance heat and cold (which referred not only to temperatures but also to various kinds of foods, emotions, and medical conditions) (Farquhar 1994).

54. Kleinman 1985, 1988.

55. Suárez-Orozco 1989.

56. De Vos 1973, 1983.

57. Lan and Fong 1999; Wang Zheng 1999; Wolf 1968, 1972.

58. Studies of family life in many 1980s and 1990s Chinese cities have shown that elderly parents in stem families were likely to have little real power, and experience powerlessness, frustration, and dependency (Ikels 1990c; Jankowiak 1993; Kleinman 1986:118–120; Whyte and Parish 1984:183).

59. Whyte 1997.

60. Cohen 1998.

61. Herzfeld 1990; Herzfeld 1997:109–114.

62. See Yunxiang Yan's longitudinal study of a Chinese village (2003) for a detailed account of how the policies of socialist modernization led to the steadily increasing disempowerment of the elderly.

## CHAPTER 5

1. United Nations 1997a.
2. Blake 1981, 1989; Claudy 1984; Cooper et al. 1984; Falbo 1984a, 1984b; Falbo and Polit 1986; Feiring and Lewis 1984; Groat, Wicks, and Neal 1984; Hawke and Knox 1977; Henderson 1991; Laybourn 1994; McKibben 1998; Polit and Falbo 1987, 1988.
3. Chen, Rubin, and Li 1994; Falbo and Poston 1993; Feng Xiaotian 1992; Poston and Falbo 1990.
4. Shanghaishi Youerjiaoyu Yanjiushi [Shanghai Preschool Education Study Group] 1980, 1988.
5. Tao and Chiu 1985; Tao et al. 1995; Tseng et al. 1988.
6. Chen Kewen 1988; Wu Naitao 1986.
7. Jiao, Ji, and Jing 1986.
8. Bian 1987.
9. Bian 1987:207.
10. This study was led by Wang Jisheng, a professor at the Chinese Academy of Social Sciences (Tang Yuankai 2001).
11. Wang Yuru 1999:325.
12. Dominic Boyer found a similar tendency to make much of small statistical differences in the German media and social science literature on differences between East Germans and West Germans (Boyer 2000:466). Boyer argued that "this kind of intellectual labor is spinning golden knowledge of generalizable difference and semantic determinance from the straw of, at best, partial and ambiguous associations" (Boyer 2000:466). Boyer's point was not that the literature on differences between East Germans and West Germans was inaccurate, but rather that the obsessive focus on these differences was itself indicative of broader cultural concerns. I would argue that a similar process was at work in the discourse on "spoiled only children" in China after the one-child policy, as well as in the United States during the early twentieth century.
13. American studies conducted during the late nineteenth and early twentieth centuries (Bohannan 1896, 1898; Bossard 1953; Fenton 1928; Smith 1907; Solomon, Clare, and Westoff 1956) focused on the undesirable effects of singleton status. In their reviews of American attitudes toward singletons as expressed in surveys, academic articles, and the popular press prior to the 1970s, Judith Blake (1981; 1989), Toni Falbo (1984b), and Vaida D. Thompson (1974). found that singletons were frequently portrayed as spoiled and maladjusted.
14. Day et al. 1993; Falbo 1984b; Falbo and Poston 1993; Hawke and Knox 1977; Laybourn 1994; McKibben 1998; Polit and Falbo 1988; Polit, Nuttal, and Nuttal 1980; Veenhoven and Verkuyten 1989.
15. Parents' tendency to provide their children with expensive diets associ-

ated with the First World has been observed in many areas of China during the 1990s (Chee 2000; Gillette 2000b; Guo Yuhua 2000; Jing 2000a; Lozada 2000; Watson 2000; Yan 1997a).

16. The "Three Years of Natural Disasters" (*san nian ziran zaihai*) was a common euphemism for the famine caused by the Great Leap Forward (1959–1961).

17. Ariès 1996; Small 2001; Zelizer 1994.

18. Baxter 1997; Burggraf 1997; Hartmann 1994; Hewitt 1993; Hochschild and Machung 1989; Nakhaie 1995.

19. China Peking Opera Troupe 1972:2, 46–48.

20. U.S. Bureau of the Census 1999.

21. Krause 2001; Schneider and Schneider 1996.

22. Krause 2001:592.

23. Riding 2002, Plesset 2002.

24. Miyazaki 2003.

25. Peak 1991.

26. Allison 1996a:107.

27. Allison 1996a:89.

28. White 1988, 1993.

29. White 1993:106.

30. Csikszentmihalyi, Rathunde, and Whalen 1993:3. Reprinted with the permission of Cambridge University Press.

31. Csikszentmihalyi, Rathunde, and Whalen 1993:3.

32. Schneider and Stevenson 1999.

33. The Sloan Study drew respondents from a diverse array of ethnic, socioeconomic, and academic backgrounds, in grades six, eight, ten, and twelve of 33 schools in 12 U.S. locations (Hoogstra 2000).

34. Asakawa, Hektner, and Schmidt 2000:45.

35. Ortner 1998:429.

36. Schneider and Stevenson 1999:245–264.

## CONCLUSION

1. Lu Hsun 1978:64. Lu Hsun's name is now more commonly spelled "Lu Xun."

2. Jiang Zemin 1996a, 1996b.

3. Becker 1997; Gore 1997.

4. See Ronald Dore (Dore 1976), Randall Collins (2002), Alex Inkeles (1974), and Alejandro Portes (1976) for discussions of problems caused by diploma inflation in a wide range of societies.

5. Wallerstein 1998, 1999.

# Works Cited

Abu-Lughod, Lila. 1986. *Veiled Sentiments: Honor and Poetry in a Bedouin Society*. Berkeley: University of California Press.

———. 1993. *Writing Women's Worlds: Bedouin Stories*. Berkeley: University of California Press.

Ahern, Emily M. 1973. The Power and Pollution of Chinese Women. In *Women in Chinese Society*, ed. Margery Wolf and Roxane Witke. Stanford: Stanford University Press.

Aird, John S. 1990. *Slaughter of the Innocents: Coercive Birth Control in China*. Washington, D.C.: AEI Press.

Allison, Anne. 1994. *Nightwork: Sexuality, Pleasure, and Corporate Masculinity in a Tokyo Hostess Club*. Chicago: University of Chicago Press.

———. 1996a. *Permitted and Prohibited Desires: Mothers, Comics, and Censorship in Japan*. Boulder, Colorado: Westview Press.

———. 1996b. Producing Mothers. In *Re-Imaging Japanese Women*, ed. Anne E. Imamura, 135–155. Berkeley: University of California Press.

Anagnost, Ann. 1988. Family Violence and Magical Violence: The "Woman-as-Victim" in China's One-Child Family Policy. *Women and Language* 1, no. 2: 16–22.

———. 1995. A Surfeit of Bodies: Population and the Rationality of the State in Post-Mao China. In *Conceiving the New World Order: The Global Politics of Reproduction*, ed. Faye D. Ginsburg and Rayna Rapp, 22–41. Berkeley: University of California Press.

———. 1997a. Children and National Transcendence in China. In *Constructing China: The Interaction of Culture and Economics*, ed. Kenneth G. Lieberthal, Shuen-fu Lin and Ernest P. Young, 195–222. Ann Arbor: Center For Chinese Studies at the University of Michigan.

———. 1997b. *National Past-Times: Narrative, Representation, and Power in Modern China*. Durham: Duke University Press.

Appadurai, Arjun. 1993. Number in the Colonial Imagination. In *Orientalism and the Postcolonial Predicament: Perspectives on South Asia*, ed. Carol A. Breckenridge and Peter van der Veer, 314–339. Philadelphia: University of Pennsylvania Press.

———. 1996. *Modernity at Large: Cultural Dimensions of Globalization*. Minnesota University Press.

Ariès, Philippe. 1996. *Centuries of Childhood*. London: Pimlico.

Arnold, Fred, and Liu Zhaoxiang. 1986. Sex Preference, Fertility, and Family Planning in China. *Population and Development Review* 12, no. 2: 221–246.

Asakawa, Kiyoshi, Joel Hektner, and Jennifer Schmidt. 2000. Envisioning the Future. In *Becoming Adult: How Teenagers Prepare for the World of Work*, ed. Mihaly Csikszentmihalyi and Barbara Schneider, 39–64. New York: Basic Books.

Attane, Isabelle, and Sun Minglei. 1999. Birth Rates and Fertility in China. How Credible Are Recent Data? *Population: An English Selection* 11: 251–260.

Badinter, Elisabeth, and Francine du Plessix Gray. 1981. *Mother Love: Myth and Reality: Motherhood in Modern History*. New York: Macmillan.

Banister, Judith. 1987. *China's Changing Population*. Stanford: Stanford University Press.

———. 1990. Trends and Implications of Population Aging and the Status of the Elderly. In *Changing Family Structure and Population Aging in China: A Comparative Approach*, ed. Zeng Yi, Zhang Chunyuan and Peng Songjian, 268–308. Beijing, China: Peking University Press.

Bauer, John, Feng Wang, Nancy E. Riley, and Xiaohua Zhao. 1992. Gender Inequality in Urban China: Education and Employment. *Modern China* 18, no. 3: 333.

Baxter, Janeen. 1997. Gender Equality and Participation in Housework: A Cross-National Perspective. *Journal of Comparative Family Studies* 28, no. 3: 220–247.

Becker, Gary. 1981. *A Treatise on the Family*. Cambridge: Harvard University Press.

Becker, Jasper. 1997. Beijing Clears the Way to Washington. *South China Morning Post*, 9.

Behar, Ruth. 1995. Rage and Redemption: Reading the Life Story of a Mexican Marketing Woman. In *The Dialogical Emergence of Culture*, ed. Bruce Mannheim and Dennis Tedlock, 148–178. Urbana: University of Illinois Press.

Bhabha, Homi K. 1991. "Race," Time, and the Revision of Modernity. *Oxford Literary Review* 13: 193–219.

Bian, Yanjie. 1987. A Preliminary Analysis of the Basic Features of the Life Styles of China's Single-Child Families. *Social Sciences in China* 8: 189–209.

———. 1994. *Work and Inequality in Urban China*. Albany: State University of New York Press.

Blake, Judith. 1981. The Only Child in America: Prejudice Versus Performance. *Population and Development Review* 7: 43–54.

———. 1989. *Family Size and Achievement*. Berkeley: University of California Press.

Bledsoe, Caroline, Fatoumatta Banja, and Alan G. Hill. 1998. Reproductive Mishaps and Western Contraception: An African Challenge to Fertility Theory. *Population and Development Review* 24, no. 1: 15–57.

Bledsoe, Caroline, John B. Casterline, Jennifer A. Johnson-Kuhn, and John G. Haaga, eds. 1998. *Critical Perspectives on Schooling and Fertility in the Developing World*. Washington, DC: National Academy Press.

Bledsoe, Caroline H. 2001. The Bodily Costs of Childbearing: Western Science through a West African Lens. In *Children and Anthropology: Perspectives for the 21st Century*, ed. Helen B. Schwartzman, 57–82. Westport, Connecticut: Bergin and Garvey.

Bledsoe, Caroline H., and Fatoumatta Banja. 2002. *Contingent Lives: Fertility, Time, and Aging in West Africa*. Chicago: University of Chicago Press.

Bohannan, E. W. 1896. A Study of Peculiar and Exceptional Children. *Pedagogical Seminary* 4, no. 1: 3–60.

———. 1898. The Only Child in a Family. *Pedagogical Seminary* 6, no. 2: 475.

Bongaarts, John, and Susan Cotts Watkins. 1996. *Social Interactions and Contemporary Fertility Transitions*. Working Papers [Population Council. Research Division]; No. 88. New York: Population Council.

Borneman, John. 1992. *Belonging in the Two Berlins: Kin, State, Nation*. Cambridge: Cambridge University Press.

Bossard, James Herbert. 1953. *Parent and Child*. Philadelphia: University of Pennsylvania Press.

Bourdieu, Pierre. 1977. *Outline of a Theory of Practice*. Translated by Richard Nice. Cambridge: Cambridge University Press.

———. 1984. *Distinction: A Social Critique of the Judgement of Taste*. Cambridge, Mass.: Harvard University Press.

———. 1998. *Practical Reason: On the Theory of Action*. Cambridge, UK: Polity.

Bourdieu, Pierre, and Jean-Claude Passeron. 1977. *Reproduction in Education, Society, and Culture*. Translated by Richard Nice. Cambridge: Cambridge University Press.

Boyer, Dominic. 2000. On the Sedimentation and Accreditation of Social Knowledges of Difference: Mass Media, Journalism, and the Reproduction of East / West Alterities in Unified Germany. *Cultural Anthropology* 15, no. 4: 459–491.

Brenner, Suzanne April. 1998. *The Domestication of Desire*. Princeton: Princeton University Press.

Broaded, C. Montgomery, and Chongshun Liu. 1996. Family Background, Gender and Educational Attainment in Urban China. *The China Quarterly* 145: 53–86.

Burggraf, Shirley P. 1997. *The Feminine Economy and Economic Man: Reviving the Role of Family in the Post-Industrial Age*. Reading, Massachusetts: Addison-Wesley.

Caldwell, John C. 1982. *Theory of Fertility Decline*. London: Academic Press.

Caldwell, John C., I.O. Orubuloye, and Pat Caldwell. 1992. Fertility Decline in Africa: A New Type of Transition? 18, no. 2: 211–243.

Casson, Ronald W. 1983. Schemata in Cognitive Anthropology. *Annual Review of Anthropology* 12: 429–462.

Chan, Kam Wing, and Xueqiang Xu. 1985. Urban Population Growth and Urbanization in China since 1949: Reconstructing a Baseline. *China Quarterly* 104: 583–613.

Chang, Jung. 1991. *Wild Swans: Three Daughters of China.* New York: Simon & Schuster.

Che Xing. 1999. *Chang Huijia Kankan [Visit Home Often].* Hebei: Hebei Sheng Juyuan [Hebei Province Theater].

Chee, Bernadine W. L. 2000. Eating Snacks, Biting Pressure: Only Children in Beijing. In *Feeding China's Little Emperors*, ed. Jun Jing, 48–70. Stanford: Stanford University Press.

Chen Kewen. 1988. Dushengzinü Yu Feidushengzinu Xingwei Tedian He Jiating Jiaoyu De Bijiao Yanjiu: Dui Beijing Shichengxiang Qianming Ertong De Diaocha Baogao [Comparative Research on the Behavior Particularities and Family Education of Singletons and Non-Singletons: A Report on 1000 Children from Rural and Urban Areas of Beijing]. In *Dushengzinü De Xinli Tedian Yu Jiaoyu [Singletons' Psychological Particularities and Education]*, ed. Beijing Shifan Daxue Jiaoyu Kexue Yanjiusuo [Beijing Normal University Educational Science Research Center], 133–148. Beijing: Nongcun Duwu Chubanshe [Rural Reading Materials Publisher].

Chen Muhua. 1979. For the Realization of the Four Modernizations, There Must Be Planned Control of Population Growth. *Population and Development Review* 5, no. 4: 723–730.

Chen, Nancy N., Constance D. Clark, Suzanne Z. Gottschang, and Lyn Jeffery. 2001. *China Urban: Ethnographies of Contemporary Culture.* Durham: Duke University Press.

Chen, Xinyin, Kenneth H. Rubin, and Bo-shu Li. 1994. Only Children and Sibling Children in Urban China: A Re-Examination. *International Journal of Behavioural Development* 17: 413–421.

Cheng, Nien. 1986. *Life and Death in Shanghai.* London: Grafton.

Cheng, Tiejun, and Mark Selden. 1994. The Origins and Social Consequences of China's Hukou System. *China Quarterly* 139: 644–668.

China Peking Opera Troupe. 1972. *The Red Lantern: A Modern Revolutionary Peking Opera [May 1970 Script].* Peking: Foreign Languages Press.

China Population Information and Research Center. 2001. *Four Periods of Population Aging Forecast in China.* National Bureau of Statistics, People's Republic of China. Available from http://www.cpirc.org.cn/e-aging2.htm.Website accessed June 25, 2001.

Chinese State Council Information Office. 2000. China's Population and Development in the 21st Century. *China Daily*, December 20, 1.

Choe Minja, Hao Hongsheng, and Wang Feng. 1995. Effects of Gender, Birth

Order, and Other Correlates on Childhood Mortality in China. *Social Biology* 42: 50–64.

Chow, Gregory C. 2002. *China's Economic Transformation.* Malden, Massachusetts: Blackwell Publishers.

Chow, Tse-Tsung. 1960. *The May Fourth Movement: Intellectual Revolution in Modern China.* Cambridge: Harvard University Press.

Chu, David S. K. 1984. *Sociology and Society in Contemporary China, 1979–1983.* Chinese Sociology and Anthropology; V. 16, No. 1–2. Armonk, N.Y.: M. E. Sharpe.

Chu, Henry. 2001. India Joins China as Member of the Billion-Population Club. *Los Angeles Times,* March 29, 2001, 9.

Chu Jun. 1999. Nu Zhongxuesheng Wo Gui Zisha De Qianqian Houhou [Before and after a Female Middle School Student Killed Herself by Lying on the Train Tracks]. *Dusheng Zinu Jiankang [Only Children's Health],* 4–6.

Clark, Gracia. 1999. Mothering, Work, and Gender in Urban Asante Ideology and Practice. *American Anthropologist* 101, no. 4: 717–729.

Claudy, John G. 1984. The Only Child as a Young Adult: Results from Project Talent. In *The Single-Child Family,* ed. Toni Falbo, 211–252. New York: Guilford Press.

Clifford, James, and George E. Marcus. 1986. *Writing Culture: The Poetics and Politics of Ethnography.* Berkeley: University of California Press.

Coale, Ansley J., and Judith Banister. 1994. Five Decades of Missing Females in China. *Demography* 31, no. 3: 459–479.

Coale, Ansley J., and Shengli Chen. 1987. *Basic Data on Fertility in the Provinces of China, 1940–82.* Honolulu: The East-West Population Institute. Papers of the East-West Population Institute, 104.

Coale, Ansley, and Susan Cotts Watkins, eds. 1986. *The Decline of Fertility in Europe.* Princeton: Princeton New Jersey Press.

Cohen, Joel E. 1995. *How Many People Can the Earth Support?* New York: Norton.

Cohen, Lawrence. 1998. *No Aging in India: Alzheimer's, the Bad Family, and Other Modern Things.* Berkeley: University of California Press.

Cohen, Myron L. 1976. *House United, House Divided: The Chinese Family in Taiwan.* New York: Columbia University Press.

Collins, Randall. 2002. Credential Inflation and the Future of Universities. In *The Future of the City of Intellect: The Changing American University,* ed. Steven Brint, 23–46. Stanford: Stanford University Press.

Comaroff, Jean, and John L. Comaroff. 1991a. *Of Revelation and Revolution: Christianity, Colonialism, and Consciousness in South Africa.* Chicago: University of Chicago Press.

———. 1991b. *Of Revelation and Revolution: The Dialectics of Modernity on a South African Frontier.* Chicago: University of Chicago Press.

———. 1993. *Modernity and Its Malcontents: Ritual and Power in Postcolonial Africa.* Chicago: University of Chicago Press.

Cooney, Rosemary Santana, and Jiali Li. 1994. Household Registration Type and

Compliance with the "One Child" Policy in China, 1979–1988. *Demography* 31, no. 1: 21–32.

Coontz, Stephanie. 1997. *The Way We Really Are: Coming to Terms with America's Changing Families*. New York: Basic Books.

Cooper, Catherine R., Harold D. Grotevant, Mary Sue Moore, and Sherri M. Condon. 1984. Predicting Adolescent Role Taking and Identity Exploration from Family Communication Patterns: A Comparison of One- and Two-Child Families. In *The Single-Child Family*, ed. Toni Falbo, 117–142. New York: Guilford Press.

Coronil, Fernando. 1996. Beyond Occidentalism: Toward Nonimperial Geohistorical Categories. *Cultural Anthropology* 11, no. 1, 1996.

———. 1997. *The Magical State: Nature, Money, and Modernity in Venezuela*. Chicago: University of Chicago Press.

Croll, Elisabeth. 2000. *Endangered Daughters: Discrimination and Development in Asia*. London: Routledge.

Croll, Elisabeth J. 1995. *Changing Identities of Chinese Women: Rhetoric, Experience, and Self-Perception in Twentieth-Century China*. Hong Kong: Hong Kong University Press.

Croll, Elisabeth J., Delia Davin, and Penny Kane. 1985. *China's One-Child Family Policy*. New York: St. Martin's Press.

Csikszentmihalyi, Mihaly, Kevin Rathunde, and Samuel Whalen. 1993. *Talented Teenagers: The Roots of Success and Failure*. New York: Cambridge University Press.

Dalian Shi Jiaoyu Weiyuanhui [Dalian City Educational Committee]. 1999. *Dalian Shi Jiaoyu Tongji Xinxi [Dalian City Educational Statistics]*. Dalian, China: Dalian Shi Jiaoyu Weiyuanhui [Dalian City Educational Committee].

Dalian Shi Jiaoyu Zhi Bian Zuan Bangongshi [Dalian City Education Records Compilation Office]. 1999. *Dalian Jiaoyu Yaolan 1997–1998 [a Survey of Dalian Education 1997–1998]*. Dalian: Dalian Shi Jiaoyu Zhi Bian Zuan Bangongshi [Dalian City Education Records Compilation Office].

Dalian Shi Shi Zhi Bangongshi [Dalian City Archives Office]. 1990. *Dalian Nianjian [Dalian Yearbook], 1987–1989*. Dalian: Dalian Chubanshe [Dalian Publisher].

———. 2000. *Dalian Nianjian [Dalian Yearbook], 1999*. Dalian: Dalian Chubanshe [Dalian Publisher].

———. 2001. *Dalian Nianjian [Dalian Yearbook], 2000*. Dalian: Dalian Chubanshe [Dalian Publisher].

———. 2002. *Dalian Nianjian [Dalian Yearbook], 2001*. Dalian: Dalian Chubanshe [Dalian Publisher].

D'Andrade, Roy G. 1995. *The Development of Cognitive Anthropology*. Cambridge; New York: Cambridge University Press.

D'Andrade, Roy G., and Claudia Strauss. 1992. *Human Motives and Cultural Models*. Cambridge, England: Cambridge University Press.

Davin, Delia. 1985. The Single-Child Family Policy in the Countryside. In

*China's One-Child Family Policy*, ed. Elisabeth Croll, Delia Davin and Penny Kane. New York: St. Martin's Press.

———. 1999. *Internal Migration in Contemporary China*. New York: St. Martin's Press.

Davis, Deborah. 1983. *Long Lives: Chinese Elderly and the Communist Revolution*. Cambridge: Harvard University Press.

———. 1988. Unequal Chances, Unequal Outcomes: Pension Reform and Urban Inequality. *China Quarterly*, no. 114: 223–242.

———. 1989. Chinese Social Welfare: Policies and Outcomes. *The China Quarterly* 21: 21.

———. 1992. "Skidding": Downward Mobility among Children of the Maoist Middle Class. *Modern China* 18, no. 4: 410–437.

———. 2000. *The Consumer Revolution in China*. Berkeley: University of California Press.

Davis, Deborah S. 1993. Financial Security of Urban Retirees. *Journal of Cross-cultural Gerontology* 8, no. 3.

Davis, Deborah, and Julia S. Sensenbrenner. 2000. Commercializing Childhood: Parental Purchases for Shanghai's Only Child. In *The Consumer Revolution in China*, ed. Deborah Davis. Berkeley: University of California Press.

Davis-Friedmann, Deborah. 1985. Old Age Security and the One-Child Campaign. In *China's One-Child Family Policy*, ed. Elisabeth Croll, Delia Davin and Penny Kane, 149–161. New York: St. Martin's Press.

Day, Lincoln H., Barbara Byrd, Arnold DeRosa, and Stephen C. Craig. 1993. The Adult Who Is an Only Child. *Journal of Genetic Psychology* 73: 171–177.

De Vos, George. 1973. *Socialization for Achievement: Essays on the Cultural Psychology of the Japanese*. Berkeley: University of California Press.

———. 1983. Achievement Motivation and Intra-Family Attitudes in Immigrant Koreans. *Journal of Psychoanalytic Anthropology* 6, no. 1: 25–71.

DeMause, Lloyd. 1974. *The History of Childhood*. New York: Psychohistory Press.

Desai, Sonalde. 1995. When Are Children from Large Families Disadvantaged? Evidence from Cross-National Analysis. *Population Studies* 49, no. 2: 195–210.

di Leonardo, Micaela. 1998. *Exotics at Home: Anthropology, Others, American Modernity*. Chicago: University of Chicago Press.

Dore, Ronald. 1976. *The Diploma Disease: Education, Qualification, and Development*. London: George Allen and Unwin.

Douglas, Mary, and Steven Ney. 1998. *Missing Persons: A Critique of Personhood in the Social Sciences*. Berkeley: University of California Press.

Downey, Douglas B. 1995. When Bigger Is Not Better: Family Size, Parental Resources, and Children's Educational Performance. *American Sociological Review* 60, no. 5: 746–761.

Dressler, William W. 1982. *Hypertension and Culture Change: Acculturation and Disease in the West Indies*. South Salem, New York: Redgrave.

———. 1990. Lifestyle, Stress, and Blood Pressure in a Southern Black Community. *Psychosomatic Medicine* 52: 182–198.

Dressler, William W., and James R. Bindon. 2000. The Health Consequences of Cultural Consonance: Cultural Dimensions of Lifestyle, Social Support, and Arterial Blood Pressure in an African American Community. *American Anthropologist* 102: 244–260.

Dressler, William W., Jose Ernesto Dos Santos, Philip N. Gallagher Jr., and Fernando E. Viteri. 1987a. Arterial Blood Pressure and Modernization in Brazil. *American Anthropologist* 89: 389–409.

Dressler, William W., Alfonso Mata, Adolfo Chavez, and Fernando E. Viteri. 1987b. Arterial Blood Pressure and Individual Modernization in a Mexican Community. *Social Science & Medicine* 24: 679–687.

Dutton, Michael Robert. 1998. *Streetlife China*. Cambridge: Cambridge University Press.

Dwyer, Kevin. 1982. *Moroccan Dialogues: Anthropology in Question*. Prospect Heights, Illinois: Waveland Press, Inc.

Easterlin, Richard A. 1978. The Economics and Sociology of Fertility: A Synthesis. In *Historical Studies of Changing Fertility*, ed. Charles Tilly, 57–113. Princeton: Princeton University Press.

Easterlin, Richard A., and Eileen M. Crimmins. 1985. *The Fertility Revolution: A Supply-Demand Analysis*. Chicago: University of Chicago Press.

Elman, Benjamin A. 1990. *Classism, Politics, and Kinship: The Ch'ang Chou School of New Text Confucianism in Late Imperial China*. Berkeley: University of California Press.

———. 1991. Political, Social, and Cultural Reproduction via Civil Service Examinations in Late Imperial China. *The Journal of Asian Studies* 50, no. 1: 7–28.

Escobar, Arturo. 1995. *Encountering Development: The Making and Unmaking of the Third World*. Princeton Studies in Culture / Power / History. Princeton, N.J.: Princeton University Press.

Esherick, Joseph. 1987. *The Origins of the Boxer Uprising*. Berkeley: University of California Press.

Esherick, Joseph, and Mary Rankin. 1990. *Chinese Local Elites and Patterns of Dominance*. Berkeley: University of California Press.

Essock-Vitale, Susan M., and Michael T. McGuire. 1988. What 70 Million Years Hath Wrought: Sexual Histories and Reproductive Success of a Random Sample of American Women. In *Human Reproductive Behaviour: A Darwinian Perspective*, ed. Laura L. Betzig, Monique Borgerhoff Mulder and Paul Turke, 221–235. Cambridge: Cambridge University Press.

Fabian, Johannes. 1995. Ethnographic Misunderstanding and the Perils of Context. *American Anthropologist* 97, no. 1, 1995.

Falbo, Toni. 1984a. Only Children: A Review. In *The Single-Child Family*, ed. Toni Falbo, 1–24. New York: Guilford Press.

———. 1984b. *The Single-Child Family*. New York: Guilford Press.

Falbo, Toni, and Denise Polit. 1986. Quantitative Review of the Only Child Literature. *Psychological Bulletin* 100: 176–189.

Falbo, Toni and Dudley L. Poston, Jr. 1993. The Academic, Personality, and

Physical Outcomes of Only Children in China. *Child Development* 64, no. 1: 18.

Farquhar, Judith. 1994. *Knowing Practice: The Clinical Encounter of Chinese Medicine*. Boulder: Westview Press.

———. 2002. *Appetites: Food and Sex in Post-Socialist China*. Durham: Duke University Press.

Farrer, James. 1998. *Opening Up: Youth Sex Culture and Market Reform in Shanghai*. Chicago: University of Chicago Press.

Feeney, Griffith, and Feng Wang. 1993. Parity Progression and Birth Intervals in China: The Influence of Policy in Hastening Fertility Decline. *Population and Development Review* 19, no. 1: 61–101.

Feeney, Griffith, Feng Wang, Mingkun Zhou, and Baoyu Xiao. 1989. Recent Fertility Dynamics in China: Results from the 1987 One Percent Population Survey. *Population and Development Review* 15, no. 2: 297–322.

Feeney, Griffith, and Jianhua Yuan. 1994. Below Replacement Fertility in China? A Close Look at Recent Evidence. *Population Studies* 48, no. 3: 381–394.

Fei, Hsiao-tung. 1953. *China's Gentry: Essays on Rural-Urban Relations*. Chicago: University of Chicago Press.

Feiring, Candice, and Michael Lewis. 1984. Only and First-Born Children: Differences in Social Behavior and Development. In *The Single-Child Family*, ed. Toni Falbo, 25–62. New York: Guilford Press.

Felmlee, Diane H. 1993. The Dynamic Interdependence of Women's Employment and Fertility. *Social Science Research* 22, no. 4: 333–360.

Feng Xiaotian. 1992. *Dusheng Zinu: Tamen De Jiating, Jiaoyu, He Weilai [Only Children: Their Families, Education, and Future]*. Pei-ching: Shehuikexue Wenxian Chubanshe [Sociological Contributions Publisher].

Fenton, Norman. 1928. The Only Child. *Journal of Genetic Psychology* 35: 546–547.

Ferguson, James. 1999. *Expectations of Modernity: Myths and Meanings of Urban Life on the Zambian Copperbelt*. Berkeley: University of California Press.

Fong, Vanessa L. 2002. China's One-Child Policy and the Empowerment of Urban Daughters. *American Anthropologist* 104, no. 4: 1098–1109.

Foucault, Michel. 1977. *Discipline and Punish: The Birth of the Prison*. New York: Pantheon Books.

Fox, Vivian C., and Martin H. Quitt. 1980. *Loving, Parenting, and Dying: The Family Cycle in England and America, Past and Present*. New York: Psychohistory Press.

Fricke, Thomas E. 1994. *Himalayan Households: Tamang Demography and Domestic Processes*. New York: Columbia University Press.

Friedman, Thomas. 2000. *The Lexus and the Olive Tree: Understanding Globalization*. New York: Anchor Books.

Frisancho, A. Roberto, Jane E. Klayman, and Jorge Matos. 1976. Symbiotic Relationship of High Fertility, High Childhood Mortality and Socio-Economic Status in an Urban Peruvian Population. *Human Biology* 48, no. 1: 101–111.

Fukuyama, Francis. 1992. *The End of History and the Last Man*. New York: Free Press.

Gao Yuan. 1987. *Born Red: A Chronicle of the Cultural Revolution*. Stanford: Stanford University Press.

Garro, Linda C. 2000. Remembering What One Knows and the Construction of the Past: A Comparison of Cultural Consensus Theory and Cultural Schema Theory. *Ethos* 28, no. 3: 275–319.

Gates, Hill. 1991. "Narrow Hearts" and Petty Capitalism: Small Business Women in Chengdu, China. *Marxist Approaches in Economic Anthropology*: 13–36.

———. 1993. Cultural Support for Birth Limitation among Urban Capital-Owning Women. In *Chinese Families in the Post-Mao Era*, ed. Deborah Davis and Stevan Harrell, 251–274. Berkeley: University of California Press.

———. 1996. *China's Motor: A Thousand Years of Petty Capitalism*. Ithaca: Cornell University Press.

———. 1997. Footbinding and Handspinning in Sichuan: Capitalism's Ambiguous Gifts to Petty Capitalism. In *Constructing China: The Interaction of Culture and Economics*, ed. Kenneth G. Lieberthal, Shuen-fu Lin and Ernest P. Young. Ann Arbor: Center for Chinese Studies, University of Michigan.

Gerson, Kathleen. 1985. *Hard Choices: How Women Decide About Work, Career, and Motherhood*. Berkeley: University of California Press.

Gewertz, Deborah B., and Frederick Karl Errington. 1996. On Pepsico and Piety in a Papua New Guinea Modernity. *American Ethnologist* 23, no. 3: 476–493.

Gillette, Maris. 2000a. *Between Mecca and Beijing: Modernization and Consumption among Urban Chinese Muslims*. Stanford: Stanford University Press.

———. 2000b. Children's Food and Islamic Dietary Restrictions in Xi'an. In *Feeding China's Little Emperors*, ed. Jun Jing, 71–93. Stanford: Stanford University Press.

Gold, Thomas B., Doug Guthrie, and David Wank. 2002. *Social Connections in China: Institutions, Culture, and the Changing Nature of Guanxi*. Cambridge: Cambridge University Press.

Goldstein, Alice, and Feng Wang. 1996. *China: The Many Facets of Demographic Change*. Boulder, Colorado: Westview Press.

Goode, William J. 1970. *World Revolution and Family Patterns*. New York: Free Press.

Gore, Albert. 1997. *Vice President Albert Gore's Remarks at Qinghua University, Beijing, China*. U.S. Embassy, China. Available from http://www.usembassy-china.org.cn/english/press/exchange/wwwhit16.html. Web page accessed July 15, 2001.

Gramsci, Antonio. 1992. *Prison Notebooks*. Translated by Joseph A. Buttigieg. New York: Columbia University Press.

Greenhalgh, Susan. 1985a. Is Inequality Demographically Induced? The Family Cycle and the Distribution of Income in Taiwan. *American Anthropologist* 87, no. 3: 571–594.

———. 1985b. Sexual Stratification: The Other Side of "Growth with Equity." *Population and Development Review* 11: 265–314.

———. 1986. Shifts in China's Population Policy, 1984–86: Views from the Central, Provincial, and Local Levels. *Population and Development Review* 12, no. 3: 491–515.

———. 1988. Fertility as Mobility: Sinic Transitions. *Population and Development Review* 14, no. 4: 629–674.

———. 1990. The Evolution of the One-Child Policy in Shaanxi, 1979–88. *The China Quarterly* 122, no. June: 191–229.

———. 1993. The Peasantization of the One-Child Policy in Shaanxi. In *Chinese Families in the Post-Mao Era*, ed. Deborah Davis and Stevan Harrell, 219–250. Berkeley: University of California Press.

———. 1994a. Controlling Births and Bodies in Village China. *American Ethnologist* 21, no. 1: 3–30.

———. 1994b. De-Orientalizing the Chinese Family Firm. *American Ethnologist* 21, no. 4, 1994.: 746–775.

———. 2001a. Fresh Winds in Beijing: Chinese Feminists Speak out on the One-Child Policy and Women's Lives. *Signs* 26, no. 3: 847–886.

———. 2001b. *Governing the Chinese Population: Techniques and Tactics of Control*. Paper delivered at the American Anthropological Association's 100th Annual Meeting in Washington, D.C., December 2.

Greenhalgh, Susan and Jiali Li. 1995. Engendering Reproductive Policy and Practice in Peasant China: For a Feminist Demography of Reproduction. *Signs* 20, no. 3: 601–642.

Greenhalgh, Susan, Li Nan, and Zhu Chuzhu. 1994. Restraining Population Growth in Three Chinese Villages, 1988–93. *Population and Development Review* 20, no. 2: 365–396.

Groat, H. Theodore, Jerry W. Wicks, and Arthur G. Neal. 1984. Without Siblings: The Consequences in Adult Life of Having Been an Only Child. In *The Single-Child Family*, ed. Toni Falbo, 253–290. New York: Guilford Press.

Gui Shixun and Li Jieping. 1996. *Dushengzinü Fumu Nian Lao Hou De Zhaogu Wenti [The Problem of Old-age Care for Parents of Singletons]*. Shanghai: Huadong Shifandaxue Chubanshe [Huadong Normal University Press].

Guldin, Gregory Eliyu. 1994. *The Saga of Anthropology in China: From Malinowski to Moscow to Mao*. Armonk, N.Y.: M. E. Sharpe.

Guo Yuhua. 2000. Food and Family Relations: The Generation Gap at the Table. In *Feeding China's Little Emperors*, ed. Jun Jing, 94–113. Stanford: Stanford University Press.

Guojia Tongji Ju [National Bureau of Statistics]. 1981. *Zhongguo Tongji Nianjian [China Statistical Yearbook], 1981*. Beijing: Zhongguo Tongji Chubanshe [China Statistics Press].

———. 1998. *Zhongguo Tongji Nianjian [China Statistical Yearbook], 1998*. Beijing: Zhongguo Tongji Chubanshe [China Statistics Press].

———. 1999. *Zhongguo Tongji Nianjian [China Statistical Yearbook], 1999*. Beijing: Zhongguo Tongji Chubanshe [China Statistics Press].

———. 2000. *Zhongguo Tongji Nianjian [China Statistical Yearbook], 2000*. Beijing: Zhongguo Tongji Chubanshe [China Statistics Press].

———. 2001. *Zhongguo Tongji Nianjian [China Statistical Yearbook], 2001*. Beijing: Zhongguo Tongji Chubanshe [China Statistics Press].

Guojia Tongji Ju Chengshi Shehui Jingji Diaocha Zongdui [National Bureau of Statistics Urban Society and Economy Research Team]. 2000. *Zhongguo Chengshi Tongji Nianjian [Urban Statistical Yearbook of China, 1999]*. Beijing: Zhongguo Tongji Chubanshe [China Statistical Press].

Han Yan. 1999. Wo Duo Xiang Wan Yi Hui'er [How Much I Want to Play for a While]. *Dalian Ribao [Dalian Daily]*, August 4, 1999, 8.

Handwerker, W. Penn. 1986. Modern Demographic Transition: An Analysis of Subsistence Choices and Reproductive Consequences. *American Anthropologist* 88, no. 2: 400–417.

Hansen, Karen Tranberg. 1997. *Keeping House in Lusaka*. New York: Columbia University Press.

———. 2000. *Salaula: The World of Secondhand Clothing and Zambia*. Chicago: University of Chicago.

Harkness, Sara, Charles M. Super, and Constance H. Keefer. 1992. *Learning to Be an American Parent: How Cultural Models Gain Directive Force*. In *Human Motives and Cultural Models*, ed. Roy G. D'Andrade and Claudia Strauss, 163-196. Cambridge, England: Cambridge University Press.

Harrell, Stevan. 1982. *Ploughshare Village: Culture and Context in Taiwan*. Seattle: University of Washington Press.

Hartmann, Heidi I. 1994. The Family as the Locus of Gender, Class, and Political Struggle: The Example of Housework. In *Theorizing Feminism: Parallel Trends in the Humanities and Social Sciences*, ed. Anne C. Herrmann and Abigail J. Stewart, 171–197. Boulder, Colorado: Westview Press.

Harvey, David. 1990. *The Condition of Postmodernity: An Enquiry into the Origins of Cultural Change*. Cambridge, Mass.: Blackwell.

———. 2000. *Spaces of Hope*. Berkeley: University of California Press.

Hawke, Sharryl, and David Knox. 1977. *One Child by Choice*. Spectrum Book; S-455. Englewood Cliffs, N.J.: Prentice-Hall.

Henderson, Zorika Petic. 1991. The Only Child Isn't Necessarily a Terror. *Human Ecology Forum* 19, no. 2: 27–29.

Hernandez, Donald J. 1986. Childhood in Sociodemographic Perspective. *Annual Review of Sociology* 12: 159–180.

Hertz, Ellen. 1998. *The Trading Crowd: An Ethnography of the Shanghai Stock Market*. Cambridge: Cambridge University Press.

Herzfeld, Michael. 1985. *The Poetics of Manhood: Contest and Identity in a Cretan Mountain Village*. Princeton: Princeton University Press.

———. 1987. *Anthropology through the Looking-Glass: Critical Ethnography in the Margins of Europe*. Cambridge: Cambridge University Press.

———. 1990. Pride and Perjury: Time and the Oath in the Mountain Villages of Crete. *Man* 25, no. 2: 305–322.

———. 1997. *Cultural Intimacy: Social Poetics in the Nation-State*. New York: Routledge.

Hewitt, Patricia. 1993. *About Time: The Revolution in Work and Family Life*. London: Rivers Oram Press.

Hirschman, Charles. 1994. Why Fertility Changes. *Annual Review of Sociology* 20: 203–233.

Hochschild, Arlie Russell, and Anne Machung. 1989. *The Second Shift: Working Parents and the Revolution at Home*. New York, N.Y.: Viking.

Hoffman, Lisa Mae. 2000. The Art of Becoming an Urban Professional: The State, Gender, and Subject-Formation in Late-Socialist China. PhD Dissertation, University of California, Berkeley.

Holland, Dorothy C., and Naomi Quinn. 1987. *Cultural Models in Language and Thought*. Cambridge: Cambridge University Press.

Holland, Dorothy, and Michael Cole. 1995. Between Discourse and Schema: Reformulating a Cultural-Historical Approach to Culture and Mind. *Anthropology and Education Quarterly* 26, no. 4: 475–489.

Hollos, Marida, and Ulla Larsen. 1992. Fertility Differentials among the Ijo in Southern Nigeria: Does Urban Residence Make a Difference? *Social Science & Medicine* 35, no. 9: 1199–1210.

Holz, Carsten A. 2003. "Fast, Clear and Accurate": How Reliable Are Chinese Output and Economic Growth Statistics? *China Quarterly* 173, no. 1–305.

Honig, Emily, and Gail Hershatter. 1988. *Personal Voices: Chinese Women in the 1980's*. Stanford, Calif.: Stanford University Press.

Hoogstra, Lisa. 2000. Envisioning the Future. In *Becoming Adult: How Teenagers Prepare for the World of Work*, ed. Mihaly Csikszentmihalyi and Barbara Schneider, 21–38. New York: Basic Books.

Hooper, Beverley. 1998. "Flower Vase and Housewife": Women and Consumerism in Post-Mao China. In *Gender and Power in Affluent Asia*, ed. Krishna Sen and Maila Stivens, 167–193. New York: Routledge.

Horowitz, Mardi Jon. 1991. *Person Schemas and Maladaptive Interpersonal Patterns*. Chicago: University of Chicago Press.

Howe, Christopher. 1973. *Wage Patterns and Wage Policy in Modern China 1919–1972*. Cambridge: Cambridge University Press.

Hymes, Robert. 1987. *Statesmen and Gentlemen: The Elite of Fu-Chou, Chiang-Hsi, in Northern and Southern Sung*. Cambridge: Cambridge University Press.

Ikels, Charlotte. 1983. The Process of Caretaker Selection. *Research on Aging* 5, no. 4: 491–509.

———. 1990a. Family Caregivers and the Elderly in China. In *Aging and Caregiving: Theory, Research and Policy*, ed. David E. Biegel and Arthur Blum, 270–294. Newbury Park, California: Sage.

———. 1990b. New Options for the Urban Elderly. In *Chinese Society on the Eve of Tiananmen: The Impact of Reform*, ed. Deborah Davis and Ezra F. Vogel, 215–242. Cambridge: Harvard University Press.

———. 1990c. The Resolution of Intergenerational Conflict: Perspectives of Elders and Their Family Members. *Modern China* 16, no. 4: 379–406.

———. 1996. *The Return of the God of Wealth: The Transition to a Market Economy in Urban China*. Stanford: Stanford University Press.

Inhorn, Marcia. 1996. *Infertility and Patriarchy: The Cultural Politics of Gender and Family Life in Egypt*. Philadelphia: University of Pennsylvania Press.

Inkeles, Alex. 1974. *Becoming Modern: Individual Change in Six Developing Countries*. Cambridge: Harvard University Press.

———. 1983. *Exploring Individual Modernity*. New York: Columbia University Press.

Institute of Population Research. 1980. Renkou Lilun [Population Theory]. In *Population Theory in China*, ed. H. Yuan Tien. White Plains, New York: M. E. Sharpe.

Jankowiak, William. 1992. Father-Child Relations in Urban China. In *Father Child Relations: Cultural and Biosocial Contexts*, ed. Barry Hewlett, 345–363.

———. 2002. Proper Men and Proper Women: Parental Affection in the Chinese Family. In *Chinese Femininities/Chinese Masculinities*, ed. Susan Brownell and Jeffrey N. Wasserstrom. Berkeley: University of California Press.

Jankowiak, William R. 1993. *Sex, Death, and Hierarchy in a Chinese City: An Anthropological Account*. New York: Columbia University Press.

Jiang Zemin. 1996a. Jiang Calls for Closer Economic, Technical Cooperation. *Xinhua News Agency*, November 25, 1996.

———. 1996b. Speech by President Jiang Zemin of the People's Republic of China at Apec Economic Leaders Meeting. Available from http://www.fmprc.gov.cn/eng/5193.html. Web page accessed July 15, 2001.

Jiao, Shulan, Guiping Ji, and Qicheng Jing. 1986. Comparative Study of Behavioral Qualities of Only Children and Sibling Children. *Child Development* 57, no. 2: 357–361.

Jing, Jun. 2000a. Introduction: Food, Children, and Social Change in Contemporary China. In *Feeding China's Little Emperors*, ed. Jun Jing, 1–26. Stanford: Stanford University Press.

———, ed. 2000b. *Feeding China's Little Emperors*. Stanford: Stanford University Press.

Johnson, Kay. 1996. Politics of the Revival of Infant Abandonment in China, with Special Reference to Hunan. *Population and Development Review* 22, no. 1: 77–98.

Kane, Penny. 1987. *The Second Billion: Population and Family Planning in China*. New York, N.Y.: Penguin Books.

Kaufman, Joan. 1993. The Cost of IUD Failure in China. *Studies in Family Planning* 24, no. 3: 194–196.

Kennedy, Bingham. 2001. *Dissecting China's 2000 Census*. Population Reference Bureau. Available from http://www.prb.org/regions/asia_near_east/DissectingChinas2000Census.html. Accessed June 25, 2001.

Kerr, Joanna, Julie Delahanty, and Kate Humpage. 1996. *Gender and Jobs in China's New Economy*. Ottawa: North-South Institute.

Kertzer, David I., and Dominique Arel, eds. 2002. *Census and Identity: The Poli-*

*tics of Race, Ethnicity, and Language in National Censuses*. Cambridge: Cambridge University Press.

Keyfitz, Nathan. 1990. Alfred Sauvy [in Memoriam]. *Population and Development Review* 16, no. 4: 727–733.

Kirsch, Stuart. 2001. Lost Worlds: Environmental Disaster, "Culture Loss," and the Law. *Current Anthropology* 42, no. 2: 167–198.

Kishor, Sunita. 1993. "May God Give Sons to All": Gender and Child Mortality in India. *American Sociological Review* 58, no. 2: 247–265.

Kleinman, Arthur. 1985. Interpreting Illness Experience and Clinical Meanings: How I See Clinically Applied Anthropology. *Medical Anthropology Quarterly* 16, no. 3: 69–71.

———. 1986. *Social Origins of Distress and Disease: Depression, Neurasthenia, and Pain in Modern China*. New Haven: Yale University Press.

———. 1988. *The Illness Narratives: Suffering, Healing, and the Human Condition*. New York: Basic Books.

Knodel, John, Napaporn Havanon, and Anthony Pramualratana. 1984. Fertility Transition in Thailand: A Qualitative Analysis. *Population and Development Review* 10, no. 2: 297–328.

Knodel, John, Napaporn Havanon, and Werasit Sittitrai. 1990. Family Size and the Education of Children in the Context of Rapid Fertility Decline. *Population and Development Review* 16, no. 1: 31–62.

Korzec, Michel and Martin K. Whyte. 1981. Reading Notes: The Chinese Wage System. *China Quarterly* 86: 248–273.

Krause, Elizabeth L. 2001. "Empty Cradles" and the Quiet Revolution: Demographic Discourse and Cultural Struggles of Gender, Race, and Class in Italy. *Cultural Anthropology* 16, no. 4: 576–611.

Lan, Hua R., and Vanessa L. Fong, eds. 1999. *Women in Republican China*. Armonk, New York: M. E. Sharpe.

Lancaster, Roger N. 1992. *Life Is Hard: Machismo, Danger, and the Intimacy of Power in Nicaragua*. Berkeley: University of California Press.

Lardy, Nicholas R. 1999. China's Economic Growth in an International Context. *The Pacific Review* 12, no. 2: 163–171.

Laslett, Peter. 1965. *The World We Have Lost*. New York: Scribner.

Lavely, William, and Ronald Freedman. 1990. The Origins of the Chinese Fertility Decline. *Demography* 27, no. 3: 357–367.

Laybourn, Ann. 1994. *The Only Child: Myths and Reality*. Edinburgh: HMSO.

Lee, James Z., and Cameron Campbell. 1997. *Fate and Fortune in Rural China: Social Organization and Population Behavior in Liaoning, 1774–1873*. Cambridge: Cambridge University Press.

Lee, James Z., and Wang Feng. 1999. *One Quarter of Humanity: Malthusian Mythology and Chinese Realities*. Cambridge: Harvard University Press.

Lee, Sing, and Arthur Kleinman. 2000. Suicide as Resistance in Chinese Society. In *Chinese Society: Change, Conflict and Resistance*, ed. Elizabeth J. Perry and Mark Selden, 221–240. London and New York: Routledge.

Lemon, Alaina. 1998. Your Eyes Are Green Like Dollars—Counterfeit Cash, National Substance, and Currency Apartheid in 1990s Russia. *Cultural Anthropology* 13, no. 1: 22–55.

Leonard, William R., Anne Keenleyside, and Evgueni Ivakine. 1997. Recent Fertility and Mortality Trends among Aboriginal and Nonaboriginal Populations of Central Siberia. *Human Biology* 69, no. 3: 403–417.

Lerner, Daniel. 1958. *The Passing of Traditional Society: Modernizing the Middle East*. New York: Free Press of Glencoe.

Leslie, Paul. 2002. Demographic Consequences of Unpredictability in Fertility Outcomes. *American Journal of Human Biology* 14, no. 2: 168–183.

Levine, Nancy E. 1987. Differential Child Care in Three Tibetan Communities: Beyond Son Preference. *Population and Development Review* 13, no. 2: 281–304.

LeVine, Robert A. 2003. A Cross-Cultural Perspective on Parenting. In *Childhood Socialization: Comparative Studies of Parenting, Learning and Educational Change*, 89–100. Hong Kong: Comparative Education Research Centre, University of Hong Kong.

LeVine, Robert A., Sarah E. LeVine, Amy Richman, F. Medardo Tapia Uribe, Clara Sunderland Correa, and Patrice M. Miller. 1991. Women's Schooling and Child Care in the Demographic Transition: A Mexican Case Study. *Population and Development Review* 17, no. 3: 459–496.

LeVine, Robert A., Sarah E. LeVine, and Beatrice Schnell. 2001. "Improve the Women": Mass Schooling, Female Literacy, and Worldwide Social Change. *Harvard Educational Review* 71, no. 1: 1–50.

LeVine, Robert A. and Merry I. White. 2003. Revolution in Parenthood. In *Childhood Socialization: Comparative Studies of Parenting, Learning and Educational Change*, ed. Robert A. LeVine, 127–143. Hong Kong: University of Hong Kong Comparative Education Research Centre.

LeVine, Robert Alan, Suzanne Dixon, Sarah LeVine, Amy Richman, P. Herbert Leiderman, Constance H. Keefer, and T. Berry Brazelton. 1994. *Child Care and Culture: Lessons from Africa*. Cambridge: Cambridge University Press.

Lewis, Jane. 1980. *The Politics of Motherhood: Child and Maternal Welfare in England, 1900–1939*. Montreal: McGill-Queen's University Press.

Li Jiali. 1995. China's One-Child Policy: How and How Well Has It Worked? A Case Study of Hebei Province, 1979–88. *Population and Development Review* 21, no. 3: 563–585.

Li Ying. 1999. Wo Shi Ge Nu Hai! [I Am a Girl!]. *Dalian Ribao [Dalian Daily]*, October 27, 1999, 15.

Li Yongping and P.eng Xizhe. 2000. Age and Sex Structures. In *The Changing Population of China*, ed. Peng Xizhe and Guo Zhigang, 64–76. Malden: Blackwell Publishers.

Liang, Jersey, and Gu Shengzu. 1989. Long-Term Care for the Elderly in China. In *Caring for an Aging World: International Models for Long-Term Care, Financing, and Delivery*, ed. Teresa Schwab, 265–287. New York: McGraw-Hill.

Lieberthal, Kenneth G. 1995. *Governing China: From Revolution through Reform*. New York: W. W. Norton.

Link, Perry, Richard P. Madsen, and Paul G. Pickowicz. 2002. *Popular China: Unofficial Culture in a Globalizing Society*. Lanham, Maryland: Rowman and Littlefield.

Litzinger, Ralph A. 2000. *Other Chinas: The Yao and the Politics of National Belonging*. Durham: Duke University Press.

Liu, Xin. 2000. *In One's Own Shadow: An Ethnographic Account of the Condition of Post-Reform Rural China*. Berkeley: University of California Press.

———. 2002. *The Otherness of Self: A Genealogy of the Self in Contemporary China*. Ann Arbor: University of Michigan.

Liu Ying. 1999. Bie Zhe Yang Ai Wo [Don't Love Me This Way]. *Dalian Ribao [Dalian Daily]*, July 21, 1999, 7.

Liu Zheng. 1981. Population Planning and Demographic Theory. In *China's Population: Problems and Prospects*, ed. Liu Zheng and Song Jian. Beijing: New World Press.

Lowe, Lisa, and David Lloyd, eds. 1997. *The Politics of Culture in the Shadow of Capital*. Durham: Duke University Press.

Lozada, Eriberto P. 2000. Globalized Childhood? Kentucky Fried Chicken in Beijing. In *Feeding China's Little Emperors*, ed. Jun Jing, 114–134. Stanford: Stanford University Press.

Lu Hsun. 1978. My Old Home. In *Selected Stories of Lu Hsun*, ed. Yang Hsien-yi and Gladys Yang, 54–64. Peking: Foreign Languages Press.

Luther, Norman Y., Griffith Feeney, and Weimin Zhang. 1990. One-Child Families or a Baby Boom? Evidence from China's 1987 One-Per-Hundred Survey. *Population Studies* 44, no. 2: 341–357.

Lutz, Catherine and Jane Lou Collins. 1993. *Reading National Geographic*. Chicago: University of Chicago Press.

MacLeod, Jay. 1995. *Ain't No Makin' It: Aspirations and Attainment in a Low-Income Neighborhood*. Boulder: Westview Press.

Mallee, Hein. 2000. Migration, Hukou and Resistance in Reform China. In *Chinese Society: Change, Conflict and Resistance*, ed. Elizabeth J. Perry and Mark Selden, 83–101. London: Routledge.

Malthus, Thomas Robert. 1809. *An Essay on the Principle of Population; or, a View of Its Past and Present Effects on Human Happiness; with an Inquiry into Our Prospects Respecting the Future Removal or Mitigation of the Evils Which It Occasions*. Washington, DC: Roger Chew Weightman.

Mandler, George. 1984. *Mind and Body*. New York: W. W. Norton.

Mankekar, Purnima. 1999. *Screening Culture, Viewing Politics*. Durham: Duke University Press.

Mao Zedong. 1958. Chairman Mao's Article for Red Flag. *Survey of China Mainland Press*, no. 1784.

———. 1961a. The Bankruptcy of the Idealist Conception of History. In *Selected Works of Mao Tse-Tung*, 4:451–459. Peking: Foreign Languages Press.

———. 1961b. Be Activists in Promoting the Revolution. In *Selected Works of Mao Tse-Tung*, ed. Central Committee of the Communist Party of China Committee for the Publication of the Selected Works of Mao Tse-tung, 5:483–497. Peking: Foreign Languages Press.

———. 1961c. On the Correct Handling of Contradictions among the People. In *Selected Works of Mao Tse-Tung*, ed. Central Committee of the Communist Party of China Committee for the Publication of the Selected Works of Mao Tse-tung, 5:384–421. Peking: Foreign Languages Press.

Marx, Karl. 1977. *Capital: A Critique of Political Economy*. New York: Vintage Books.

Marx, Karl and Friedrich Engels. 1967 [1848]. *The Communist Manifesto*. Translated by Samuel Moore. Harmondsworth: Penguin.

McDade, Thomas W. 2001. Lifestyle Incongruity, Social Integation, and Immune Function in Samoan Adolescents. *Social Science & Medicine* 53: 1352–1362.

———. 2002. Status Incongruity in Samoan Youth: A Biocultural Analysis of Culture Change, Stress, and Immune Function. *Medical Anthropology Quarterly* 16, no. 2: 123–150.

McKibben, Bill. 1998. *Maybe One: A Personal and Environmental Argument for Single-Child Families*. New York: Simon & Schuster.

Meredith, William H., Douglas A. Abbott, and Ming Zheng Fu. 1992. Self-Concept and Sociometric Outcomes: A Comparison of Only Children and Sibling Children from Urban and Rural Areas in the People's Republic of China. *The Journal of Psychology* 126, no. 4: 411.

Milwertz, Cecilia Nathansen. 1997. *Accepting Population Control: Urban Chinese Women and the One-Child Family Policy*. Richmond: Curzon.

Miyazaki, Hirokazu. 2003. The Temporalities of the Market. *American Anthropologist* 105, no. 2: 255–265.

Moore, Thomas G. 2002. *China in the World Market: Chinese Industry and International Sources of Reform in the Post-Mao Era*. Cambridge: Cambridge University Press.

Mosher, Steven W. 1993. *A Mother's Ordeal: One Woman's Fight against China's One-Child Policy*. New York: Harcourt Brace Jovanovich.

Mueggler, Erik. 2001. *The Age of Wild Ghosts*. Berkeley: University of California Press.

Murphy, Rachel. 2002. *How Migrant Labor Is Changing Rural China*. Cambridge: Cambridge University Press.

Murthi, Mamta, Anne-Catherine Guio, and Jean Dreze. 1995. Mortality, Fertility, and Gender Bias in India: A District Level Analysis. *Population and Development Review* 21, no. 4: 745–782.

Nakhaie, M. R. 1995. Housework in Canada: The National Picture. *Journal of Comparative Family Studies* 26, no. 3: 409–425.

Notestein, Frank. 1953. Economic Problems of Population Change. In *Proceedings of the Eighth International Conference of Agricultural Economists, Eighth Conference, 1952*, 13–31. London: Oxford University Press.

Office of the Federal Register. 1999. The Federal Register. 64, no. 52.

Ogbu, John U. 1983. Minority Status and Schooling in Plural Societies. *Comparative Education Review* 27: 168–190.

———. 1987. Variability in Minority School Performance: A Problem in Search of an Explanation. *Anthropology and Education Quarterly* 18, no. 3: 312–334.

Ogbu, John U., and Margaret A. Gibson. 1991. *Minority Status and Schooling: A Comparative Study of Immigrant and Involuntary Minorities.* New York: Garland Press.

Ogbu, John U., and Herbert D. Simons. 1998. Voluntary and Involuntary Minorities: Cultural-Ecological Theory of School Performance with Some Implications for Education. *Anthropology & Education Quarterly* 29, no. 2: 155–188.

Ong, Aihwa. 1999. *Flexible Citizenship: The Cultural Logics of Transnationality.* Durham, NC: Duke University Press.

Orleans, Leo A. 1979. *Chinese Approaches to Family Planning.* White Plains, New York: M. E. Sharpe.

Orlove, Benjamin S. and Arnold J. Bauer. 1997. Giving Importance to Imports. In *The Allure of the Foreign: Imported Goods in Post-Colonial Latin America,* ed. Benjamin S. Orlove, 1–29. Ann Arbor: University of Michigan Press.

Ortner, S. B. 1998. Generation X: Anthropology in a Media-Saturated World. *Cultural Anthropology* 13, no. 3: 414–440.

Oshima, Harry T. 1983. The Industrial and Demographic Transitions in East Asia. *Population and Development Review* 9, no. 4: 583–607.

Palmer, Michael. 1995. The Re-Emergence of Family Law in Post-Mao China: Marriage, Divorce and Reproduction. *The China Quarterly,* no. 141: 110–135.

Parsons, Talcott. 1971. *The System of Modern Societies.* Englewood Cliffs, New Jersey: Prentice Hall.

Pasternak, Burton. 1983. Sociology and Anthropology in China: Revitalization and Its Constraints. *AAAS Selected Symposium Westview Press* 86: 37–62.

———. 1985. On the Causes and Demographic Consequences of Uxorilocal Marriage in China. In *Family and Population in East Asian History,* ed. Susan B. Hanley and Arthur P. Wolf, 309–334. Stanford: Stanford University Press.

Peak, Lois. 1991. *Learning to Go to School in Japan: Transition from Home to Preschool Life.* Berkeley: University of California Press.

Pearson, Veronica. 1995. *Mental Health Care in China: State Policies, Professional Services and Family Responsibilities.* London: Gaskell.

Peng, Xizhe. 1994. *Recent Trends in China's Population and Their Implications.* London: Research Programme on the Chinese Economy.

Peng Xizhe. 1991. *Demographic Transition in China: Fertility Trends since the 1950s.* Oxford: Clarendon Press.

Peng Xizhe and Dai Xingyi. 1996. *Zhongguo Nongcun Shequ Shengyu Wenhua [Community Fertility Culture in Rural China].* Shanghai: Huadong Shifan Daxue Chubanshe [Huadong Normal University Press].

Peng Xizhe and Guo Zhigang. 2000. *The Changing Population of China.* Oxford: Blackwell Publishers.

Pepper, Suzanne. 1996. *Radicalism and Education Reform in 20th-Century China:*

*The Search for an Ideal Development Model*. Cambridge: Cambridge University Press.

Perry, Elizabeth J. and Mark Selden. 2000. *Chinese Society: Change, Conflict, and Resistance*. London: Routledge.

Phillips, Michael R., Xianyan Li, and Yanping Zhang. 2002. Suicide Rates in China. *The Lancet* 359, no. 9309: 835–840.

Phillips, Michael R., Huaqing Liu, and Yanping Zhang. 1999. Suicide and Social Change in China. *Culture, Medicine, and Psychiatry* 23, no. 1.

Phillips, Michael R., Gonghuan Yang, Yanping Zhang, Lijun Wang, Huiyu Ji, and Maigeng Zhou. 2002. Risk Factors for Suicide in China: A National Case-Control Psychological Autopsy Study. *The Lancet* 360: 1728–1736.

Piot, Charles. 1999. *Remotely Global: Village Modernity in West Africa*. Chicago: University of Chicago Press.

———. 2001. Of Hybridity, Modernity, and Their Malcontents. *Interventions* 3, no. 1: 85–91.

Plesset, Sonja B. 2002. Sheltering Women: Visions of Gender, Motherhood, and Marriage in Northern Italy. Ph.D. diss., Harvard University.

Polit, Denise F., and Toni Falbo. 1987. Only Children and Personality Development: A Quantitative Review. *Journal of Marriage and the Family* 49, no. 2: 309.

———. 1988. Intellectual Achievement of Only Children. *Journal of Biosocial Science* 20, no. 3: 275–285.

Polit, Denise, L. R. Nuttal, and E. V. Nuttal. 1980. The Only Child Grows Up: A Look at Some Characteristics of Adult Only Children. *Family Relations* 29: 99–106.

Portes, Alejandro. 1976. On the Sociology of National Development. *American Journal of Sociology* 82: 55–85.

Poston, Dudley L., Jr. and Toni Falbo. 1990. Academic Performance and Personality Traits of Chinese Children: "Onlies" Versus Others. *American Journal of Sociology* 96, no. 2: 433.

Quanguo Renkou Chouyang Diaocha Bangongshi [National Census Office]. 1997. *1995 Quanguo 1% Renkou Chouyang Diaocha Ziliao [Materials from the 1995 1% Population Census]*. Beijing: Zhongguo Tongji Chubanshe [Chinese Statistics Press].

Rabinow, Paul. 1977. *Reflections on Fieldwork in Morocco*. Quantum Book. Berkeley: University of California Press.

Renmin Ribao [People's Daily]. 1979. Party Secretaries Take Command in Mobilizing the Whole Party in Doing a Still Better Job in Family Planning. In *Chinese Approaches to Family Planning*, ed. Leo A. Orleans. White Plains, New York: M. E. Sharpe.

Renne, Elisha. 1993. Gender Ideology and Fertility Strategies in an Ekiti Yoruba Village. *Studies in Family Planning* 24, no. 6: 343–353.

Riding, Alan. 2002. Italian Court Rules That Son Knows Best About Leaving Home. *New York Times*, April 6, 2002, A3.

Robbins, Joel. 2001. God Is Nothing but Talk: Modernity, Language, and

Prayer in a Papua New Guinea Society. *American Anthropologist* 103, no. 4: 901–912.

Robertson, Jennifer. 1998. *Takarazuka: Sexual Politics and Popular Culture in Modern Japan*. Berkeley: University of California Press.

Robinson, Jean C. 1985. Of Women and Washing Machines: Employment, Housework, and the Reproduction of Motherhood in Socialist China. *China Quarterly* 101: 32–57.

Rofel, Lisa. 1999. *Other Modernities: Gendered Yearnings in China after Socialism*. Berkeley: University of California Press.

Rosenweig, Mark and T. Paul Schultz. 1982. Market Opportunities, Genetic Endowments, and Intra-Family Resource Distribution: Child Survival in Rural India. *American Economic Review* 72: 803–815.

Ross, Ellen. 1993. *Love and Toil: Motherhood in Outcast London, 1870–1918*. New York: Oxford University Press.

Rostow, W. W. 1990. *The Stages of Economic Growth: A Non-Communist Manifesto*. Cambridge: Cambridge University Press.

Sahlins, Marshall. 1972. *Stone Age Economics*. Chicago: Aldine.

———. 1994. Cosmologies of Capitalism: The Trans-Pacific Sector of the World System. In *Culture/Power/History*, ed. Nicholas B. Dirks, Geoff Eley and Sherry B. Ortner, 412–455. Princeton: Princeton University Press.

Salaff, Janet W. 1995. *Working Daughters of Hong Kong: Filial Piety or Power in the Family?* New York: Columbia University Press.

Sander, William. 1990. More on the Determinants of the Fertility Transition. *Social Biology* 37, no. 1–2.

Sangren, P. Steven. 1983. Female Gender in Chinese Religious Symbols: Kuan Yin, Ma Tsu, and "the Eternal Mother." *Signs* 9, no. 1: 4–25.

Sassen, Saskia. 1991. *The Global City: New York, London, Tokyo*. Princeton: Princeton University Press.

———. 2000. *Cities in a World Economy*. Thousand Oaks, California: Pine Forge Press.

Sassen, Saskia, and K. Anthony Appiah. 2000. *Globalization and Its Discontents: Essays on the New Mobility of People and Money*. New Press.

Sauvy, Alfred. 1952. Trois Mondes, Une Planète [Three Worlds, One Planet]. *L'Observateur [The Observer]*, August 14, 1952.

Scheper-Hughes, Nancy. 1992. *Death without Weeping: The Violence of Everyday Life in Brazil*. Berkeley: University of California Press.

———. 1997. Demography without Numbers. In *Anthropological Demography: Toward a New Synthesis*, ed. David I. Kertzer and Thomas E. Fricke, 201–222. Chicago: University of Chicago Press.

Schneider, Barbara and David Stevenson. 1999. *The Ambitious Generation: America's Teenagers, Motivated but Directionless*. New Haven: Yale University Press.

Schneider, Jane C., and Peter T. Schneider. 1996. *Festival of the Poor: Fertility Decline and the Ideology of Class in Sicily: 1860–1980*. Tucson: University of Arizona Press.

Schwartz, Theodore, Geoffrey M. White, and Catherine Lutz. 1992. *New Di-*

*rections in Psychological Anthropology*. Cambridge: Cambridge University Press.

Scott, James C. 1985. *Weapons of the Weak*. New Haven: Yale University Press.

Selden, Mark. 1993. *The Political Economy of Chinese Development*. Armonk, New York: M. E. Sharpe.

Shanghaishi Youerjiaoyu Yanjiushi [Shanghai Preschool Education Study Group]. 1980. Dushengzinü De Jiatingjiaoyu [Family Education of Only Children]. *Zhongguo Funü [Chinese Women]* 5, no. 17.

———. 1988. Wu Zhi Liu Sui Dushengzinü De Zhishi Mian Renshi Nengli Ji Jiating Jiaoyu De Diaocha [Investigation of the Knowledge, Understanding, and Family Education of Singletons between Ages Five and Six]. In *Dushengzinü De Xinli Tedian Yu Jiaoyu [Singletons' Psychological Particularities and Education]*, ed. Beijing Shifan Daxue Jiaoyu Kexue Yanjiusuo [Beijing Normal University Educational Science Research Center], 148–165. Beijing: Nongcun Duwu Chubanshe [Rural Reading Materials Publisher].

Shirk, Susan L. 1982. *Competitive Comrades*. Berkeley: University of California Press.

———. 1993. *The Political Logic of Economic Reform in China*. Berkeley: University of California Press.

Short, Susan E. and Zhai Fengying. 1998. Looking Locally at China's One-Child Policy. *Studies in Family Planning* 29, no. 4: 373–387.

Shorter, Edward. 1977. *The Making of the Modern Family*. New York: Basic Books.

Siu, Helen. 1990. Where Were the Women? Rethinking Marriage Resistance and Regional Culture in South China. *Late Imperial China* 11, no. 2: 32–62.

———. 1993. Reconstituting Dowry and Brideprice in South China. In *Chinese Families in the Post-Mao Era*, ed. Deborah Davis and Stevan Harrell, 165–188. Berkeley: University of California Press.

Small, Meredith F. 2001. *Kids: How Biology and Culture Shape the Way We Raise Our Children*. New York: Doubleday.

Smith, T. L., ed. 1907. *Aspects of Childhood Life and Education*. Boston: Ginn.

Solinger, Dorothy. 1999. *Contesting Citizenship in Urban China: Peasant Migrants, the State, and the Logic of the Market*. Berkeley: University of California Press.

Solomon, E. S., J. E. Clare, and C. F. Westoff. 1956. Fear of Childlessness. Desire to Avoid an Only Child, and Children's Desire for Siblings. *Milbank Memorial Fund Quarterly* 34: 160–177.

Spence, Jonathan. 1990. *The Search for Modern China*. New York: W. W. Norton and Company.

Spence, Jonathan D. 1980. *To Change China: Western Advisers in China, 1620–1960*. New York: Penguin Books.

Stafford, Charles. 1995. *The Roads of Chinese Childhood: Learning and Identification in Angang*. Cambridge: Cambridge University Press.

Stockard, Janice. 1989. *Daughters of the Canton Delta: Marriage Patterns and Economic Strategies in South China, 1860–1930*. Stanford: Stanford University Press.

Stone, Lawrence. 1977. *The Family, Sex and Marriage in England, 1500–1800*. New York: Harper & Row.

Strauss, Claudia, and Naomi Quinn. 1997. *A Cognitive Theory of Cultural Meaning*. Cambridge: Cambridge University Press.

Suárez-Orozco, Carola, and Marcelo Suárez-Orozco. 1995. *Transformations: Migration, Family Life, and Achievement Motivation among Latino Adolescents*. Stanford: Stanford University Press.

Suárez-Orozco, Marcelo. 1989. *Central American Refugees and U.S. High Schools: A Psychosocial Study of Motivation and Achievement*. Stanford: Stanford University Press.

Summerfield, Gale. 1994. Effects of the Changing Employment Situation on Urban Chinese Women. *Review of Social Economy* 52, no. 1: 40–59.

Tabah, Leon. 1991. Alfred Sauvy: Statistician, Economist, Demographer and Iconoclast [1898–1990]. *Population Studies* 45, no. 2: 353–357.

Tang, Wenfang, and William L. Parish. 2000. *Chinese Urban Life under Reform: The Changing Social Contract*. Cambridge: Cambridge University Press.

Tang Yuankai. 2001. The "Unbearable" Examination. *Beijing Review* 30: 12–20.

Tao, Kuotai, and Jing-Hwa Chiu. 1985. One-Child-Per-Family Policy: A Psychological Perspective. In *Chinese Culture and Mental Health*, ed. Wen Shing Tseng and David Y. H. Wu, 153–165.

Tao, Kuo-Tai, Jing-Hwa Qiu, Bao-Lin Li, Wen-Shing Tseng, Jing Hsu, and Dennis G. McLaughlin. 1995. One-Child-Per-Couple Family Planning and Child Behaviour Development: Six-Year Follow-up Study in Nanjing. In *Chinese Societies and Mental Health*, ed. Tsung-Yi Lin, Wen-Shing Tseng and Ying-kun Yeh, 341–374. Oxford; New York: Oxford University Press.

Teng, Ssu-yu, and John King Fairbank. 1979. *China's Response to the West: A Documentary Survey, 1839–1923*. Cambridge, Mass.: Harvard University Press.

Thompson, Vaida D. 1974. Family Size: Implicit Policies and Assumed Psychological Outcomes. *Journal of Social Issues* 30, no. 4: 93–124.

Tien, H. Yuan, ed. 1980. *Population Theory in China*. White Plains, New York: M. E. Sharpe.

Tomkins, Silvan S., and Carroll E. Izard. 1965. *Affect, Cognition, and Personality: Empirical Studies*. New York: Springer.

Topley, Marjorie. 1978. Marriage Resistance in Rural Kwangtung. In *Studies in Chinese Society*, 247–268.

Travers, S. Lee. 1982. Bias in Chinese Economic Statistics: The Case of the Typical Example Investigation. *China Quarterly* 91: 478–485.

Tseng, Wen-shing, Tao Kuotai, Jing Hsu, and Chiu Jinghua. 1988. Family Planning and Child Mental Health in China: The Nanjing Survey. *American Journal of Psychiatry* 145, no. 11: 1396–1403.

U.S. Bureau of the Census. 1999. *World Population Profile: 1998*. Washington, DC.

United Nations. 1997a. *Expert Group Meeting on Below-Replacement Fertility*. New York: Population Division, Department of Economic and Social Affairs, United Nations Secretariat.

———. 1997b. Population 2050: 9.4 Billion. *UN Chronicle* 34, no. 3: 72.

United Nations Department of Economic and Social Affairs. 1998. *World Population Prospects as Assessed in 1998*. New York: United Nations.

Veenhoven, Ruut and Maykel Verkuyten. 1989. The Well-Being of Only Children. *Adolescence* 24, no. 93: 155–166.

Verdery, Katherine. 1991. *What Was Socialism, and What Comes Next?* Princeton: Princeton University Press.

Wallerstein, Immanuel. 1974. *The Modern World System: Capitalist Agriculture and the Origins of the European World Economy in the Sixteenth Century*. New York: Academic Press.

Wallerstein, Immanuel Maurice. 1979. *The Capitalist World-Economy: Essays*. Cambridge: Cambridge University Press.

———. 1998. *Utopistics, or, Historical Choices of the Twenty-First Century*. New York: New Press.

———. 1999. *The End of the World as We Know It: Social Science for the Twenty-First Century*. Minneapolis: University of Minnesota Press.

Wallerstein, Immanuel, and Joan Smith. 1992. Core-Periphery and Household Structures. *Creating and Transforming Households: the Constraints of the World Economy*: 253–262.

Waltner, Ann. 1983. Building on the Ladder of Success: The Ladder of Success in Imperial China and Recent Work on Social Mobility. *Ming Studies* 17, no. 30–36.

Walvin, James. 1982. *A Child's World: A Social History of English Childhood, 1800–1914*. Harmondsworth, Middlesex, England: Penguin Books.

Wan, Chuanwen. 1996. Comparison of Personality Traits of Only and Sibling School Children in Beijing. *Journal of Genetic Psychology* 155, no. 377–388.

Wang Yuru. 1999. *Bu an De Taiyang: Zhongguo Di Yi Dai Dushengzinü Xinli Tansuo [Uneasy Sun: A Study of China's First Generation of Singletons]*. Shanghai: Fudan Daxue Chubanshe [Fudan University Press].

Wang Zheng. 1999. *Women in the Chinese Enlightenment: Oral and Textual Histories*. Berkeley: University of California Press.

———. 2000. Gender, Employment and Women's Resistance. In *Chinese Society: Change, Conflict and Resistance*, ed. Elizabeth J. Perry and Mark Selden, 62–82. London; New York: Routledge.

Wasserstrom, Jeffrey. 1984. Resistance to the One-Child Family. *Modern China* 10: 345–374.

Watson, James L. 1980. Transactions in People: The Chinese Market in Slaves, Servants, and Heirs. *Asian and African Systems of Slavery*: 223–250.

———. 2000. Food as Lens: The Past, Present, and Future of Family Life in China. In *Feeding China's Little Emperors*, ed. Jun Jing, 1–26. Stanford: Stanford University Press.

———, ed. 1984. *Class and Social Stratification in Post-Revolution China*. Cambridge: Cambridge University Press.

Watson, James L. and Patricia Ebrey, eds. 1986. *Kinship Organization in Late Imperial China, 1000–1940*. Berkeley: University of California Press.

Watson, Rubie. 1984. Women's Property in Republican China: Rights and Practices. *Republican China* 10, no. 1a: 1–12.

Watson, Rubie S. 1986. The Named and the Nameless: Gender and Person in Chinese Society. *American Ethnologist* 13, no. 4: 619–631.

———. 1996. Chinese Bridal Laments: The Claims of a Dutiful Daughter. In *Harmony and Counterpoint: Ritual Music in Chinese Context*, ed. Bell Yung, Evelyn Sakakida Rawski and Rubie S. Watson, 107–129. Stanford, Calif.: Stanford University Press.

Weber, Max. 1958. *The Protestant Ethic and the Spirit of Capitalism*. Translated by Talcott Parsons. New York: Charles Scribner's Sons.

Weinberg, Martin S. 1976. *Sex Research: Studies from the Kinsey Institute*. New York: Oxford University Press.

Weismantel, Mary. 2001. *Cholas and Pishtacos: Stories of Race and Sex in the Andes*. Chicago: University of Chicago Press.

White, Merry. 1987. The Virtue of Japanese Mothers: Cultural Definitions of Women's Lives. *Daedalus* 116, no. 3: 149–163.

White, Merry I. 1988. *The Japanese Educational Challenge: A Commitment to Children*. New York: Free Press; London: Collier Macmillan.

———. 1993. *The Material Child: Coming of Age in Japan and America*. New York: Free Press.

White, Tyrene. 1987. Implementing the "One-Child-Per-Couple" Population Program in Rural China: National Goals and Local Politics. In *Policy Implementation in Post-Mao China*, 157–189. Berkeley: University of California Press.

———. 1994. The Origins of China's Birth Planning Policy. In *Engendering China: Women, Culture, and the State*, ed. Christina Gilmartin, Gail Hershatter, Lisa Rofel and Tyrene White, 250–278. Cambridge: Harvard University Press.

———. 2000. Domination, Resistance and Accommodation in China's One-Child Campaign. In *Chinese Society: Change, Conflict and Resistance*, ed. Elizabeth J. Perry and Mark Selden, 102–119. London: Routledge.

Whyte, Martin K. 1979. Revolutionary Change and Patrilocal Residence in China. *Ethnology* 18: 211–227.

Whyte, Martin King. 1997. The Fate of Filial Obligations in Urban China. *The China Journal*, no. 38: 1–31.

Whyte, Martin King, and S. Z. Gu. 1987. Popular Response to China's Fertility Transition. *Population and Development Review* 13, no. 3: 471–493.

Whyte, Martin and William Parish. 1984. *Urban Life in Contemporary China*. Chicago: University of Chicago Press.

Wilson, William J. 1987. *The Truly Disadvantaged: The Inner City, the Underclass, and Public Policy*. Chicago: University of Chicago Press.

Winterhalder, Bruce, and Paul Leslie. 2002. Risk-Sensitive Fertility: The Variance Compensation Hypothesis. *Evolution and Human Behavior* 23: 59–82.

Wolf, Margery. 1968. *The House of Lim: A Study of a Chinese Farm Family*. Englewood Cliffs, New Jersey: Prentice Hall.

———. 1972. *Women and the Family in Rural Taiwan*. Stanford: Stanford University Press.

———. 1985. *Revolution Postponed: Women in Contemporary China*. Stanford: Stanford University Press.

Wolf-Phillips, Leslie. 1987. Why "Third World"? Origin, Definition and Usage. *Third World Quarterly* 9, no. 4: 1131–1139.

Wong Siu-lun. 1979. *Sociology and Socialism in Contemporary China*. London: Routledge.

Wu Naitao. 1986. Dealing with the Spoiled Brat. *Beijing Review* 29, no. 12 [May]: 26–28.

Xiao Fulan and Zhang Qibao. 1985. Guanyu Xiaoxue De Shen Zi Nu Jiao Yu Qing Kuang De Diao Cha [a Survey of the Primary School Education of the Only Child]. *Xinlixue Bao [Psychological News]* 3: 50–52.

Yan, Yunxiang. 1996. *The Flow of Gifts: Reciprocity and Social Networks in a Chinese Village*. Stanford, Calif.: Stanford University Press.

———. 1997a. McDonald's in Beijing: The Localization of Americana. In *Golden Arches East: McDonald's in East Asia*, ed. James L. Watson, 39–76. Stanford, Calif.: Stanford University Press.

———. 1997b. The Triumph of Conjugality: Structural Transformation of Family Relations in a Chinese Village. *Ethnology* 36, no. 3: 191–212.

———. 2003. *Private Life under Socialism: Love, Intimacy, and Family Change in a Chinese Village 1949–1999*. Stanford: Stanford University Press.

Yang, Bin, Thomas H. Ollendick, Qi Dong, Yong Xia, and Lei Lin. 1995. Only Children and Children with Siblings in the People's Republic of China: Levels of Fear, Anxiety, and Depression. *Child Development* 66, no. 5: 1301–1311.

Yang, Mayfair Mei-hui. 1994. *Gifts, Favors, and Banquets: The Art of Social Relationships in China*. Ithaca, N.Y.: Cornell University Press.

Ye, Weili. 2001. *Seeking Modernity in China's Name: Chinese Students in the United States, 1900–1927*. Stanford: Stanford University Press.

Yeh, Wei-Hsin. 1990. *The Alienated Academy: Culture and Politics in Republican China, 1919–1937*. Cambridge: Harvard University Press.

Yu Jingquan. 1999. Jin Xia You Xie Haizi Wu Jiaqi [This Summer Some Children Will Not Have a Vacation]. *Dalian Ribao [Dalian Daily]*, August 4, 1999, 4.

Yue Daiyun and Carolyn Wakeman. 1985. *To the Storm: The Odyssey of a Revolutionary Chinese Woman*. Berkeley: University of California Press.

Zelizer, Viviana A. Rotman. 1994. *Pricing the Priceless Child: The Changing Social Value of Children*. Princeton, N.J.: Princeton University Press.

Zeng Yi. 2000. Marriage Patterns in Contemporary China. In *The Changing Population of China*, ed. Peng Xizhe and Guo Zhigang, 91–100. Malden: Blackwell Publishers.

Zeng Yi, Tu Ping, Gu Baochang, Xu Yi, Li Bohua, and Li Yongping. 1993. Causes and Implications of the Recent Increase in the Reported Sex Ratio at Birth in China. *Population and Development Review* 19, no. 2: 283–302.

Zhang, Hong. 1998. Social Transformations, Family Life, and Uxorilocal Marriage in a Hubei Village, 1870–1994. PhD Dissertation, Columbia University.

Zhang, Li. 2001. *Strangers in the City: Reconfigurations of Space, Power, and Social Networks within China's Floating Population*. Stanford: Stanford University Press.

Zhang Weiguo. 1999. Implementation of State Family Planning Programmes in a Northern Chinese Village. *China Quarterly* 157: 202–230.

Zhang Zhen. 2001. Mediating Time: The "Rice Bowl of Youth" in Fin De Siècle Urban China. In *Globalization*, ed. Arjun Appadurai, 131–154. Durham: Duke University Press.

# Index